Microsoft® Data Warehousing: Building Distributed Decision Support Systems

Robert S. Craig
Joseph A. Vivona
David Berkovitch

Wiley Computer Publishing

John Wiley & Sons, Inc.

NEW YORK · CHICHESTER · WEINHEIM · BRISBANE · SINGAPORE · TORONTO

To our families, our readers, and the user community.
Our families keep us focused on what's really important.
Our readers are engaged with us in the great adventure we call
the software industry. If together we and our readers can help
the users derive value from the power of computers,
then we've done something worthwhile.

Publisher: Robert Ipsen
Editor: Theresa Hudson
Managing Editor: Angela Murphy
Text Design & Composition: Publishers' Design and Production Services, Inc.

Designations used by companies to distinguish their products are often claimed as trademarks. In all instances where John Wiley & Sons, Inc., is aware of a claim, the product names appear in initial capital or ALL CAPITAL LETTERS. Readers, however, should contact the appropriate companies for more complete information regarding trademarks and registration.

This book is printed on acid-free paper. ♾

Published by John Wiley & Sons, Inc.

Published simultaneously in Canada.

This publication is designed to provide accurate and authoritative information in regard to the subject matter covered. It is sold with the understanding that the publisher is not engaged in professional services. If professional advice or other expert assistance is required, the services of a competent professional person should be sought.

Library of Congress Cataloging-in-Publication Data:

ISBN 0-471-32761-1

Printed in the United States of America.

10 9 8 7 6 5 4 3 2 1

When Bob Craig first came to me with the idea of writing a book about Microsoft data warehousing, I immediately felt that a book written from the perspective of an experienced industry analyst would be a valuable addition to the data warehousing body of knowledge for several reasons.

The character of the decision support software marketplace is rapidly changing and at Hurwitz Group we believe that Microsoft will have a significant impact on the future direction of that market. One goal of Microsoft's is to bring decision support technology to a much broader audience than has been the case in the recent past. This will undoubtedly increase the competitiveness of the decision support marketplace, which will help to drive down overall implementation costs.

At Hurwitz Group we believe that Microsoft will also have a major impact as a result of the widespread acceptance of the OLE DB and OLE DB for OLAP APIs. The major desktop query and analysis vendors, with very few exceptions, are all lining up to support these interfaces, which will establish OLE DB as the de facto standard for access to both relational and multidimensional databases. Similarly, the Microsoft Repository will likely become the industry standard for metadata interoperability, which will finally bring some order out of the current chaotic state of multi-vendor database metadata. However, there are still concerns in the marketplace about Microsoft's ability to deliver and support enterprise-level business applications. The discussion of these issues in this book are what make it important, in my opinion, because it is intended to help you, the reader, understand what Microsoft has to offer and where it is most applicable.

While there are many books about data warehousing available at any good computer bookstore, many are written from the perspective of a data warehouse practitioner and tend to focus on the technical details of implementing the data warehouse. Most of these books fail to discuss the overall architecture of the data warehouse in terms that are understandable to a non-technical, business user. This book, on the other hand, develops three major themes that make it useful to a wider audience.

1. There is the in-depth discussion about the five environments that make up a complete decision support application. The concept of the five environments was first developed and fleshed out by Bob, and the other Hurwitz Group analysts on the Data Warehouse and Business Intelligence Service, and I am pleased to see that their insights will receive broader exposure through this book.

2. There is a solid and capable presentation written by Joe Vivona, an experienced practitioner that describes the process for implementing the five environments using Microsoft technology. This section of the book is technical enough to be useful to a software professional, but is also understandable by a non-technical reader.

3. In the final chapter, David Bercovitch delivers a description of a variety of effective multi-dimensional analysis scenarios. Again, the description of the various types of analysis scenarios is understandable by a non-technical user, but can also guide the software professional who needs to deliver useful applications to end users.

In keeping with the spirit of bringing decision support technology to a broader mass market this book is not intended for the data warehouse professional who wants extremely detailed, code-level examples. While there are descriptions of how to use many important features of SQL Server, the goal of this book is to help the reader conceptually understand Microsoft SQL Server 7 and its related components such as SQL Server OLAP Services, Data Transformation Services, and the Microsoft Repository. This understanding will make it easier to analyze whether SQL Server 7 will meet the business needs of an organization contemplating implementing a decision support system.

A piece of advice we regularly impart to our clients, whether they are end users or software vendors, is to always focus on the underlying business problem that the software developer is trying to solve. Without this business focus, the application is doomed to failure. A lack of business focus and end-user involvement are two of the major problems facing the data warehouse community. The question you need to ask yourself when reading this book is, "How is this going to help me (or my company) sell more orange juice tomorrow?" The authors have put together a framework for helping you, the reader, to assess whether the technology that Microsoft has brought to the market will help you answer this question.

Judith Hurwitz, CEO, Hurwitz Group, Inc.
http://www.hurwitz.com

CONTENTS

Business Reasons for Enterprise Data Warehousing

Decision makers require high-quality information in order to make timely, consistent, and reliable decisions that impact their business. Many organizations have deployed data warehouse and business intelligence software to deliver this information. There are a number of important business drivers that have led companies to take this step.

First, the organization benefits from a consolidated view of enterprise data. For example, a manufacturer may have a dozen or more different systems (sales, accounting, purchasing, customer support, etc.) that contain customer information but no mechanism for gaining insight into the customer's behavior or establishing the customer's value to the organization. A data warehouse can provide a centralized repository of uniform, comprehensive information from heterogeneous source systems (including external data, such as syndicated market data supplied by independent vendors).

A related concern is the need to maintain longitudinal, historical records. Online transaction processing (OLTP) systems often purge "old" data to archives in order to maintain acceptable performance levels. This archived data can be extremely valuable for many business purposes, such as establishing a customer's lifetime value.

Secondly, end users often need data that is buried in OLTP production databases. In a typical production environment a programmer is required to write a custom report to extract the data in a usable format. The result, in most large organizations, is a significant backlog of report requests. Often, by the time the IT organization produces the data, it no longer meets the user's needs. Ad hoc queries can be difficult to construct for OLTP databases, especially if the database is non-relational and does not support SQL.

A third, related, issue is that OLTP systems are designed to handle many short, brief transactions. They do not have the data structures required to respond quickly and easily to business intelligence queries. Consequently, if users are allowed to run queries in a transactional environment, the database's performance will be severely reduced for the mission-critical OLTP system.

Lastly, given the increasingly distributed nature of today's business environment, progressive companies need cost-effective, secure methods for delivering access and analysis capabilities to both centralized and remote decision-makers.

These business drivers—the need to consolidate diverse data sources, the need to enable users to analyze their own data, the need to provide ad hoc access to data, and the need to broadly deliver information to all decision makers—have led to the deployment of data warehouse/data mart systems. A data warehouse solution, combined with user-friendly OLAP tools, enables end users to analyze the wealth of information in their data warehouse without requiring significant involvement from IT and while simultaneously preserving the performance of mission-critical OLTP systems.

The Evolution of Decision Support

Those companies that began to develop and deploy data warehouses in the early to mid-1980s have discovered that a modern decision support environment provides them with a new form of competitive advantage.

This advantage comes from two factors. One is the delivery of consolidated, high-quality, time-oriented data that has been collected from various internal and external systems. This data is scrubbed and restructured to ensure that it is clean, correct, and consistent. The second is the ability to deploy this data in a form that is amenable to analysis and query by end users. The explosion of reporting, query, analysis and data mining tools that has occurred in the 1990s has enabled companies to improve their business processes, enhance the quality of their products and services, and strengthen their relationship with their best customers.

Most of the vendors who have been significant players in the decision support marketplace have based their technology on the Unix operating system. Other technological elements have included relational database management systems and proprietary multi-dimensional databases. While these products have been successful, they have tended to be extremely expensive, and to require significant internal IT resources such as experienced Unix system administrators, and relational database administrators.

According to a survey of 50 companies reported by the consulting firm PriceWaterhouseCoopers LLP,* 70 percent of the data warehouse projects cost more than $1 million, and 37 percent cost more than $5 million.

Beginning in the mid-1990s, Microsoft Corporation recognized that there was an opportunity to provide a new generation of decision support software to companies that would enable them to deliver relatively inexpensive decision support solutions that were easier to design, deploy, and use. As a result, Microsoft embarked on an effort to leverage its core competency in graphical user interfaces, operating systems, and databases to create an integrated platform for delivering these solutions to customers.

The Microsoft DSS Architecture

In this book we describe the process of designing, building, deploying, and managing a modern, distributed decision support architecture, based on Microsoft technology. Microsoft decision support technology can be used to build large-scale, distributed, decision support databases that contain a mix of transaction-level detail data and aggregated, summary data. These databases can be deployed to meet the analytical needs of users in various corporate functions, such as accounting and finance, human resources, customer management, shipping and logistics, and marketing and sales.

The architecture we will describe in this book is flexible, extensible, easy to design, deploy and maintain, and moves analytical data closer to the users who need it. One of the big advantages of this architecture is that a company can begin to deploy discrete, focused, decision support databases using the concepts described in this book, with the assurance that metadata integration and consistency will enable them to expand the system incrementally as business needs dictate. The alternatives are

*Information Management Center Report 6, December, 1997.

to build a single, mammoth data warehouse, which is risky, expensive and time-consuming; or to build separate, non-integrated independent data marts, which results in data inconsistency and duplication of effort.

The technology elements that make up this architecture consist of:

- SQL Server 7
- SQL Server OLAP Services
- Data Transformation Services
- Microsoft Repository
- The OLE DB, OLE DB for OLAP, and ActiveX Data Objects (ADO) application programming interfaces (API)
- Microsoft Management Console
- Desktop tools, such as English Query, Access, and Excel

Why This Book?

Our intent in this book is to provide you with a realistic, balanced perspective regarding where these technologies make sense, and where they don't.

Our belief is that companies will want to use this approach in a variety of scenarios, depending on their size, scope, and internal skill sets. Once you have read this book, you'll be able to determine if this technology is appropriate for your company, division, or group. If it is, and we believe it will be, then this book will describe the process of designing, implementing, deploying, and managing enterprise-wide decision support systems, based on technology from Microsoft and its major partners.

IT managers and end users can all benefit from a clear understanding of how decision support systems work, and how they can best utilize a new generation of powerful, easy-to-use, and inexpensive DSS tools, such as Microsoft SQL Server and SQL Server OLAP Services, to establish and maintain competitive advantage.

This book is intended to demonstrate how to deploy a scalable, enterprise-wide DSS solution, based on the Microsoft decision support framework. It is designed to help IT managers and other IT professionals, such as database designers, understand the role of DSS systems in an overall information architecture. While many of the concepts described in this book are technical in nature, we will endeavor to make this information applicable to, and useful for, non-technical readers as well.

The specific theme of the book is how to build a decision support system based on Microsoft's Data Warehouse Framework. We will discuss the definition of a decision support environment and then describe in some detail how to utilize the combined Microsoft decision support products and services to build and maintain a distributed DSS system.

Acknowledgments

I'd like to extend a special thanks for the support and encouragement of Judith Hurwitz, Dave Kelly, Steve Foote, Phil Russom, Ellen Gutter, Jane Boston, and the analyst and support staff at Hurwitz Group, Inc. Much of the material in the first five chapters of this book is based on research and analysis developed at Hurwitz Group, and I gratefully acknowledge the profound debt I owe Judith and the outstanding organization at Hurwitz Group.

I also owe a special thanks to Ralph Kimball for the rich insights I've gleaned from his two books *The Data Warehouse Toolkit* and *The Data Warehouse Life-cycle Toolkit*, his columns in *Intelligent Enterprise* magazine, and several conversations we've had. The depth and breadth of Ralph's experience has been a source of inspiration to me throughout the process of writing this book. When you've finished reading this book, go out and buy Ralph's books!

I'd be remiss if I didn't thank Jim Ewel, Steve Murchie, Doug Leland, Phil Bernstein, Stewart MacLeod, Corey Salka, Brian Welcker, and Goetz Graefe of Microsoft and Kate Phillippay at Waggner Eggstrom. They were always available to answer questions, despite the pressures of managing a major product launch, and were willing to help in any way they could to ensure that the information in this book is complete and accurate. However, I take full responsibility for any errors or omissions.

Finally, I'd like to thank my wife Carol and my two young children Emma and Ben, for their patience, and forbearance. I know they were sick and tired of seeing the back of my head, but I couldn't have completed this project without their love and affection to sustain me along the way.

—Robert Craig

With loving thanks to my wife Faith and my daughter Christina Joy, without your support and understanding I would never have been able to participate in this book. You enable me to do great things, everyday. Also, to my friend and mentor Mike Nugent, who has provided me countless guidance and advice over the years: Thanks for being there and listening. Finally, to my family—your support and help has meant the world to me—I can only say one thing. Thanks.

—Joe Vivona

I would like to acknowledge my wife Sari and my daughter Dayna, as well as the entire team at The Sierra Consulting Group, each of whom have contributed in their own ways.

—David Bercovitch

Robert Craig brings 15 years of experience in the software industry to this book. His background includes being an industry analyst, software project manager, and software marketing executive. Robert is Vice President of Marketing at WebEngine. Prior to joining WebEngine he was Vice President of Application Architectures at Hurwitz Group, where he managed the Hurwitz Data Warehousing and the Internet Business Strategy Services. Before joining Hurwitz, Robert was a Vice President at Science Applications International Corporation where he directed system integration projects in the commercial healthcare market. He also has extensive experience as an independent high-tech marketing consultant, as Director of Sales and Marketing for a small high-tech startup, and close to ten years in a variety of software engineering and product marketing positions at Digital Equipment Corp.

Joseph Vivona has more than ten years experience in applications development and business reengineering. Joe is currently the Vice President of Applications Development and Delivery at KPI Technologies Inc., where he focuses on building decision support systems using OLAP technologies for the Customer Relationship Management market. Prior to joining KPI Technologies, he was a Product Development and Services Manager for one of the leading Enterprise Asset Management software companies in the world. Over the years he has worked for numerous Fortune 100 companies, including Exxon USA and Tosco Corporation as a software developer and IT project manager.

David Bercovitch is a ten-year veteran at implementing decision support technology. His insight stems from a solid grasp of the business issues related to technology, derived from various under-graduate and postgraduate business degrees, and on-the-job experience. David co-owns The Sierra Consulting Group, a team of professionals dedicated to developing an Information Centric Office (an environment where information is at the hub of all decision making). Specifically, Sierra involves itself in developing information-capturing technology, data warehousing, business intelligence technology, and facilitating the implementation and support of the entire process.

The 5 Environments

This book is divided into two parts. In Part One we present a framework for analyzing the key elements and processes required to implement a decision support system. The framework is based on the concept of five environments, which we will describe and define in detail. We discuss the key issues that designers and developers need to consider in each environment, present some of the best practices that we are aware of for dealing with those issues, and close with a description of the data warehouse lifecycle. Part Two will focus on how to implement the five environments using Microsoft technology.

Decision Support Architectures

Establishing Competitive Advantage

It has become axiomatic that companies are competing in a fast-paced market environment. Today's business environment features a number of powerful agents that are driving rapid changes. Global competition has created a need to manage product, marketing, and sales issues on a worldwide basis. The competitive landscape is constantly shifting and changing due to mergers, acquisitions, and the emergence of new players. Users are becoming much more sophisticated and diverse in their requirements and have increasingly higher expectations. Technology is creating new opportunities, challenges, and venues, such as the Internet, for addressing the needs of end users, customers, suppliers, distributors, and others in the corporate value chain.

To compete in the complex, shifting maelstrom that makes up the global marketplace, companies need to work smarter, not harder. Organizations are undertaking numerous information technology (IT) initiatives to improve their competitiveness, such as implementing enterprise resource planning (ERP) packages, and widely deploying client/server and Internet technologies.

Decision support software (DSS) is an increasingly important enabling technology that companies are adopting for competitive advantage. Decision support software systems are used to bring timely, up-to-date information to managers throughout the organization with the goal of enabling them to make faster, better decisions on behalf of the business.

Why Decision Support?

A DSS system is designed to help an organization answer the six questions that consume the attention of all managers: who, what, when, where, why, and how? Different managers in different industries have different detailed versions of these questions, but some universal examples of these questions that are of vital concern to managers include:

- Who are our customers? Which customer base are we missing?
- What are they buying from us? From our competition? What should we be selling to them that we aren't? What unmet needs do they have that we are capable of fulfilling?
- When and where are they buying?
- Why do they buy our products or our competitors products? Why do they respond to certain marketing initiatives and not others?
- How do we reach our customers and establish value-added relationships with them? How do we reach our new prospects? How do we find out who our best customers are and how to keep them? How are customers and prospects serviced—by us and our competition? How do they perceive our company, our competitors, and our industry?

These are the questions that keep senior executives and managers up at night. By answering these questions, they can better understand how to differentiate their companies and products from the plethora of competing products and offerings available in the marketplace.

A Brief History of Decision Support

Decision support is the delivery of information to end users who require data for making business decisions. This simple requirement has spawned a multibillion-dollar industry and has resulted in a significant restructuring of the computer industry. Even the major ERP vendors, such as SAP, PeopleSoft, J.D. Edwards, and Baan, have all recognized the need to provide products and services that enable end users to analyze business information for the purposes of making decisions and effecting changes in their organizations.

Originally, companies created management reports, which were delivered on reams of green-bar paper. Over time, however, it became apparent that this means of delivering management information to end users was insufficient for several reasons.

The process of creating a report in a traditional third-generation language (3GL) environment is complex and cumbersome. A programmer had to work with a user and try to understand the data the user needed and define the appropriate report format—headers, footers, control breaks, and so on. Then the programmer had to design, code, and test the report. If the user was lucky, it would be available in a few days, but in most instances this process typically took weeks, even months.

The lengthy process for defining and programming a report made it impossible for the user to participate in an iterative feedback loop with the programmer. No mechanism existed to develop ad hoc reports easily and quickly that address new business conditions or opportunities, so often the data was stale by the time it reached the user. Also, if a report was defined to meet the needs of one category of user such as marketing, another category, like sales support, may want a slightly different variant, which required another design, develop, debug loop for each instance of additional reports. Finally, users were typically only able to obtain reports that accessed data on a single system. Few programmers had the time or the expertise to consolidate data from multiple systems in a single report.

The cumbersome process for report development is flowcharted in Figure 1.1.

Some companies attempted to get around this problem by creating Executive Information Systems (EIS) which were designed to support top management with automated decision support. However, the cost, complexity, and inflexibility of these systems reduced their overall effectiveness and made them useful only for senior managers. Others in the company, such as product or production managers, didn't have access to these systems and were unable to benefit from the data they contained.

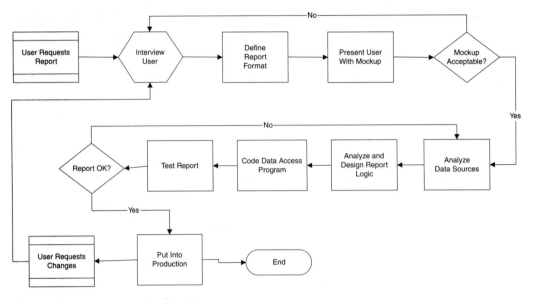

Figure 1.1 Report creation flowchart.

With the advent of client/server technology in the late 1980s, new tools appeared that were designed to allow end users to create their own reports. However, it quickly became apparent that these tools had serious limitations. They required that the user learn the data structures of the database that contained the information they required. Many business users had neither the inclination nor the time to learn all about relational databases and SQL. The users had to invest in a steep learning curve to understand the tool itself.

IT also discovered that these tools had the ability to create what is known as the query from hell. As a result of opening up access to online transaction processing (OLTP) databases, end users began to create queries without understanding the performance implications of some of the business questions that they asked. A simple query to analyze the relationship between customers and products could result in a massive table scan and multi-way table join. This often resulted in a major performance drain on the OLTP system, with unacceptable effects on response time for online, interactive users.

One other effort that many companies tried was to make copies of the OLTP databases and make them available to users for queries. However, these solutions still failed to provide a good decision support solution because the database structures were not designed with decision support queries in mind, nor could the users access data that was not in the original source database.

As a result of this, companies began to deploy specialized databases that were designed to enable users to analyze information without impacting production users. One category of databases became the data warehouse, while the second became the online analytical processing (OLAP) database.

The Data Warehouse

The data warehouse is intended to address many of the shortcomings of the transaction processing systems when applied to decision support. (See Table 1.1.) Microsoft's database for data warehousing is SQL Server. A data warehouse provides several significant advantages for a company struggling to provide its business users with an effective decision support solution.

First, a data warehouse provides a common platform for consolidating information stored in heterogeneous business systems. This is a crucial feature in a world where companies have a wide variety of systems developed internally and acquired from vendors. The ability to consolidate data

Table 1.1   Transaction Processing versus Decision Support Databases

DATABASE ATTRIBUTE	TRANSACTION PROCESSING SYSTEMS	DECISION SUPPORT SYSTEMS
Data Structure Optimization	Normalized, optimized for rapid access and update	Redundant, optimized for query and analysis
Data Volume	Relatively small	Large to huge
Data Timeliness	Current state of the business	Historical record
Transaction Load	Many, small (200 KB) transactions	Fewer, large (multiple MB) queries
Performance Requirements	Rapid response to transactions	Intermediate, depending on query complexity
Changes, Adds, Deletes	Done in place	Create new record

Data Warehouse Business Driver

A large teaching hospital in a major metropolitan area needed to consolidate patient billing information from its various autonomous departments, such as radiology and pediatrics. These departmental solutions were purchased individually, so the various departments used different practice management systems, each with its own patient billing and reporting functions. A data warehouse enabled the enterprise to improve the management of its outstanding receivables and improve cash flow.

from multiple platforms, regardless of operating system, database, or programming language, is a major improvement in decision support. By consolidating data into a data warehouse, companies can—often for the first time—gain a deeper understanding of the relationship between various business functions such as accounting and customer service.

The second key advantage of a data warehouse is that it is optimized for decision support. The data structures of most OLTP applications are not designed to meet the requirements of high performance decision support. In fact, the exact opposite is often the reality. Most databases designed for transaction processing have difficulty meeting the needs of users who ask questions such as, "Who were my top 50 customers in the Northeast region last quarter, and how much did their business grow from the same period the previous year?" A data warehouse, or multi-dimensional database, can be structured to respond efficiently to these types of questions with reasonable performance.

Another important feature of the data warehouse is that it is a historical record. Most transaction processing systems capture the current state of the business. Many organizations enhance transaction-processing performance by purging data at regular intervals and reorganizing the database to reduce disk-head movement. The purged data disappears into offline storage media, such as tape libraries, often never to be seen again. Many organizations recognize that this historical information is extremely valuable, and use data warehousing to capture its value.

The data warehouse contains longitudinal data. This means that the DSS database doesn't delete, purge, or update records. For example, if a customer moves, an OLTP database would update the customer record with the current address in place, overwriting the old address of a customer. A DSS database, on the other hand, would keep both the old and current address. This would enable an analyst, such as a marketing manager, to understand the movement of customers over time.

The other related side effect is that a data warehouse is a time-oriented database. Many of the inquiries that end users submit to the data warehouse are related, in one form or another, to the movement of information—customers, products, markets—over time.

A Decision Support System Architecture

When an organization creates a decision-support database, it typically consists of more than simply a data warehouse. Put another way, the data warehouse is the foundation for a decision support system. Companies often make the mistake of assuming that a data warehouse is a single entity and fail to realize that a decision support system requires more than a simple data warehouse.

At the same time, companies must also understand that data warehousing is a process, not a thing. We discuss the data warehouse lifecycle and process in greater detail in Chapter 7.

An end-to-end decision support solution requires a data warehouse architecture that provides services that address the needs of businesses in five environments, as outlined in Table 1.2.

Table 1.2   Five Decision Support Environments

ENVIRONMENT	PURPOSE
Source	Contains data sources and systems responsible for preparing the data for the data warehouse.
Storage	Contains decision support databases such as relational databases, multi-dimensional cubes, or data marts that stage engines and report servers.
Desktop	Contains end-user reporting tools, query and analysis tools, data mining tools, and decision support applications.
Design and Development	Contains software used to design and implement the software in the Source, Storage, and Desktop environments.
Operations and Management	Contains software used to manage performance, security, capacity planning, data integrity and reliability, and other operational functions.

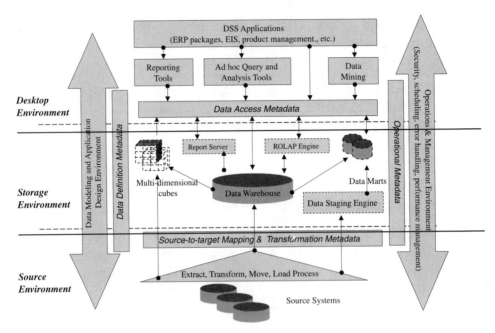

Figure 1.2 Decision support system architecture.
(Source: Hurwitz Group)

The next five chapters describe these environments, which are illustrated in Figure 1.2, in more detail.

The Role of OLAP

OLAP technology is designed to make it easier for users to query and analyze the data, whether it's stored in a data warehouse or a data mart. An OLAP database is not a data warehouse. An OLAP database is a specialized data store that has a hierarchical or multi-dimensional structure typically referred to as a *cube*. This is in sharp contrast with the structure of a relational DBMS, which organizes its tables into columns (fields) and rows (records).

OLAP databases have a number of advantages over relational databases. The hierarchical, multidimensional structure of an OLAP database makes it easier for users to navigate the data. Relational databases, particularly those that are designed for high performance transaction processing, typically have a much more complex structure, which makes it difficult for the end user to analyze the data. The star schema was designed for relational databases to simplify navigation of a relational decision support database.

Because OLAP databases have a multi-dimensional structure, they store summary (or aggregate) information at higher levels in the hierarchy. This concept, which is explained in greater depth in Chapter 3, enables the OLAP databases to provide fast response time. Many business users are interested in analyzing summary data like orange juice sales in the Northeast region during the third calendar quarter, and the OLAP environment summarizes much of the data when the database is updated. In addition, OLAP tools typically have powerful calculation engines to provide additional business statistics, such as standard deviation, mean, maximum, minimum, along with profit and cost analysis, comparisons between dimensions such as sales compared to budget, or to same-store sales the prior year, and so forth.

The Role of Metadata

Metadata is the glue that binds the five environments together into a coherent, intelligible system. The role of metadata and the various categories of metadata are the subject of some heated debate in the data warehouse world. In this book we discuss metadata in terms of its role in the five environments listed in Table 1.2.

Source Environment Metadata

In the source environment the major role of metadata includes descriptive information and specifications for source databases, data transformation, and consolidation.

Source specifications include items such as COBOL copybooks, relational database schemas, proprietary or nonrelational database schemas, and flat file—both fixed and variable-length—formats. Descriptive information includes data security attributes, access information such as usernames and passwords, network access paths, and update and extraction schedules.

Source environment metadata also includes extraction and transformation logic, such as the mapping of an input field into a modified value required for an output field. Data transformation includes name and address validation and verification, as well as other data cleaning/data quality processes. If fields from heterogeneous databases are consolidated, this information is captured in the metadata that describes this process. Finally, this metadata describes the source-to-target mapping between the source database(s) and the target database(s). As we will see, this mapping can be one-to-one, many-to-one, one-to-many, or many-to-many.

Storage Environment Metadata

The metadata in the storage environment describes the structure and schemas of the storage database. In a relational data warehouse, this metadata is contained in the relational DBMS data dictionary, where it describes database, table, and field attributes. Some of these attributes include logical database information, such as primary key/foreign key relationships and security restrictions. Other attributes are more physical, such as table partitions, column data type, and length. Multidimensional OLAP databases contain much of this same information but also describe the hierarchical relationships between the data levels as well as aggregation and calculation formulas.

Desktop Environment Metadata

The metadata in the desktop environment is mainly concerned with enabling the end user to locate the data required for query and analysis. This metadata layer maps business terms to specific data elements, enabling a user to develop a query using a tool such as English Query, which can generate code that a database, such as SQL Server, can interpret correctly.

In some instances, the end user requires information about the sources for the data in the decision support database, how the data was transformed or modified for the decision support environment, and when the most recent update occurred. This information can be valuable for assessing the reliability and timeliness of the data in question.

Design and Development Metadata

As you can see in Figure 1.2, the design and development environment spans the prior three environments. Thus, developers working in the source, storage, and desktop environments need to be able to analyze, develop, and deploy metadata that is used in those three environments.

Unfortunately, no one tool can be used to facilitate this task; the developer must use the appropriate tools for each environment to create the metadata for that environment. Thus, the source environment metadata is created using the tool that is used to extract data from a source system and run it through the transformation process. In the Microsoft world, this metadata is managed by Data Transformation Services (DTS), which is part of the SQL Server 7 product. The DTS transformation data is stored in the Microsoft Repository.

Likewise, in the storage environment, the developer is concerned with creating the metadata used to design the decision support databases, which can be relational, multi-dimensional, or some combination of both. In addition, if the developer creates a report server, metadata requirements are necessary for producing reports and making them available to users.

Finally, in the desktop environment, the developer is concerned with presenting the end user with a business-oriented description of the database. This requires mapping database structures to business terms, such as customer, product, sales channel, and so on. It also requires, in many instances, defining calculations that are important to users, such as profit. While the concept of profit is well understood—profit equals revenue minus costs—companies and industries have different business rules for calculating profit, because they have different rules for identifying how costs are allocated. For example, a business manager may need to analyze profit by different dimensions, such as profit by customer, profit by product, profit by geography, profit by channel, and so on. These derived measures need to be clearly defined and implemented in the decision support metadata architecture.

Operations and Maintenance Metadata

Once the decision support system has been implemented and put into production, operations and maintenance personnel must tend to the care and feeding of the system. These individuals are responsible for ensuring that the ETML process (see Chapter 3) completes the process of moving data to the decision support database without interruption or error. The scheduling and coordination of these activities can be extremely complex, particularly in a large, mission-critical production environment, and solid scheduling and coordination metadata can be extremely helpful.

Operations personnel, such as database administrators, must concern themselves with the overall performance of the system. They need to collect and analyze data about query complexity, number of queries, overall system throughput, and end-user response time. They must define and manage security processes and procedures and also concern themselves with system issues, such as security breaches and backup/ recovery processes and procedures. These data are all described in some form of metadata.

Microsoft Data Warehouse Framework

In this book we'll discuss how to build a distributed, enterprise-wide set of federated decision support databases, based on the Microsoft data warehouse framework. (See Figure 1.3.) The Microsoft data warehouse framework consists of a set of products and services designed to provide support for the end-to-end process of building distributed data marts, including OLAP cubes. The framework defines a set of components used to create an architecture for defining, building, and managing distributed data warehouses and data marts. This architecture is based on the NT operating system, running on either Intel or Alpha processors. The major components of the framework are shown in Table 1.3 and Figure 1.3.

Table 1.3   Microsoft Framework Components and Roles

COMPONENT	ROLE
Repository	Metadata and database schema, DTS packages
SQL Server 7	Relational decision support database
SQL Server 7 OLAP Services	Multi-dimensional database for decision support
Data Transformation Services	Data consolidation and transformation
Universal Data Access	OLE DB, OLE DB for OLAP, and ActiveX Data Objects (ADO) provide access to a variety of data sources, including Decision Support Services.
Microsoft Management Console	Scheduling, security, event management
English Query, Excel, Access, third-party tools	Desktop data query and analysis

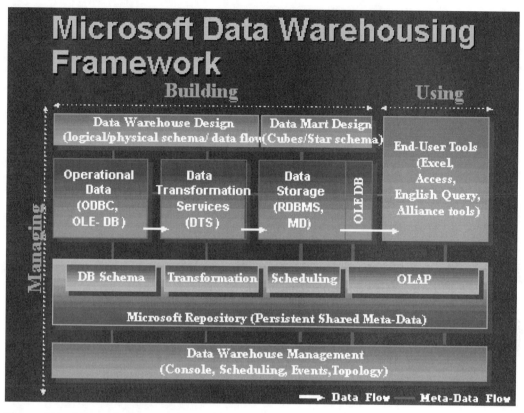

Figure 1.3   Microsoft data warehouse framework.

In the following chapters, we explore the five environments and their association to the Microsoft Framework, and describe the process for building a distributed, enterprise-wide decision support system using the Microsoft framework products. For areas in which Microsoft lacks products or services, we either describe the products available from third-party vendors, or we outline the requirements for products so you can identify the attributes of compatible products.

2

The Source Environment

A decision support system must obtain data from one or more source systems. This essential task is performed by designing and implementing a data extract, transform, move, and load (ETML) process. This process is critical to the success of any DSS database, whether it's an enterprise-wide data warehouse, a departmental data mart, or a multi-dimensional OLAP cube.

Companies that build data warehouses and other decision support systems find that the ETML process is one of the most complex phases of the data warehouse lifecycle. This is because of two factors. One is the variety of source systems and databases that must be accessed. The other is the variety of transformation and data quality issues that must be addressed to prepare the data for the data warehouse.

Designers and developers need to plan for this process as carefully as they plan for other parts of the data warehouse lifecycle. If the ETML process is not carefully designed and implemented, the result will be a decision support system that doesn't meet the needs of end users, either because the right data isn't in the warehouse or because the data is inconsistent with the other systems to which users have access. If users find the warehouse data isn't consistent with the sources they know and trust they won't accept the warehouse.

Sources include both internal and external data and systems. Commonly used internal source systems include functional systems, such as accounting, human resources, manufacturing management, procurement, order processing, customer service, help desk, shipping and logistics, and others. Packaged applications, particularly ERP packages, such as SAP R/3, PeopleSoft, and Baan, are an increasingly popular source for decision support systems. External data sources include data in the public domain such as government statistics, purchased data such as point-of-sale data provided by market analyst organizations, or data supplied by business partners such as inventory management systems for suppliers or customers.

Many companies implement the ETML process using customized application software. While this may be a reasonable solution for a relatively simple, single source-to-target environment, when multiple sources are used to populate multiple targets, the best recourse is to use a tool. In some cases in which specialized processing is required, multiple tools may be needed.

ETML Tool Architectures

Two major categories of tools—code generators and transformation engines—are available on the market. IT managers who build an ETML solution need to make a careful assessment regarding whether they are better served by a code generation package or an engine-based package. Developers need to assess the flexibility of the tool, and its ability to support complex, multi-stage transformation logic. The tool should have a developer-friendly user interface. The developer also needs to consider the variety of sources that the tool can access, including non-relational, mainframe-based legacy data sources. IT managers need to asses operational issues such as the degree of flexibility the tool provides for scheduling batch runs, its ability to detect and manage runtime errors, and how the process can be restarted in the event of a failure. A sophisticated tool will have support for checkpoints that enable the system operator to restart a failed job at the last checkpoint, rather than running the entire job again.

Code generation tools are often selected when the source system is a mainframe with COBOL data files or non-relational databases, such as Adabas or IMS. Newer generations of these tools are capable of generating multiple languages, including C/C++, Adabas, ABAP4 for SAP R/3 sources, and Java.

In the code generation environment, the transformation logic is typically executed on the host platform as part of the generated application logic, and the data is then moved to the target platform. In some cases, the environment may require multi-step transformations and data merges.

Code generators are typically more flexible in terms of how they are configured. They can also access a wider variety of legacy data sources natively. This greater flexibility is offset by the need to employ developers with higher levels of expertise and training to design and develop the transformation process.

The engine-based tools rely on TCP/IP sockets to establish a connection to the source system and then use SQL to extract data from the source databases. If the source database does not have native support for SQL, an ODBC driver can be used. In situations in which neither SQL nor ODBC is available the system administrator may need to write a specialized routine using a 3GL that will dump the required data into a flat file that the engine can retrieve. The engine systems perform most manipulations on the engine itself, using a staging area, before forwarding the data to the target machine(s).

Engines are usually easier to work with and have a richer set of predefined functions and capabilities, but they are not as flexible in terms of their legacy data access. Most rely on third-party products to access non-relational legacy data.

As we mentioned in Chapter 1, Data Transformation Services (DTS), Microsoft's data transformation software, is an engine-based data transformation and movement tool. It uses OLE DB to access source data on platforms with support for OLE DB or ODBC, and relies on gateways such as SNA Gateway to interface with legacy mainframe systems. DTS is discussed in greater detail in Chapter 9.

The ETML Process

The ETML design and development process consists of

- Capturing source target definitions for platforms, operating systems, data files or databases, and interfaces

- Defining and coding transformation workflow and logic, which includes algorithms for data quality, validation, and verification

- Mapping the transformed data to the target DSS databases

As the software is moved into production, integration with scheduling and application packages becomes important.

A modern graphical user interface (GUI) is a requirement for most shops, and support for a component-based application architecture encourages reusable, modular development processes. The tool should provide a user-friendly interface to its metadata repository along with basic configuration management controls if the software is developed in a team environment. Finally, sophisticated testing and error-checking features will help ensure a solid design and validate the control and transformation logic.

If the tool is a code-generation product, it should provide seamless, transparent code-module movement and deployment features that will make it easy for the developer to install the code on the target platform.

Data mapping is facilitated by the tool's ability to generate the data definition language (DDL) code for relational targets. If the target database is a multi-dimensional database (MDD), the tool should support the MDD product's metadata catalog so that data can be easily mapped to the appropriate structures.

Data Extraction

The first thing the software needs to do is to extract data from the source systems. (See Figure 2.1.) The plural tense is used here because it is relatively rare for a DSS database of any consequence to be populated from a single source. The product needs to be able to retrieve data from hardware environments, operating systems, file systems, and databases. Many of the legacy databases aren't relational, so the software must be able to understand COBOL files, IMS or VSAM files, as well as Progress, Pick, Adabas, M/Mumps, and other non-relational database formats. Some tools depend on the system administrator to run a batch job that moves data into a flat file for the tool to pick up, but it is preferable for the tool itself to extract the data in a single pass.

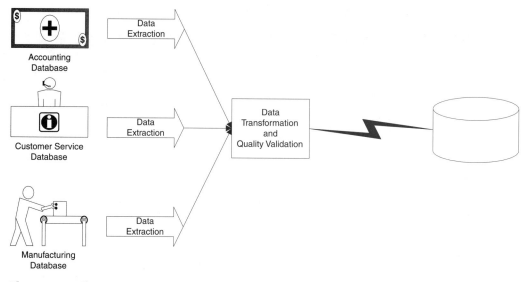

Figure 2.1   The ETML process.

Change Data Capture

An important feature to look for in the software is *change data capture (CDC)*. CDC is the ability to incrementally extract changed data. As databases change, the tool should provide a mechanism to extract the incremental data that changed since the last extraction run. Otherwise the data warehouse will need to be rebuilt from scratch every time it is refreshed. This can have a significant impact on the source systems and the network, and requires the data warehouse to be offline for a considerable period of time.

Change data capture can be implemented using a variety of techniques as shown in Table 2.1. One technique is to read database transaction log files that require that the extract/read process must be synchronized with the closing and opening of transaction log files. Also, the job that reads the log files must treat deletes as a separate case, since the fact that a database record has been deleted from a transaction database doesn't necessarily mean it is desirable to delete it from the decision support database. If the data warehouse is populated from multiple databases, the synchronization may need to occur simultaneously on all of the affected systems.

Table 2.1   Change Data Capture Approaches

APPROACH	PROS	CONS
Read database transaction logs	• Captures all changes—adds, deletes, updates—logged by the database • Doesn't require application changes • Easy to implement	• Deletes must be filtered, otherwise they are applied to data warehouse • Cannot easily capture changes in distributed database environment • Log file open/close must be synchronized with extract jobs
Application writes changes to change file	• Ensures all logical transactions are captured • Change file can be customized to meet extract job requirements	• Requires changes to application • Data warehouse may require data changes that the application doesn't write to the change file
Scan database for timestamps	• Captures all changes marked by time-stamp • Doesn't require changes to application if time-stamps are already implemented	• Extract software must keep track of start/stop of extract runs • May require changes to application or creation of database trigger • Consumes database space • Different databases have different time formats, extract code will need to reformat to decision support database format • Only captures most recent update • May require expensive full table scan with every run
Compare database snapshots	• Doesn't require changes to applications • Minimal synchronization required	• Processing time and resources required to compare two large databases • Disk space requirements
Data Replication	• Captures all data changes • Works with multiple databases • Doesn't require application changes	• May require special logic to filter deletes • Storage requirements of replicated database

A related approach is for the application to write changes directly to a change file (as opposed to a database transaction log file) that can be read by the change-data-capture routine. This requires changes to the application code, which may not be feasible in a turnkey environment. Also, the changes to the application must be coordinated with the data requirements of the decision support database. If the database developer decides additional data is required, the application may need to be changed multiple times.

A variant on this theme is to create a database trigger or stored procedure that writes out incremental changes to a change file. Both these methods can have a significant impact on database performance because of the extra CPU and I/O processing involved.

Another CDC technique is to scan the source database for timestamps. This method requires the ETML tool to remember when it last performed an extract so it can skip past records that have been read. Scanning for timestamps also requires that the application that populates the source database put a timestamp in the database as part of its transaction processing. This can be done with either application logic or a post-processing database trigger. This technique may miss changes if the same record has been updated multiple times since the most recent extraction is run or if the record has been deleted. Scanning can also represent a significant load on the source database, and scanning a large database may require considerable time. This overhead can be reduced if the timestamp column is indexed. The designer must carefully consider the processing, computer resources, and time requirements of this approach, particularly if the source database becomes very large. Finally, if multiple source databases are scanned using this technique, the database designer needs to take into account the various time formats used by different database vendors. Differing time formats must be restructured into the native format for the target database if time-related data is used, which is often the case with decision support databases.

A fourth way to implement CDC is to perform a differential comparison between two or more copies of the database that were saved at different times—a method that is also called a *snapshot differential*. This obviously requires close scheduling coordination between the programs responsible for the database snapshot and the ETML tool. Another consideration is the disk space required to store two complete copies of the database. Referential integrity may also be an issue if a logical record spans two or more physical databases and the different databases are not snapshot at the same time.

A final approach is to use a replication tool to capture changes to a database as they occur and pass them on to another database. Most companies use replication as a way of distributing data for higher performance and availability, but this information can also be used to capture incremental data changes. This approach is similar to the database log file approach in that it requires the extraction process to filter out deletes.

Transform

The transformation process prepares the data for the target database. This can be as simple as changing a gender field from 1 to M or as complex as writing a program in a procedural or nonprocedural language. In some instances a multi-step transformation process is required, with the output of one stage being the input for the next stage.

The transformation product should provide the developer with a rich set of built-in transformation functions, such as string, math, lookup, and time-related functions. It should provide a programmable scripting environment, preferably using a standard, nonproprietary language. Another related feature is the ability to call external code modules. Developers may also consider using specialized products for address verification or detailed data cleansing. Just think about the many ways a name can appear in a database record. The tool that developers select should be able to perform these functions or have the ability to interoperate with a tool that does.

An important architectural consideration is the transformation processing location. Some products, primarily the code generation tools, execute transformation logic on the host platform, while others move it to an intermediate staging area for further processing. The important thing to consider is how easy it is to move transformation logic to various platforms to maximize the overall throughput and management of the process.

The developer also needs to consider the process of handling data errors. We are all aware of fields that should never be NULL but which are, or address fields that contain invalid or non-existent addresses. The ETML tool developer should consider all the assorted and sundry ways errors can creep into the source data and he or she should devise algorithms to handle the most commonly encountered ones. The alternative, of course, is to simply dump the erroneous data into a holding file, along with the appropriate error message, and let a human being determine how to fix it.

The data transformation logic should be readily accessible to end users who need to know where the data came from and what was done to it to prepare it for the warehouse. This implies either a metadata navigation tool supplied by the vendor or a metadata repository with public APIs that are supported by the desktop tools that the organization deploys.

Data Movement

Data must be moved, preferably as fast as possible and with as little disruption as possible, to the mission-critical production environment. Bulk data movement is preferable to dribbling data across the wire one record at a time, unless the DSS database is updated with real-time data feeds. The movement of large volumes of data may cause significant network congestion, so one thing that developers need to do is coordinate with the network management team to ensure that the network configuration is adequate. Often a network or router upgrade may be required, or the network topology will need to be modified to reduce the impact of the movement process from the rest of the network.

It is crucial to consider encryption and other security measures, such as authorization and authentication, if data moves across an insecure or public network. For example, if the vendor only supports ftp, critical corporate secrets may be transmitted in the clear. Also, if the data resides on a mainframe, look for support for high-speed, mainframe-class connectivity.

Data Load

Once the data is on the target machine, it must undergo a preparatory process before it's loaded. Again, for high performance, look for bulk loader support. The faster that data can be stuffed into the data warehouse, the better. The load process may include pre-processing, such as data sorting, which is typically best done outside the database. In addition, developers should factor in time for post-processing activities, such as building indexes and aggregate tables. Look for a platform that won't require the database administrator (DBA) to completely rebuild database indexes every time the database is updated. The DBA also needs to factor in the time to ensure the database is functionally ready for end-user access, which is usually done by running a logical integrity checker routine.

Management

The ETML process is put into production after the code extraction and transformation logic have been defined and tested, the target databases are available, and the production schedule has been established. The ETML runtime environment should support the enterprises' existing production cycles, processes, procedures, and scheduling management software, if at all possible. Systems administrators should be able to effect seamless integration of the new ETML scheduling software into their pre-existing production environment.

The ETML production system must provide a mechanism for the system administrator to start, monitor, stop, pause, abort, or restart the ETML process. It should have sophisticated functions for error detection and management. If a transformation fails, or the source data is inconsistent like a NULL field was detected that should have data, the administrator should have a variety of options from which to choose. These could include stopping the run, logging the error, processing the data using an alternative code path, inserting a default value, and so forth. The ability to send a message to an operational specialist by way of pager or email is desirable in a lights-out environment.

The tool should enable the administrator to analyze performance data and manage overall throughput by moving transformation logic to the most appropriate platform. The ability to load balance the ETML workflow manually is essential for a large production shop, while automatic load balancing is a plus.

The ETML production environment should also honor all corporate security policies that have been implemented on both the source and target system, as well as provide for secure transmission of data in a distributed environment.

Developers require ETML tools that are flexible, open, and that interface with their source and target systems. Flexible means that the ETML process can be easily configured and modified as new source/target systems become available. It also means that the developer should be able to use internal functions, create new functions, or call out to pre-existing code using standard APIs. Openness refers to interoperability with other tools that are used in different phases of the data warehouse life cycle, such as query and analysis, or application design tools. The tool should publish APIs and support the leading metadata standards, such as the Metadata Coalition MDIS standard, or emerging standards, such as the upcoming Microsoft Repository. Ideally, the tool is well integrated with a suite of tools, all using a common metadata repository.

ETML Development Process

Once an organization has selected the appropriate set of tools to implement its ETML process, it enters a development process that is similar in many respects to database integration processes.

The development process consists of several steps.

1. Identify source databases and fields, select candidate data for the decision support database(s), and capture source metadata.
2. Model target data structures.
3. Build source-to-target data mappings.
4. Analyze and define data transformation and data quality verification logic.
5. Select data transformation platform(s).
6. Test and debug data extract, transform, move, and load logic.
7. Define and implement production-scheduling process.
8. Document the transformation process and train operations staff.

Step 1: Identify Source Data and Metadata

Important source metadata includes data attributes (primarily type and length—fixed or variable), legal values, out-of-bound values, and relationships between various data elements. (See Table 2.2.) The map of data relationships is particularly important in two instances. The first is when a primary key/foreign key relationship exists between two tables in the database. The decision support designer needs to ensure that referential integrity is preserved when these data elements are moved to

Table 2.2   Source Metadata Examples

METADATA	EXAMPLES
Attributes	Type = char, int, tinyint, real, BLOB
	Length = fixed number of characters, variable (maximum allowed length)
Legal values	Sex = M, F, U
	Age = >1 yr., <110 yr.
Out-of-bound values	Balance > $10,000,000 or Balance < $0.00
	Serum Potassium > 10 MEq/L
	NULL in non-NULL field
Relationships	`Customer_id` in Accounting system is functional equivalent to `Client_Number` in customer support system. (Note these two data items may have very different attributes and valid values.)
	Individual customer record is related to a household record.

the target decision support database. The second instance is when two or more data elements from heterogeneous, previously disconnected systems are brought together.

An example can be the relationship between customer accounting data—invoice and payment records—from the finance department and customer satisfaction data—customer support and service calls—from the service department. In this instance, referential integrity at the database level is not a constraint; in the classic sense, however, it is a business constraint because the combined data must be consistent and make sense to the end user.

Heterogeneous Sources

Capturing data and metadata definitions from disparate, heterogeneous source systems creates a number of special problems that are not encountered in the typical application or database development environment.

Often the platform that hosts the source data is not directly accessible through standard interfaces or tools. Inaccessibility can manifest itself in a number of ways. The host platform may be a turnkey system, without any published APIs or report writer capabilities. These bounded applications, typically provided by an independent software vendor (ISV), are not usually designed to support access through any means except the turnkey application itself. If the application doesn't include a report writer or query engine, data extract will not be possible via the application. On some platforms the database may have published APIs or support SQL, but the data structures are regarded by the vendor as proprietary and confidential. In this case, the vendor may refuse to supply a data dictionary or data map to customers.

Sometimes no easy mechanism exists for extracting the data to a common medium. Data can be transferred either via a network or via sneakernet. In the case of a network, if both machines are online, and both support the same network transport protocol, such as ftp, then the data can be transferred. Network security, availability, and bandwidth are factors that must be considered when designing the process of moving the data.

If there is no common network, the data must be transferred either on diskette or tape. Given the wide variety of media available in the typical IT environment, this can be a serious problem.

Access to source data on an IBM mainframe environment can also be complicated. Third-party data extraction tools are available to obtain data from IBM mainframe databases—principally DB2, IMS, VSAM and IDMS—but many shops implement a gateway for data access and write customized COBOL code to extract the data to a flat file, where it is available for transfer.

Data Access Nightmare

One of the authors worked on designing a technical architecture for a planned decision support system in which the source systems, which were at various locations on an urban campus, were not on a common network. They included two VAXs with reel-to-reel tape—one running M/MUMPS databases, the other hosting a Model 204 database, a PC running SCO Unix which supported tar on 5¼" diskettes, an AS/400 running DB/400 with 8" floppies, and a Novell file server with DAT tape cartridges. The target system was a Sun machine running Solaris with 8 mm tape cartridges.

The incompatible media made it impossible to physically move the data from the various sources to the target. The site was forced to invest in a substantial expansion of its internal network to accommodate the systems at their various locations.

Another consideration is the variety of data formats on heterogeneous source systems. Date and time fields are a particular problem because no commonly accepted standard exists for formatting chronological data. Special consideration must be given to understanding the native date/time formats of the source systems and also to the work needed to convert them to a common format that will be acceptable to the target databases.

Step 2: Model Target Data Structures

The second step in the development process is defining the data structures for the target database(s). This process, known as *data modeling*, must be completed in order to understand where the data is going to go. In the case of a relational DBMS, modeling consists of defining three levels of database structure—database, table, and column. In the case of a multi-dimensional database, modeling consists of defining database names, array names, and levels. In both cases, modeling also consists of determining required field values, relationships, aggregates, calculations, and indexes.

Modeling Relational Databases

Three variants of database schemas are used for relational DBMS: entity-relation schemas or third normal (3NF), star schemas, and snowflake schemas. These models are discussed in greater detail in Chapter 3.

The *entity-relation schema* is the one most database designers are familiar with. The goal of a traditional entity-relation schema is to eliminate data redundancy and to maintain referential integrity in a high-performance, transaction-processing environment. Many designers use an entity-relation schema to implement a data warehouse database if the database is directly queried by end users. This is because the entity-relation structure provides a high degree of performance while conserving disk space. However, these advantages are offset by the complexity of the entity-relation structure, and the increased difficulty of providing end users with a view of the database that is easy for them to navigate.

Ease of navigation is the primary benefit of implementing a *star schema*. The star schema has a core fact table surrounded by multiple dimensional tables, hence the term *star*. The star provides users with a multi-dimensional view of a relational database, and emulates much of the navigational structure of an OLAP database.

Some decision support databases have a structure that is too complex to model with a star. In this situation, modelers often elect to design a *snowflake*. In a snowflake schema model, additional dimensional tables are linked to the primary dimensional tables in the star. Another variant of the snowflake includes multiple fact tables.

In all three schemas, the data modeler relies on primary key/foreign key relations to provide the mechanism for the user (or a SQL generation tool) to navigate the tables.

Modeling Multi-dimensional Databases

Modeling a multi-dimensional target database is very different then modeling a relational DBMS. Whereas the relational DBMS has an underlying structure—tables with rows and columns—a multi-dimensional database is relatively unstructured. An array is the closest thing to a logical structure that a multi-dimensional database possesses. Unlike the relational logic underlying relational databases, multi-dimensional databases don't have a mathematical calculus that defines the logic for managing the array structures.

Unfortunately, none of the current commercial tools can model both relational and multi-dimensional databases, so the developer is left to select discrete tools for this process. In the Microsoft environment, the multi-dimensional database modeled is the SQL Server OLAP Services database, which is sourced by the SQL Server relational database. Microsoft does provide a Cube Wizard and a Cube Designer to facilitate the modeling and definition of an SQL Server OLAP Services cube.

SQL Server is also *star-aware*, which means it can be implemented using a star schema model. Designing and implementing a SQL Server OLAP Services database is discussed in greater detail in Chapters 8 and 9.

Step 3: Build Source-to-Target Data Mappings

The third step in the process is to map the source data to the target data. Two levels of source-to-target data mappings are inherent in the Microsoft decision support database environment. One level is from source (transaction) system to the SQL Server data warehouse. The second

Table 2.3 Source-to-Target Mapping Types

MAPPING CATEGORY	MAPPING MATRIX	EXPLANATION
Linear	One-to-one mapping	Each source data field is mapped to one, and only one, target data field.
Fan-out	One-to-many mapping	Each source data field is mapped to multiple target data fields or target databases.
Consolidate	Many-to-one mapping	Multiple source data fields are mapped to a single target data field.
Multi-linear	Many-to-many mapping	Multiple source data fields are mapped to multiple target data fields or target databases.

level is from the data warehouse to one or more SQL Server OLAP Services cubes.

Four categories of source-to-target mappings exist and need to be considered. They are shown in Table 2.3.

In any complex decision support environment, a variety of mappings must be identified and managed for each stage of the data movement between the data sources and final targets. For example, customer source data, such as customer purchases from a sales database, credit status from an accounting database, and satisfaction measures from a customer-service database may be consolidated into a single customer record in the data warehouse. This represents a many-to-one mapping. However, if the data is required for two data marts—one for customer profitability analysis, and one for product profitability—the mapping matrix becomes multi-linear.

Step 4: Define Data Transformation and Data Quality Logic

Defining the data transformation logic is the fourth step in the ETML process. Data transformation, as discussed previously, can be very simple or extremely complex depending on the needs of the system. The goal of the data transformation software is to modify the incoming data fields to make them consistent and acceptable to the target database. Consistency is particularly important when data from multiple systems is being consolidated. The data consistency effort that is part of the data warehousing process is often the first time the corporation has had data with a uniform format available for analysis.

One of the most common data consistency issues is to establish uniform identifiers for business entities, such as customer, product, supplier, or distributor as shown in Figure 2.2. An organization with a variety of turnkey applications that carry out routine functions, such as customer support, accounting, sales force automation, shipping and logistics, and product management, will likely discover that each package has its own method for determining the identifier for the business entities it creates and manages. As a result, a particular customer may be associated with multiple identifiers in the accounting, shipping, and support databases. In fact, in many organizations the same customer has multiple identifiers and, therefore, multiple records in the *same* database. This is usually because the users or the application failed to check to see if the customer was already in the database, before creating a new record.

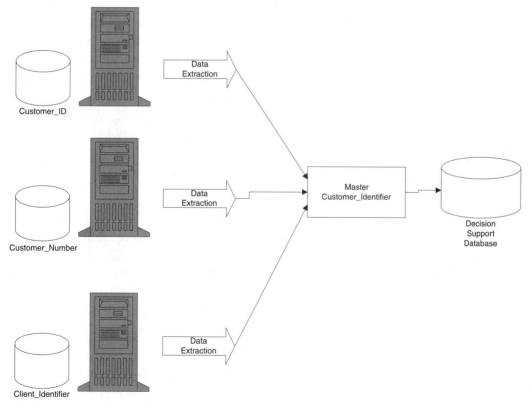

Figure 2.2   Defining master customer identifier.

This type of data duplication represents a serious data-quality problem. For example, a healthcare system must go to great lengths to ensure that all clinical and prescription data for a patient are associated with a single, unique patient identifier. Otherwise, a physician may unknowingly prescribe a medication that is contraindicated due to an unrecognized clinical problem. A less extreme example is direct mail. Companies that have duplicate records in their marketing databases often send duplicate mailings to the same household, or even the same individual due to poor data quality. This results in significant costs that cannot be eliminated without undertaking a serious data-quality effort.

The effort to bring data from these systems into a single data warehouse requires that the developer understand these various identifiers and how they are assigned, and develop a scheme for mapping them into a common, unique identifier.

Another consideration is how to identify the customer when it is a multi-part entity. If a company sells a product to a customer, is the customer the party that authorized the purchase (purchasing manager), the party that that received the shipment (ship-to address), the party that consumes the product, or the party that pays the invoice (bill-to address)? These are thorny questions that cannot be answered by IT alone. They require the business users of the system to understand clearly and define who or what a customer is. Once that business definition has been established, IT can design and implement a repeatable algorithm for allocating an identifier to the customer fields.

A related issue is names. Consider the ubiquitous John Doe. Different systems may identify this individual as John Doe; J. S. Doe; Doe, John; or John S. Doe. If Mr. Doe has additional attributes, such as a fiduciary role as a trustee, his name may become John Doe, Trustee under the Uniform Gifts to Minors Act for Jane Doe, a minor. Again, data consolidation requires that organizations develop a common, uniform method of managing names. The most common is to parse the name and decompose it into its various elements such as surname, first name, middle name or initial, prefix (Dr., Mr., Ms.), postfix (M.D., II, Jr.), and relation (Trustee, Parent). Then the name can be reconstructed into a consistent uniform format.

Data quality addresses the question, "Is the data correct?" This is a serious problem in organizations, particularly in legacy environments, in which the quality of the data may have degraded during the life of the system. In many environments, for example, users subvert the database design by using a field for purposes other than those intended by the original designer. Or the data may be a typo that was entered incorrectly. Or, the application software may not have properly or completely validated the data before it was entered into the database. This may not be a serious issue when the scope of the data is limited to a single transaction, but it can become a major headache when the data is consolidated with other data into a data warehouse.

Two major questions must be considered when evaluating data quality.

1. Is the data formatted correctly?
2. Is the data valid?

The first question tries to uncover if the data has been entered incorrectly, while the second question tries to determine if the data correctly represents something in the real world. For example, a correct U.S. address field should contain a ZIP+4 postal code. Application software can algorithmically check to see if the ZIP field contains five integers, a + character, followed by four integers. This indicates the data is correctly formatted. On the other hand, the data may have a ZIP code of 99999+9999, which doesn't exist and is, therefore, invalid. A user may have entered this value to mean, "we don't have the correct zip code for this address, but the application forced me to enter something into this required field."

This type of data quality problem cannot be corrected algorithmically. It often requires a lookup table, such as valid ZIP codes, to verify the correctness. The size of the lookup table will, of course, vary with the cardinality of the potential universe of correct entries. A lookup table of names for the population of the world is impractical, since it would contain five billion rows, most of which are not of interest to the average corporate data warehouse. However, a lookup table of U.S. postal codes would contain approximately one million rows, and would be very helpful to validate the postal code field of an address. Similarly, a lookup table of U.S. households could contain approximately 103 million rows by the year 2000 that for certain customer-oriented applications, such as credit-card usage, would be extremely useful.*

*Projections of the Number of Households and Families in the United States: 1995 to 2010, U.S. Bureau of the Census, Current Population Reports, P25-1129, U.S. Government Printing Office, Washington, D.C., 1996.

Step 5: Select Transformation Platform

The physical location of the transformation logic is another important consideration. Data transformation can occur on the source platform, on a staging engine, or at the target platform. Considerations include native platform transformation capabilities, maximizing system throughput, the effort required to schedule and synchronize activities across platforms, and the corporation's basic information management architecture.

Microsoft's DTS software typically runs on the same platform as SQL Server, therefore in most environments the data transformation software will be running on the same platform as the target database. However, it is possible to run DTS on another system when moving and transforming data from source systems. This is desirable in some environments where the administrator needs to relieve a data warehouse that is busy handling queries from the additional burden of data transformation and validation. It is also attractive in a one-to-many or many-to-many setting in which the transformed data is sent to multiple targets.

Step 6: Test ETML Logic

Testing and debugging the ETML process is usually done in two stages—unit testing and integration testing. The unit test phase involves configuring each step of the ETML process and testing the individual components of the step. For example, the extract step would involve simulating various extraction scenarios and verifying that the scripts extracted the correct data and did not extract data that should not be extracted, such as data that is not used for decision support. This test should be performed first on simulated data, and then on real data.

Similarly, the transform step can be tested independently from the extraction step. This step should test the robustness of the transformation logic by exposing the transformation software to unexpected data formats and verifying that it handles these anomalous data appropriately. Some examples of anomalous data include fields containing NULL data, date fields with invalid dates, and invalid name and address fields. This software should also correctly manage the consolidation of multiple data sources if it is going to be placed in a many-to-one transformation scenario.

Integration testing requires, however, that all the software which is tested and debugged be brought together to simulate various scenarios of the entire process. Again, the integration scenario can be run using simulated data or real, production-quality data. The integration test is primarily a test of the interfaces between the data stages in the process. It is also an opportunity to test and validate assumptions about overall system throughput. Integration testing provides designers with the opportunity to identify potential or actual choke points in the overall flow of data through the system.

Step 7: Production Scheduling

Every shop that has a production environment has a process—formal or informal—for placing new software and systems into production. This may be simply a telephone call from the designer to the system administrator, or it can be a scheduled meeting that reviews the project status and transfers authority from the development department to the production department.

The administrator must schedule the batch jobs that are responsible for the ETML process and implement operational procedures for managing the entire process. In the Microsoft decision support environment, these jobs are scheduled with the NT scheduler and, possibly, the Microsoft Management Console, or a third-party scheduling package. The operational procedures include the

- Identification of routine jobs using a unique job stream identifier.
- Creation and maintenance of a log that indicates when each job started, stopped, and its termination status. Since the ETML process is a multi-step process, the log should indicate this information for each step in the job stream.
- Determination of when the jobs should be run and the expected run-time interval.
- Coordination of activities that are internal and external to the job stream. Internal activities include those that must occur to ensure data consistency, such as closing/opening log files or shutting down production databases. External activities include coordinating the job stream with other production job streams, such as not

running the data warehouse build until a routine data warehouse database backup has been performed.

- Determination of what steps the system operators should take in the event of known and unknown failure scenarios. In a known failure scenario, such steps could include what to do in the event the data warehouse database fills up all available disk space. For an unknown failure scenario that could include a completely unanticipated error, the steps to consider may be, for instance, what to do if a construction accident severs a key communications link.

- Identification of the operator or operational role responsible for ensuring that the ETML process is run correctly and to completion. Identify support and engineering staff who should be notified in the event of a failure, with an escalation process to ensure the IT organization meets its service level agreements with the end user departments that are dependent on the decision support database.

Step 8: Documentation and Training

Finally, the entire process must be documented and the operations staff trained in the processes and procedures required to successfully implement the ETML process.

Documentation must contain information such as the source data location and attributes, the transformation, consolidation and validation logic applied to the data, and the target data location and attributes. It should also include information about how the process should be run, how operators should handle errors and exceptions that appear during the process, and under what circumstances the operators should cancel or restart the run. If the process is a multi-step one, the documentation should clearly outline the process flow, and specify all applicable coordination and scheduling requirements.

Operator training, which is discussed in further detail in Chapter 7, is designed to ensure the operation staff has a full understanding of the ETML process. It should cover the source-to-target data mapping design, the data transformation and data quality steps, and provide a complete review of the scheduling and error handling process. The goal of the training is to enable the operations staff to function independently of the development staff, except in a situations where the

ETML process has failed due to a software bug or design flaw. Where there is a failure, the operations staff should be competent to identify the source of the error, assess whether or not the job should be restarted and, if it is restarted, whether it should restart at the beginning or at the failure point.

Metadata

No description of the ETML process in the source environment is complete without describing the role of metadata in the process.

Source Environment Metadata

Several categories of metadata are used in the decision support life cycle. The ETML process in the Source environment (see Figure 2.1) is concerned with the following categories of metadata.

1. Data access metadata
2. Data manipulation metadata
3. Source-to-target mapping metadata

Data access metadata describes the attributes of the source system and the source data. The attributes of the source system include the hardware and operating system configuration, and how the transformation process is going to access the source data. For example, access is typically through a TCP/IP socket, but other tools and middleware approaches may be more appropriate. The data source may have an ODBC driver available, or the transformation process may need to use a proprietary API to get at the data. If no API is available, then the developer is going to have to create a program that can export the required data to a flat file. The location of the file and the method for accessing and copying it to the transformation platform are part of the data access metadata.

Data access metadata also includes the metadata stored in the source database catalog. This metadata identifies the data attributes such as data type, length, NULL/non-NULL and primary key/foreign key relationships.

Data definition metadata identifies the manipulations that the data is subject to before it is loaded into the decision support database. These include date/time transformations, consolidation of data from multiple sources, parsing and decomposition of fields, field value changes, and so forth.

Source-to-target mapping metadata identifies where the data came from and the target databases and fields that are the destination of the data.

In the Microsoft environment, these various categories of metadata are stored in the Microsoft Repository, which is discussed in further detail in Chapter 9.

CHAPTER 3

The Storage Environment

The storage environment consists of the software and server systems that contain decision support data. The role of the storage environment is to store data extracted from transactional applications and databases in the source environment for delivery to decision support applications and tools in the desktop environment. Desktop decision support applications and tools are discussed in Chapter 4.

It can be useful to evaluate the ability of a decision support solution to support business requirements based on the attributes of an application. These attributes include:

- Degree of data sparseness (dense, intermediate, sparse)
- Usage patterns (ad hoc/sporadic, routine/predictable)
- Data volume (highly indexed, raw data)
- Number of users
- User distribution
- Update frequency (weekly, daily, near real-time)

Based on these attributes, data warehouses tend to fall into one of four major categories: financial, product, customer, and transactional as shown in Table 3.1. Vendors and industry experts have done a poor job

41

Table 3.1 Data Warehouse Characteristics

DATA ATTRIBUTES	DATA WAREHOUSE CATEGORIES			
	FINANCIAL	PRODUCT	CUSTOMER	TRANSACTIONAL
Data Sparseness	Dense	Medium	Sparse	Sparse
Usage Pattern	Routine	Routine & Dynamic	Dynamic	Routine & Dynamic
Data Volume	Moderate	Large	Massive	Massive
Number of Users	Small	Moderate	Moderate	Large
User Distribution	Centralized	Centralized	Distributed	Distributed
Update Frequency	Monthly	Daily or Weekly	Daily	Very Frequent

of articulating the fact that these different data warehouse categories require unique product architectures to address end users' requirements for performance, reliability, throughput, scalability, and analysis. Because vendors are eager to position their products as solving all problems, confusion is predominant in the marketplace.

Financial Data Warehouses

Financial data warehouse systems focus on capturing and analyzing financial and accounting data, such as general ledger, accounts receivable/payable, budgeting and forecasting, and cash flow.

The data tend to be relatively small in volume—megabytes or small numbers of gigabytes—and usually have a fairly uniform format (financial numbers) with little variability. Due to the nature of the information—that is in an ongoing business every fiscal interval will have relevant financial data—the data are relatively dense. Also, because of the multi-dimensional, hierarchical structure of business organizations, these warehouse systems tend to have a large proportion of aggregated or calculated data stored in the database, which tends to be a multi-dimensional database.

The user base is relatively small—finance, purchasing, and senior management. Users tend to be geographically centralized at corporate headquarters, and system utilization patterns are uniform and predictable. Access occurs primarily during normal business hours, with noticeable utilization spikes at the end of key fiscal periods such as month-end, quarter-end, and year-end.

Users do not typically require access to data in real-time because they are more interested in analyzing routine reports that cover a specific interval, such as a month or fiscal quarter. Consequently, most data can be loaded at regular, scheduled intervals, such as end of day or end of week. To access the database, users will often use financial tools, such as spreadsheets, rather than specialized ad hoc query and analysis tools.

These requirements are easily addressed by a desktop or server-based multi-dimensional database (MDD) system. SQL Server OLAP Services, like other MDDs, is well suited to support this type of application with its small volume of relatively dense data and centralized user population with predictable usage patterns.

Product Data Warehouses

Product data warehouses, the second category of OLAP systems, consolidate information from sources such as inventory, pricing, and point-of-sale (POS) systems. The retail and consumer packaged goods (CPG) industries are prime examples of segments with these types of systems.

A product data warehouse is most often used by store or product managers, inventory analysts, and marketing personnel. The purpose of the warehouse and its supporting OLAP tools is to allow multiple groups and departments to make more timely, effective decisions that spur the movement of products. The goal is to improve inventory turnover, increase top-line revenue through higher sales, and enhance the effectiveness of marketing.

The data in these systems tend to be larger in volume ranging from tens of gigabytes to a terabyte or more, and they also tend to have a less uniform format with regard to product attributes such as size, color, packaging, and weight and sales figures. A typical system may track up to 10 thousand products throughout hundreds or thousands of locations by fiscal periods.

Since not every product of each attribute type—size, color, package— is sold at every location or outlet during every sales interval, data sparseness is intermediate. Analysis of the information tends to be oriented by time—sales this quarter compared with the prior-year quarter, geography—store locations, states, regions, countries, and product attribute—sales of red shoes compared with blue shoes.

Like the financial systems discussed previously, product data systems tend to have a large amount of aggregated, summarized data stored at various levels in the hierarchy. The user base is larger and incorporates a more diverse population such as product managers, store managers, sales managers, purchasing, product marketing, and senior management that may be geographically distributed. In other instances, remote business partners—suppliers and distributors—may have access to the system through an intranet. System utilization patterns are relatively variable, particularly during periods of intensive promotional activity when managers track the effect of product advertising and promotional campaigns.

Access occurs primarily during normal business hours, with end-of-period and seasonal utilization spikes. While users do not require access to data in real-time, they do require timely data with data updates and refreshes often performed at the end of the day. In many instances, the sales refresh occurs overnight as POS data is downloaded from individual store locations. An example of the kind of application this database supports is market-basket analysis, which attempts to identify products that sell together. Knowing this information enables the retailer to promote products with this type of affinity or to rearrange store displays to put the products in close proximity, which will hopefully result in higher sales. Analyses tend to be a mix of routine and exception reports delivered by triggers or software agents or because of user request.

The larger data volumes, higher degree of sparseness, and relatively dynamic nature of end-user queries make it difficult for desktop or server-based MDDs to address the needs of this type of data warehouse. These applications require flexible and scalable analysis software, which is usually addressed by deploying a relational OLAP solution. SQL Server OLAP Services is also suitable for this type of application when it is used in a relational OLAP configuration based on a star schema.

Customer Data Warehouses

Customer data warehouses represent the third type of system. Banking, retail, health care, insurance, and telecommunications are examples of industries that adopt customer-centric data warehouses.

This type of data warehouse is often used for customer relationship management. The goal of these databases is to analyze customer behavior in an effort to improve marketing efficiency and effectiveness. The databases are extensively used for customer acquisition/retention programs. For example, customer churn is a significant factor in the retail banking and telecommunications industries. Many of these warehouses are designed to enable a company to capture and analyze every interaction it has with a customer. One example of this type of analysis is customer lifetime value, which attempts to assess the overall profitability of an individual or group. Therefore, a wide mix of marketing analysts, executive staff, product managers, and customer service representatives use the warehouse.

The data in these systems tend to be much larger—hundreds of gigabytes to multiple terabytes—in volume, and more heterogeneous in nature. These databases commonly contain customer profiles, buying histories, and external syndicated data. A typical system may track hundreds of thousands or even millions of customers or prospects and their buying behavior. Since not every customer purchases a product during a sales cycle, data tends to be extremely sparse. Analysis is typically oriented toward understanding customer attributes such as a comparison between customers who purchase heavily and customers who purchase infrequently.

System utilization patterns can be highly variable, particularly during periods of intensive promotional activity, as managers build, manage, and assess the results of large marketing campaigns. Users tend to run, or have agents deliver, a mix of predefined and exception-based queries and reports. Access is mostly during normal business hours, with end-of-period and promotion utilization spikes; however, large international enterprises require 24-hour availability. The increasingly global nature of the companies that build these systems provides a relatively small window of opportunity for bulk data loads, and time also needs to be reserved for system maintenance, such as backups, reorganizations, purging, and other "housekeeping" activities.

The larger data volumes, higher degree of sparseness, and relatively dynamic nature of end-user queries require a multi-tier architecture. The most successful systems have been based on a combined relational and OLAP architecture, with the data warehouse and the OLAP engine stored on separate platforms for maximum overall throughput and reliability.

Transactional Data Warehouses

Data warehouses have traditionally been viewed as read-only resources. However, in the past few years we have seen an increasingly large number of transactional data warehouses appear that are designed to be updated by users. Transactional data warehouse systems enable organizations to learn how different events affect customer loyalty, profitability, and efficiency. The data warehouse focuses on gathering information from numerous, industry-dependent sources, ranging from treatments and diagnoses to shipping and customer retention.

For example, a health-care or insurance provider can perform outcome analysis. This process is designed to assess the effectiveness of a series of prescriptions, hospital or doctor visits, or therapies to determine which is most beneficial for the patient, taking the cost of the procedure or visit into consideration. Or a telecommunications company may need to track record-level call data to understand the changing nature of how their customers use their phone systems. This enables them to detect changing call patterns that are significant. For instance, a transaction data mart could detect that a customer's calling pattern has switched from relatively short—less than five minutes—to relatively long calls—greater than one hour—that are initiated at night. This information may indicate that the customer has started to use an Internet Service Provider and is spending long periods surfing the net. This type of customer may be amenable to an offer for a second phone line, an ISDN line, or if the company itself is an ISP, a special Internet access offer. This type of system can also alert managers to activities that deviate from given trends and that may indicate fraud or mismanagement, such as a sudden surge of credit card spending or large simultaneous credit card purchases from different locations. Or, a surge of credit card transactions may indicate the card holder just purchased a new home, which opens up other marketing opportunities.

The data tends to be very large in volume and extremely sparse, with a high degree of variability in format. Because of the nature of the analysis, systems require detailed transactional data to be stored in the warehouse. Complex analysis is necessary to evaluate trends over time according to customer expectations and profitability.

The user base is relatively large—senior management, marketing, operations, and customers—and geographically decentralized world-

wide. System utilization patterns are continual and predictable.
must have timely information to make a correct analysis of perfc
ance. Individuals using the system will be much less experienced wi
the data warehouse and will require an interface that directs their attention to areas that need attention or that simply builds ad hoc reports
with minimal key strokes. For example, end users may be doctors
analyzing the cost and effectiveness of new treatments, or they may be
customers evaluating their options for payment and delivery of time-
dependent goods.

These descriptions represent examples of some of the more common
types of data warehouse applications that are currently deployed. Other
types of data warehouses are also deployed, such as in the scientific field
for genetic analysis, or in support of specialized EIS applications, such
as Balanced Scorecard which is discussed further in Chapter 4.

Data Warehouse or Data Mart?

Many people refer to the systems in the storage environment as either
data warehouses or data marts. The decision support industry is still
debating where it's appropriate for an organization to consider deploying an enterprise data warehouse or where it should consider a data
mart architecture.

It's generally accepted that a data warehouse is defined as a decision
support database that supports multiple corporate functions or business units, whereas a data mart is defined as a decision support database that is limited in scope to support a single business function or
unit. Although a data warehouse does not require a relational database
management system (RDBMS), most data warehouses are built using
relational technology. Some well-known products available on Windows 2000 include Microsoft SQL Server, Oracle8, Informix, Sybase,
IBM DB2, and NCR Teradata. Data marts, on the other hand, are
typically built using either a RDBMS or, in many instances, a multi-
dimensional database.

It's important to emphasize that the size or volume of the data contained in the database does not define a data mart. The authors are
aware of systems with more than one terabyte (TB) of raw data that are
defined as data marts because of the limited business scope and objectives of the system. For example, AT&T has a system that contains close

yte of data, which we would define as a data mart. The sys-
arn management system that is used primarily to identify
who may be vulnerable to offers from competitors. The
data is customer call data, and the scope of the business
customer retention.

are attractive for a variety of reasons. Compared to data
warehouses, and notwithstanding various examples of large-scale implementations, in general data marts are relatively quick and easy to
implement. They require less coding, and simple data marts can be
deployed quickly, in some instances in as little as 90 days compared to
the one or two-year deployment period that is typical of a warehouse.
Data mart tools extract only the information relevant to solving specific
business problems, which reduces their impact on operational systems.
Because data marts are typically smaller than a data warehouse, query
performance is often better, all other factors being equal, than a large
data warehouse.

Costs can be lower with a data mart. On average, the data mart itself is
usually relatively small—gigabytes instead of terabytes, thus requiring
less investment in hardware and maintenance personnel. Often a data
mart project can be funded from a departmental budget. However, this
cost advantage can be offset if a company suffers from proliferating data
marts. We believe centralized control is optimal for purchasing and
management of data marts.

Data Mart Architectures

There are three fundamental data mart architectures: independent, dependent, and federated as shown in Figure 3.1.

Independent Data Mart

An independent data mart is usually built by a business unit driven to
solve an immediate problem, where the overriding consideration is
"just do it," rather than get IT involved. In many instances, IT learns
about the data mart when the department submits a request for data
or other resources that IT controls. However, IT is not involved in the
design, implementation, or management of the mart. From a corporate
perspective, independent data marts are usually a bad idea. If the data
mart is successful it acquires a life of its own, and, sooner or later users

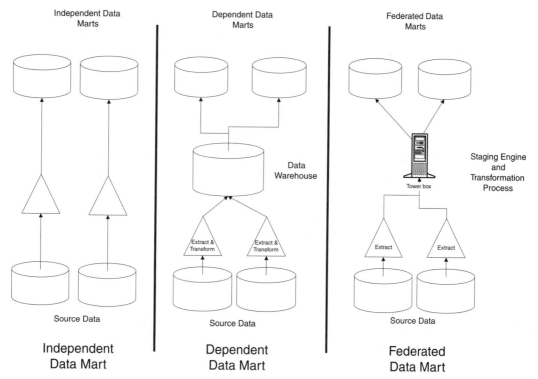

Figure 3.1 Data mart categories.

in other departments want to share its benefits. Or, if the organization goes through a business change, such as a merger or a new management initiative, the mart will need to be integrated with other systems. Before long, the mart gets stretched beyond its design parameters, and it can't scale up to meet changing requirements.

Dependent Data Mart

A dependent data mart is populated from data stored in a data warehouse. This approach is probably the most popular in those large organizations that have gone through the effort to deploy a packaged application, especially if the packaged application vendor provides a data warehouse solution set.

There are several reasons why an organization builds a dependent data mart rather than simply let users launch queries against a data warehouse. For one reason, performance is often better. The limited scope of the data mart database tends to make end-user navigation easier. Or, a business unit may have additional requirements for data or functionality that the corporate data warehouse does not address.

The primary advantages of a dependent data mart architecture are data consistency and investment protection. The developers of the corporate data warehouse have already gone through the effort to ensure the consistency and quality of the warehouse data, so the data mart developers do not need to reproduce that effort. For example, common data names and key naming elements, such as CUSTOMER_ID, are all defined as part of the process for building an enterprise data warehouse. Because this information is all captured in the data warehouse metadata, the developers of a dependent data mart can reuse it. Also, they will benefit from the consistency of the data if they need to integrate data across marts. In particular, this means that dimension keys will be consistent between the data marts, which will enable a user to launch a query that goes against two or more data marts, with some reasonable assurance that the response will have referential integrity.

Federated Data Mart

An emerging category of distributed data mart architecture is the federated data mart. The federated data mart replaces the data warehouse with a platform for managing data movement, transformation, consolidation, aggregation, and metadata management. However, this platform functions more like a staging area than a decision support platform. Once the data is prepared, it is forwarded to the target databases, where it is restructured into decision support data.

The federated data mart approach enables a company to build distributed decision support databases in an incremental manner, with the assurance that they can scale up either horizontally or vertically. Horizontal scalability is accomplished by using query tools and middleware that enable a desktop user to analyze data from two or more databases while preserving the illusion that only a single database is used. Common metadata standards and table key definitions are essential for this approach to be feasible. Vertical scalability is achieved by using an underlying database and platform architecture that can scale up to support the attributes described in "A Word on Scalability."

Decision Support Database Architecture

The distinction between data warehouses and data marts is relatively artificial and provides little analytical value from an information architecture perspective. The decision about which architecture to implement should be based on business requirements and not on the basis of what are, at best, technology buzzwords.

We believe the single, enterprise-wide data warehouse has become too unwieldy and complex for most organizations to rely on for all decision support decisions. Similarly, the approach of independent departmental, uncoordinated decision support databases is not sustainable in any reasonably-sized organization.

Consequently, organizations will increasingly implement either a dependent decision support database or a federated decision support database architecture. Those companies that deploy a dependent data mart solution will rely on the data warehouse primarily for data storage, not decision support. The data marts will contain the data with which the users interact when they are performing analytical tasks.

Conversely, companies that adopt the federated data mart approach will use the data marts both for data storage and for decision support. The core of the success of the federated approach is a shared metadata repository, which contains information about the transformation and source-to-target data mappings as well as the navigation metadata that will enable users to launch queries that join information from multiple databases.

Companies that deploy Microsoft SQL Server can use either the dependent or federated architectures effectively. Later in this book we describe how the combination of distributed query APIs, such as OLE DB for OLAP and metadata management provided by Microsoft Repository, enable designers to build discrete distributed decision support solutions on distributed platforms, without limiting enterprise-wide data access.

Decision Support Databases

Now that we have discussed the distinction between data warehouses and data marts, let's focus on the basic types of decision support databases. Decision support databases can be divided into two categories: relational and multi-dimensional.

Table 3.2 A Comparison of Relational and Multi-Dimensional Databases

FEATURE	RELATIONAL DBMS	MULTI-DIMENSIONAL DATABASE
Query language	SQL	Proprietary language or API—Many multi-dimensional databases now support the OLE DB for OLAP API
Query-and-analysis tool availability	Many—any tool that generates SQL	Limited to tools that support the database's API
Data structure	Table with rows and columns	Hierarchical, tree-like structure
Data volume scalability	Excellent	Limited
Design-and-development tool availability	Many—any tool that generates data definition language (DDL)	Limited, mostly proprietary tools
Data navigation	Undirected navigation using nonprocedural language	Directed navigation using GUI to traverse database tree structure
Ease of navigation	Relatively poor (see discussion on star schema in this chapter)	Excellent
Query limitations	Any available data	Limited to data stored in pre-defined hierarchy

Relational databases such as SQL Server are primarily used for data warehouses and dependent or federated decision support databases. Multi-dimensional databases, such as SQL Server OLAP Services, however, are rarely used to build a data warehouse. Table 3.2 illustrates some of the differences between relational and multi-dimensional decision support databases.

The Relational Decision Support Database

Most organizations depend on a relational DBMS to store data in a data warehouse for a variety of reasons. First, relational technology is familiar to most shops because their client/server OLTP database applications were based on it.

Second, the scalability of relational databases is superior, overall, to multi-dimensional databases.

A Word on Scalability

Developers need to consider three measures of scalability when they select a product for implementing a decision support database. These measures are data scalability, usage scalability, and query scalability.

1. *Data scalability* refers to the actual volume of data the database can support. Most relational DBMSs, including SQL Server, can support data—including indexes, aggregate tables, and other non-atomic data—in excess of a terabyte. However, be wary of vendors that brag about reference sites that are bigger than a terabyte. Often a detailed examination reveals that the vendor is counting RAID storage with redundant disks, temp table space, and unused capacity to arrive at that figure. What really matters is how much raw—row-level, denormalized—data the system can handle. Once you have computed that figure (see Chapter 7), then add indexes and aggregate tables, plus temporary table and system table space, to arrive at the final database size. RAID, which is important for high availability, must figure into the total system size, but it is not part of the underlying database size calculation.

2. *Usage scalability* refers to the number of online, interactive, simultaneous users. Usage scalability is controlled by a number of factors including the operating system, available system memory, maximum number of concurrent client connections the database can manage, application complexity, and database concurrency control features. Developers often use intermediate transaction servers or monitors to multiplex client connections to the database. Concurrency control is usually managed through the use of database locks to ensure that two or more users are prevented from simultaneously updating the same data. Naturally, the database must have a lock table large enough to manage all of the concurrent outstanding locks. A complex application can consume significant system resources, especially if application logic is running on the server. This is the case when the application is running on the web, or if significant functionality is embedded in frequently executed stored procedures.

3. *Query scalability* refers to the ability of the database to manage complex queries. A database with high query scalability can respond to complex, multi-part SQL queries with consistent response times. Join performance, sophisticated indexing algorithms, and transparent support for aggregation tables are all essential for high-performance decision support. Microsoft has rewritten the query processor with the release of SQL Server 7.0 to improve its ability to handle complex queries.

Third, relational technology uses SQL, which is the industry standard language for query and analysis, whereas multi-dimensional databases have typically relied on a proprietary API for data access and analysis. That is changing, however. The Microsoft OLE DB for OLAP API will rapidly become the de facto standard API for programmatic access to multi-dimensional databases. We do not believe the competing multi-dimensional API, the MD-API published by the OLAP Council (see www.olapcouncil.org/), will become a significant factor in the decision support industry. In our opinion, the Microsoft standard will be supported by all the major desktop query and analysis vendors, which will give it critical mass in the marketplace. The MD-API, on the other hand, is supported by a relatively small number of vendors.

Fourth, relational databases have a variety of features such as triggers and stored procedures, that enhance the usefulness and practicality of the system. However, it should be noted that multi-dimensional databases typically have stronger calculation and aggregation features than relational databases because they are not dependent on the lack of calculation features in the SQL language.

Compared with multi-dimensional databases, the biggest drawback from which relational databases suffer (compared to multi-dimensional databases) is query performance. The original generation of relational databases was designed to meet the needs of high-performance transaction processing applications. This design goal meant the system had to be very good at locating a specific record or a relatively small set of records linked with a primary key/foreign key relationship. The database located the record and returned it to the application, which would typically perform an update or delete on that record. If no record was found, the system would insert a new one.

Since the design goal of these original systems was to support hundreds or thousands of relatively small concurrent transactions, concurrency control (locks) between large numbers of users became crucial for performance, as well as the ability to manage many, relatively small records. Buffer management algorithms were developed to enable the system to reduce disk I/O and improve performance of tables with shared data. The volume of data in the traditional, transaction-processing environment is also relatively small, often less than 100 GB. In many production environments, older data are purged from the database to offline media such as tape or computer output to laser disk, and the database is reorganized to maintain high-performance transaction processing.

In comparison, a decision support application has very different requirements that have a profound impact on the characteristics required for a decision support database. First, an enterprise decision support database may need to support an extremely large volume of data. It is not uncommon to hear of databases that are in the range of tens of terabytes, and we are beginning to hear about databases with hundreds of terabytes that will be deployed before the year 2000.

Most multi-dimensional databases are designed to support, at most, a few dozens or hundreds of gigabytes (GB) of summary and aggregated data, not detailed transaction-level data. A relational data warehouse, on the other hand, can store hundreds or even thousands of gigabytes of data, including both detail and summary data. This larger volume of data can result in a longer response time, especially if the user submits a complex SQL query or if the DBA has not optimized the database for the particular query the user is executing.

Second, decision support queries tend to be more complex than those traditionally associated with OLTP queries. Query complexity increases as a result of the need to iteratively refine a data search using subqueries and complex WHERE clauses. A corollary to this query complexity is the need to support ad hoc queries rather than the predefined queries seen in the transaction-processing world.

Third, decision support queries often scan and join huge tables. Performing a join in a relational table can be extremely resource intensive. Most transaction-processing applications require few, if any, table joins. Even when several tables in a transaction-processing application are joined, relatively few rows return in the result set. Decision support applications, by contrast, may join as many as 10 or 15 tables, and thousands of rows may be returned in the result set.

A related issue is the impact a large, table scan has on buffers. All database management systems, including SQL Server, try to reduce disk I/O by allocating an in-memory data cache. A scan of a large table can quickly fill up the cache. As the cache fills up, "older" pages are discarded, or written to disk if they have been modified. If a transaction-processing application is running, the users may suffer from disk thrashing as the pages they update are prematurely flushed from the cache. Thrashing can significantly reduce performance.

The growth of the decision support marketplace in the late 1990s has motivated the major vendors, including Microsoft, to make significant modifications to their optimizers for decision support. These modifications allow rapid scanning of large numbers of records, improve the performance of multi-table joins, and speed up summarization and aggregation of columns of interest.

To deliver decision support performance at acceptable levels a relational data warehouse must provide support for four attributes: parallelism, partitioning, indexing, and aggregation.

Parallelism

Parallelism is the ability to distribute the workload of a DBMS across multiple CPUs, either on a single machine or multiple machines. A database with a high degree of parallelism can support a larger number of users that execute more complex queries than one that is designed for a serial-processing environment. Parallelism is also useful to reduce the time required to load data, build indexes, and regenerate aggregates as part of the update process.

A relational DBMS performs many functions or tasks that can be improved with parallelism. Loading data using multiple job streams, for example, can accelerate data warehouse updates. This capability is particularly important if the data warehouse contains large index or aggregate tables. Rebuilding or updating these tables can be time-consuming when not done in parallel.

Queries can return results more quickly when the functional elements of the query are deconstructed into logical units that work independently of each other. These elements include table scans, index scans, and multi-table joins. How a database deconstructs and manages multi-table joins is of critical importance in a data warehouse environment because relatively few queries in a decision support environment are limited to a single table.

Partitioning

Partitioning is data distribution done in parallel. Databases are partitioned in a number of ways, depending on the granularity of the partitioning schema. The simplest, most elegant and technically challenging, is by random distribution of the entire database across the complete set of available storage units. The level of granularity is the database block or page. This architecture, which is the functional equivalent of disk striping, means any disk has an equal likelihood of satisfying any requested database page. This type of architecture, however, can require a database rebuild if you add additional disk capacity to the system.

The next more coarse level of partitioning granularity is within a table. Microsoft SQL Server supports two types of table-level partitioning: horizontal and vertical.

Horizontal partitioning (also called row storage) segments a table at the row level, based on a primary key. For example, a table can be broken into one segment for each month of the year, based on a primary key value. Thus each sub-table will contain fewer rows, and queries that are constrained by month are limited to the tables that are keyed by month. However, the downside is that UNION queries that are not constrained by month may result in slower performance since the table(s) will need to be joined.

Vertical partitioning (also called columnar storage) segments a table by columns. Columns that are frequently referenced can be placed in one table, while infrequently accessed columns can be moved to a different table. This partitioning scheme can also improve performance, as long as the query doesn't result in a UNION of tables in a large partition.

The more coarse level of database partitioning is the table itself. Most commercial DBMSs enable the DBA to confine data within a table to a set of named disks or data volumes. SQL Server supports the concept of filegroups. A filegroup is a collection of distinct files that contain the tables within a database. Different files within a filegroup can be placed on individual disk drives to improve overall I/O throughput, or to enable data growth.

Indexing

Indexing is used to speed up access to data within a table. An index is a structure that inverts one or more columns within a table. Some sophisticated databases allow more than one type of index to be applied to a single column, and the optimizer selects the appropriate index based on the query attributes.

Indexes improve performance because a relational DBMS, almost by definition, does not store data in any sorted order that is accessible by an end user. An index provides a mechanism for rapidly locating a record based on the data value of a field (column).

SQL Server does allow data to be stored in sorted order by using a clustered index. Since a clustered index enforced the physical storage of data, a table can only have one clustered index. You would design a clustered index where you expect most queries to request data that falls within some range of values, such as a date or product identifier. A clustered index will create additional overhead when you add data to the table, since the rows in the table are kept in sorted order.

The big advantage of an index is that it reduces the number of rows that must be searched to locate the desired records. For example, a query that is searching a table for data within a certain range can use an index to provide quick location of the applicable records rather than scanning the entire table, which can improve query performance by orders of magnitude.

One of the most common tasks undertaken by a DBA is to determine which columns to index and what type of index to apply to them. Indexes take up disk space and require maintenance. For example, when new data is added to the database, the index must also be updated. In some instances it is better to update the index in place, whereas in other instances it is easier simply to drop the entire index and rebuild it from scratch. Because of this maintenance load, it is not always appropriate to index all columns in all tables. Although it's outside the scope of this book to go into a great deal of detail about the various index types that are used in a relational decision support database, designers should become familiar with the most important indexes such as B-tree (binary tree), bitmapped, and hash.

B-tree indexes are most useful for applications in which the application doesn't search a large number of records or perform a search that joins multiple tables. While various vendors provide diverse implementations of a B-tree index, the underlying principle is that a B-tree index stores pointers to data in sorted order in a binary structure that enables the searching software to discard half the records with each level it searches. This is called a binary search, and the structure that implements it is a binary tree, or B-tree. Both clustered and non-clustered indexes in SQL Server are implemented using B-trees.

A bitmap index, on the other hand, creates a set of one or more bitmaps. A bitmap is a set of binary digits that represent the rows in the target table. The bits that represent a desired value are set to 1, while the rest are set to 0. To find the rows in the table with the required attribute, the optimizer performs a bit-wise search, which is a relatively fast operation for two reasons. First, bitmaps are relatively small and often can be held in memory, so almost no disk access is required to perform the search. Second, computer instruction sets contain low-level, bit-wise operators, so the search is performed efficiently by the CPU.

The real value of the bitmap-index approach can be seen when joining multiple tables using bitmaps. In this scenario, the search can be performed quickly by simply performing an AND, OR, NOT, or COUNT operation on the bitmaps. The result set can be manipulated quickly to locate the rows that match. SQL Server does not currently implement bitmap indexes.

A hash index uses a specialized mathematical algorithm to hash the value of the column and maintain it in a specialized data structure. A hash index provides the fastest method for direct access to a row since the system only needs to run the hash algorithm to identify the target row. A hash index works best when hash of the column value guarantees a unique hash key. If multiple rows hash to the same value, a *hash collision* results, which forces the database to store the hash value in a linked list. This significantly reduces the performance benefit of a hash index. SQL Server does not support hash indexes.

Aggregation

Aggregation is probably the most important method for improving performance in a decision support database. The basic notion behind aggregation is that, in many scenarios, decision support users are interested in summary data. Some examples include sales of merchandise (product) by fiscal period (time) or by sales location (geography). If the data in which the user is interested has already been aggregated, the database can respond quickly. If, on the other hand, that data has not been aggregated, the database must search for and summarize the results dynamically. This process can be extremely time-consuming and resource intensive, particularly if the table that must be searched is very large.

However, aggregated data results in data redundancy. For example, a product-oriented decision support database may contain information about juice sales along several sets of attributes. The database contains aggregates for juice sales by product—orange, apple, grape, tomato, lemon; package—gallon, half-gallon, quart, pint, half-pint, individual serving; time—week, month, quarter, year; location—neighborhood, city, state, region, country, continent; and channel—vending machine, super-market, sports events, distributor. Each aggregate level contains data that also exist in other aggregate levels or dimensions. This configuration enables a marketing manager to analyze sales data in different ways with fast response time.

The DBA needs to consider which aggregate tables to define. It doesn't make sense to define every possible aggregate for the same reason that it doesn't make sense to define every possible index. Aggregate tables can consume considerable disk space—as much as three to five times the space required for the record-level detail data. Aggregate tables also require time and resources, primarily CPU, to build and maintain. It makes little sense to build an aggregate table that contains data that are rarely or never used by a query.

Companies embraced the concept of the multi-dimensional, or OLAP, database primarily because it was designed to supply aggregate data. It wasn't until the concept of the star schema was developed that database designers had a model for building aggregates for relational databases. Microsoft SQL Server OLAP Services is Microsoft's multi-dimensional database. Later in this book we describe the process of designing, building and deploying a multi-tier decision support architecture which uses SQL Server to store transaction-level detail records, and SQL Server OLAP Services to store aggregate, multi-dimensional data.

To Star or Not to Star

The data warehouse community continues to debate whether a data warehouse or data mart should use an aggregated, de-normalized structure, such as a star schema (or a related design, such as a snowflake), or whether it should use a normalized database schema, such as a third normal form (3NF).

In a normalized database, the goal is to reduce data redundancy as much as possible, consistent with good performance. Primary key/foreign key relations are used primarily to enable the query processor to locate tables that are logically linked, and secondarily to maintain referential integrity. A normalized customer database might look something like Figure 3.2. It is important to understand that the 3NF structure has no core table. The architecture is akin to a web, where each nexus (table) is as important as any other table. The complexity of the 3NF structure can

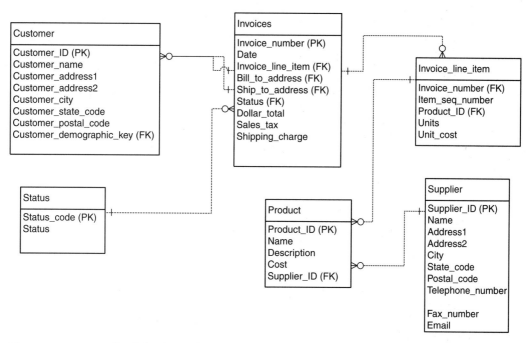

Figure 3.2 Normalized database design.

be daunting to a naïve user, making it difficult for them to know where to begin.

A star schema consists of a central *fact* table, which is surrounded by one or more *dimension* tables. This model is simpler for end users to navigate, and it reduces the number of complex multi-table joins that are required to answer any query.

Each row in the fact table contains multiple keys (one for each dimension) along with one or more columns containing various facts about the data stored in the row. Figure 3.3 illustrates a star schema design.

Note the differences between the two schemas. The primary difference is that the `Product_sales` table, which is the fact table, has a multi-part primary key. Each of the key components is related to a dimensional table. Each dimensional table has a single primary key. The combination of keys in the fact table creates a composite multi-part key that is unique to the transaction record. Note also that in the star schema the `Product_sales` table is similar to the `Invoice_line_item`

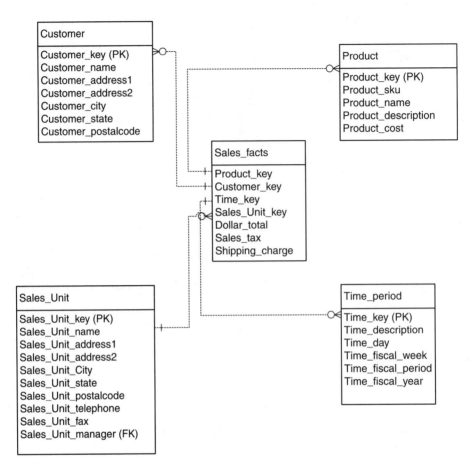

Figure 3.3 Star schema design.

table in the normalized design. This similarity occurs because the fact table records are at the lowest level of granularity that is interesting to the users of the decision support database. The granularity of the fact table is an important design consideration because it limits the levels of the dimension tables. A user can define any number of aggregate dimensional data structures once the appropriate level of granularity has been defined for the fact table.

The star schema has several advantages over a normalized database structure. From the perspective of the end user, probably the most important advantage is ease of navigation. If end users are going to access the database, the database should probably be designed as a star. The typical normalized database, with its hundreds or thousands of tables, is too complicated for most end users to understand. They will get lost in the complexity of the database and be unable to formulate meaningful business queries. Because it is inherently dimensional, a star provides the basis for enabling users to navigate the database using concepts that are already familiar to them, such as product, time, customer, or whatever is the subject matter of the database.

The other big advantage of the star is in the area of performance. A typical query against a star results in far fewer table joins than would be the result in a normalized database. In a star schema, the dimension tables are usually relatively shallow and wide (few entries, but lots of attributes), whereas the fact table is usually deep and narrow (many records with relatively few columns). This structure makes joins across dimension tables even more efficient. By querying the dimension tables and using the resulting answers to obtain the appropriate fact table rows, the database designer can significantly enhance query response time, relative to a normalized structure. This enhancement occurs because the combination of keys from multiple dimension tables can be resolved with an intelligent query optimizer into one pass through the fact table index. The ability to resolve an arbitrary number of N-way joins to a single pass is extremely powerful, especially in a large database.

Dimensional Modeling

Dimensional modeling is the implementation of a star schema within a relational DBMS. The dimensional modeler must deal with four related data structures: fact tables, dimension tables, aggregate tables, and indexes.

Fact-Table Modeling

A fact table contains the lowest level of transaction information that is of interest to the end users. This information is termed the *grain* of the fact table. As pointed out by Kimball,* the most useful facts are those that are numeric, continuously valued, and additive.

Numeric data elements belong in the fact table. Non-numeric data elements such as color, size, brand, shape, location, and name belong in the dimension tables.

---

*See Ralph Kimball's two books, *The Data Warehouse Toolkit* (John Wiley & Sons, 1996) and *The Data Warehouse Lifecycle Toolkit* (John Wiley & Sons, 1998) for an in-depth discussion of dimensional modeling.

Continuously valued facts are consecutive numbers. The best type of continuously valued, numeric fact is money. Units sold is another example of a continuously valued fact. Stock-keeping unit (SKU) numbers, however, do not qualify as a fact because SKUs, although numeric, are not continuous.

Additive means that the numbers can be summed to produce a meaningful result. Thus revenue, costs, and units can be summed, but SKUs, for example, cannot. An important design feature that derives from the additive rule is that data within fact tables can be used to create aggregate tables.

Dimension-Table Modeling

A dimensional table contains a single primary key that points to a fact table key, and one or more columns that contain textual data about the dimension. For example, a time dimension table can contain both a time key and a description column that contains the text description of the time such as "May" or "Quarter 1." A product dimension will contain information about "brand", "category", "unit size", "color", "flavor", or SKU.

The dimension tables are the entry points into the fact table. An interesting observation is that properly defined dimensions can become row headers in a query. As Kimball* points out, "the precise definition of drilling down is to add a row header."

Users who browse the data warehouse will want to use the dimension tables to get started with their analysis, and extend the analysis by adding more dimensions. It is important to have clear-text descriptors in the dimension columns, since these are the attributes the users will search for and analyze.

It is worthwhile to point out that there are two dimensions that are particularly important in most data warehouse environments. They are time and peoples names and addresses.

The time-dimension table needs special attention because almost every data warehouse has a time element in the data. The time dimension is used to track how a business changes and it provides the basis for comparison across weeks, months, quarters, years, and fiscal periods.

*Kimball, Ralph, *The Data Warehouse Lifecycle Toolkit* (John Wiley & Son, 1998), p. 167.

The data in the time-dimension table should be at a level of granularity that enables the greatest degree of analytical flexibility. This is usually at the date level. Storing data at the date level enables the user to summarize data to higher levels of aggregation. Storing time data at a higher aggregate level like week or month, eliminates essential analytical flexibility.

People's names and addresses present special data quality problems. Most transaction-processing systems have very poor name validation and verification algorithms. However, especially in customer-oriented decision support databases, quality names are essential. The process for validating name quality should be delegated to the ETML software that loads data into the data warehouse. In the Microsoft environment, this is the DTS software. The DTS process should, at a minimum, parse names and addresses into their individual constituents, and then re-assemble them into a standard format.

Aggregate-Table Modeling

Aggregate tables are the most significant approach to improving query performance in a relational decision support database. An aggregate table contains summarized facts, such as product category total sales by month, by sales region, or by any other measure that makes business sense. DBAs build aggregate tables to reduce the number of rows that must be scanned to return summed facts in a large fact table. The SQL functions SUM, AVG, COUNT, COUNT(*), MAX, and MIN are used to return aggregate results from a single users query. These *functions* should not be confused with aggregate *tables* that can be used by multiple queries or users.

For example, if a manager needed to analyze total product sales by sales region per month, the system would have to scan the fact table looking for all product sales within a region and then sum the sales for each region and the sales for each month. In a large decision support database with millions of records, this type of query may be unacceptably slow for the end user. If the DBA designs the appropriate aggregate tables, the system can respond to the query in a manner that is orders of magnitude faster than would be otherwise possible.

The DBA needs to consider the impact of aggregate tables on database size. Aggregate tables, which should be separate tables distinct from the fact table, can cause a tremendous increase in the volume of data stored in the DBMS. As Kimball points out, the accumulation of data in aggregate tables will be a multiplication of the various facts based on the dimensions we want to aggregate. Thus if we decide to create an aggregate table of product (10,000 products) by store (1,000 stores) by week (100 weeks, or 2 years), we will have an aggregate table with $10,000 \times 1,000 \times 100$, or 1,000,000,000 (one billion) records. However, it is unlikely that all stores will sell all products in all weeks. This reality means that the data are sparse, and a sparsity factor needs to be factored into the equation. Thus, if we determine that 10 percent of all products are sold in all stores in all weeks, we reduce the number of records in the aggregate table to 100,000,000 (one hundred million). This is still a relatively large table, and if we consider that we may need to create anywhere from five to 50 tables to support a reasonable number of aggregates, we find a substantial increase in the volume of data being created. It is not unusual to find that a star schema database with multiple aggregate tables may expand fivefold over the base table model.

Another issue that the data modeler needs to consider is the ability of the end-user query tool to take transparent advantage of the presence of one or more aggregate tables. End users cannot be expected to navigate the database and uncover the presence of an aggregate table, so the DBA has to provide an aggregate navigation capability. This functionality can be provided by building the aggregate tables in the DBMS and then defining a link between the aggregate table(s) and the fact table, and it is another form of database metadata that is specific to a relational data warehouse.

The aggregate navigator needs to effect transparent interception of the desktop SQL query, analyze it by comparing the requested tables in the query with the aggregate table directory, and substitute the appropriate aggregate table cells, before submitting the query to the DBMS optimizer. Microsoft SQL Server 7.0 relies on SQL Server OLAP Services to deliver aggregate data to the end-user, not an aggregate navigator.

The Multi-Dimensional Decision Support Database

An important component of most decision support environments is a multi-dimensional database. Multi-dimensional databases, also known as online analytical processing (OLAP) databases, are hierarchical databases that are designed to provide end users with a user-friendly view of business data. SQL Server OLAP Services is Microsoft's OLAP database.

A Word about OLAP

OLAP is a term whose meaning has changed considerably since it was first introduced. OLAP stands for online analytical processing, which refers to the process for analyzing multi-dimensional data. Over time it has also become synonymous with the specialized, multi-dimensional databases that were implemented by various vendors, such as Essbase (from Hyperion Solutions), Express (from Oracle), and TM1 (from Applix). The key to understanding OLAP is realizing that OLAP provides a multi-dimensional data structure that end users can easily and quickly analyze without requiring any programming knowledge.

The term OLAP was originally coined by E.J. Codd, who also originated the concept of the relational database. Codd wrote a white paper in 1993 that described the concept of OLAP as a multi-dimensional data model that contrasts with the two-dimensional relational database model. In that paper (which is available on-line at http://warehouse.chime-net.org/software/datastore /dataware/coddc0.html) he outlined 12 rules for OLAP systems. An extension of these rules is also available from The OLAP Report (see www.olapreport.com).

An important distinction must be drawn between data warehousing and OLAP. Data warehousing is the process of collecting, correcting, and consolidating enterprise data into a single system environment. Most enterprises use relational databases for data warehousing. OLAP is the restructuring of enterprise data into a multi-dimensional format that is optimized for analysis by end users.

A multi-dimensional database stores data in a hierarchy structure. The hierarchical structure of the multi-dimensional database contains *dimensions*, which represent business structures. For example, a typical product-sales multi-dimensional database would have dimensions for product, time, and geography.

Multi-dimensional, or OLAP, databases have two key advantages over a data warehouse. First, the multi-dimensional database provides the end user with a natural hierarchical view of business data that makes it easier for the user to navigate the data. This often easily maps to the users' perspective of the world. Of course, this can be simulated using a star schema in a RDBMS, but in the multi-dimensional database, it is a natural result of the database structure.

Second, the multi-dimensional database stores and aggregates data at multiple levels in a hierarchy, which enables fast performance as users move up and down the hierarchy. Again, this can be done in a RDBMS, using aggregate tables, but it requires implementing many—usually dozens, often hundreds—of tables. As we discussed earlier, this is a nontrivial problem that can also result in a substantial increase in the volume of data that is stored.

A multi-dimensional database contains only one data structure—the array—and it contains all the summarized data at higher levels in the array. In addition, most OLAP databases also provide logic for performing complex calculations, especially time-oriented computations, such as moving averages. The results of this data can also be stored in the dimensional structure and made available to the user who wants to compare results across dimensions.

Each dimension contains some number of *levels*, each level representing an aggregation. For example, the highest level of the geography dimension is Country, and the lowest level is Store. The time dimension starts at Fiscal Year and goes down to the level of Day.

The power of the multi-dimensional database is its ability to provide users with a cross-dimensional perspective, enabling the user to analyze data across multiple dimensions. For example, a product manager may be interested in product sales (Orange Juice) by time (first week in June) and by region (Northeast).

The process of querying the database at lower levels of aggregation is called *drill-down*, while the process of moving up the dimensional hierarchy to higher levels is called *drill-up*.

The multi-dimensional database structure enables users to query across dimensions. Thus, a product manager can analyze juice sales in the

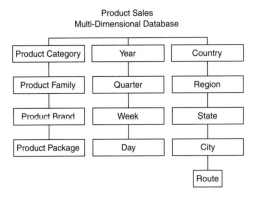

Figure 3.4 Logical multi-dimensional database structure.

northeast region during the week of a promotional campaign and compare those results with prior weeks' sales or against sales in other regions in which no campaign occurred.

Multi-dimensional databases are not problem free. The structure of a multi-dimensional database typically needs to be created by a specialized programmer. Microsoft makes this task somewhat easier by supplying both a Cube wizard and a Cube Editor with SQL Server OLAP Services. If users need data that are not part of the hierarchical structure of the multi-dimensional database, they will need to find some other data source or revert to a programmer to add the new dimension to the database. Some multi-dimensional databases, including Microsoft's OLAP Services, enable users to *drill-through* to an underlying relational data warehouse to obtain data that is not in the multi-dimensional database structures.

Multi-dimensional databases also suffer from a problem known as the data explosion problem. Each additional dimension, with its aggregate levels, results in an exponential increase in the number of cells, or dimensional intersections. In some scenarios, such as a customer-centric data warehouse, the multi-dimensional database may be called on to create many cells for which no data are provided. For instance, a large retail chain may have one thousand locations with ten thousand products at each location, and one million identified customers. If the organization attempted to build a multi-dimensional database with all these data points, most of the cells would be empty because not every customer purchased every product at every location on every day.

Multi-Dimensional Database Categories

Multi-dimensional databases fall into three major categories.

1. The first category is the pure multi-dimensional, or MOLAP, database. A MOLAP database contains the entire multi-dimensional database in a specialized structure that can only be accessed using a specialized query language or tool. MOLAP databases are available from vendors such as Oracle, Hyperion Solutions, Applix, and Speedware.

2. The second category is the pure relational, or ROLAP, database. This is an OLAP database based entirely on a relational DBMS using either a star or snowflake database schema. Usually a specialized server product sits between the client and the ROLAP database. This server intercepts queries from the client, generates SQL for the RDBMS, and

returns the result set to the client. These servers are also responsible, in many instances, for aggregations, calculations, or other manipulations that are not performed by the relational DBMS. Companies such as Information Advantage, Informix, and MicroStrategy provide ROLAP solutions.

3. The third category is the hybrid, or HOLAP, database. This type of multi-dimensional database stores some summarized or aggregated data in the multi-dimensional database itself, while other data, such as detailed transaction data, is stored in an underlying, related RDBMS. The user can navigate the multi-dimensional database analyzing the summary data, but if the user requires data that is not stored in the multi-dimensional database, the system automatically generates SQL to retrieve the data from the back-end RDBMS and then loads that data into the multi-dimensional database. Crystal Software and Gentia deliver HOLAP solutions.

Microsoft has taken a uniquely different approach with SQL Server OLAP Services. The database designer can decide to implement a distributed OLAP architecture that can be either purely multi-dimensional, relational, or a blend of the two. Thus, data can be stored on a separate OLAP server or in the SQL Server database as a star schema, or some data can be stored in the OLAP server with the remainder in the relational database.

Metadata Management

Similar to the other environments discussed in this book, the storage environment has special metadata requirements. The metadata in the storage environment is used primarily to organize the data into structures that can be populated by the activities in the source environment as described in Chapter 2, and queried by users or applications in the desktop environment. (See Chapter 4.) In addition, as described in Chapter 1, this metadata is created by developers in the design and development environment and is managed by users in the operations and management environment.

In the storage environment metadata is used primarily to describe data attributes and relationships. Attributes include such things as data type (integer, variable-length string, fixed-length string, boolean, date/time), and maximum size (in bytes). Relationships describe the linkages between fields, such as primary key and foreign key relationships. In the multi-dimensional Microsoft OLAP Services environment, metadata describes the hierarchical relationship between higher levels of aggregation (such as Year) and lower levels (such as Month or Week). It is also used to handle the calculations that are an integral part of OLAP analysis. For example, profitability analysis or budgeting and forecasting analysis are heavily dependent on calculations of varying complexity. These calculations are performed using the features of the OLAP engine, and are stored in the engine's metadata.

Security Metadata

Another important category of metadata is focused on data security and access controls. Access to data can be restricted to four modes: no access, read-only access, read/write access, or read/write/delete access as shown in Table 3.3.

Data access can be maintained at several levels of granularity, both within the database and outside it. Outside security refers to access to the system itself at the operating system level, or the network connecting the client with the server. It can also refer to the ability to gain access to the disk or file system that contain the database files. In most instances, once users gain authorized access to the machine hosting the database, they can only access data through a database server process. Users have no direct access to the database files, which are secured using the account of the DBA or system administrator.

Within the database, further levels of security granularity are available. The user can be granted varying levels of access, with varying privilege levels, to the database, table, row, or column.

Table 3.3 Security Modes

SECURITY MODE	MEANING
No access	User has no access to the data.
Read-only	User can view the data but has no right to modify it.
Read/write	User can view data and can modify existing data or add new data.
Read/write/delete	User has the additional privilege to remove data from the database.

Table 3.4   Security Matrix

	READ-ONLY	READ/WRITE	READ/WRITE/DELETE
Operating system	X		
Database	X		
Table	X	X	
Row/Column	X	X	X

Access control enables the DBA to provide fine-grained security that results in a matrix that looks like Table 3.4.

This table indicates the user can only write to a specific set of one or more tables, but can only delete a specific set of rows or columns.

One or more users can also be granted varying levels of access based on a continuum ranging from individual to group. An individual user can be granted specific access to a particular object or resource by means of a username/password combination. The user can also be made a member of a group that has a different level of security access. Or, the user who is a member of a group may be granted a role which can supersede the security profile of the group. For example, a sales manager may be granted read/write access to sales data based on membership within the sales group but may also be extended read access to accounting data based on his or her role as a senior executive.

Views

Views is an important category of metadata within a relational decision support database. A relational DBMS does not typically provide an easy mechanism for the user to navigate the data, which is one reason OLAP databases and star schemas have become so popular. Both are attempts to provide the user with a hierarchical view of the data that makes sense from the perspective of the user.

An argument can be made for deploying only a fully normalized relational structure. A normalized RDBMS has no duplication of data, which conserves disk space. Although the cost of a disk drive has decreased at a rapid pace, the growth of data has accelerated at an even greater clip. An extra 10 bytes per row in a million-row table adds up to 10 megabytes. Most de-normalized star schema structures create a significant additional storage load on the system.

However, system administrators have the ability to provide users with the power and flexibility of a fully normalized relational DBMS while simultaneously providing them with the ease of use and navigability of a de-normalized OLAP database. In the Microsoft environment, this can be accomplished in two ways: by implementing an OLAP or hybrid-OLAP database using SQL Server OLAP services, or by creating a view of an SQL Server database that implements a star schema.

CHAPTER 4

The Desktop Environment

From the era of the earliest computers, the automated generation of reports has been a priority function of computerized information systems. This tradition continues in modern decision-support systems, with reporting now complemented by query, analysis, data mining, and other functions. The massive green-and-white printouts of ancient line printers have acceded to interactive client applications. Report *readers*—who until relatively recently read data from paper—are now report *users*, reading interactive reports online in viewing tools.

The Users' Domain

The report has evolved into a kind of application that report consumers use to explore their organization's data. In addition to the tables and charts of traditional reports, the new online reports typically include executable data queries (ad hoc or parameterized), analytic data functions (pivot and drill down/up), and advanced visualization (compound graphs and data maps). These are all available online, which permits the user/reader to interact with the data. Analogous to editing a document in a word processor, the user submits a query to change the data content, pivots the result set to find a dimension of interest, or recharts the data to effect a dramatic presentation.

These data collection, analysis, and presentation tasks are accomplished with client software running in the desktop environment which is clearly the domain of the end-user—whether a producer or consumer of reports. This layer contains reporting, query, analysis, and data mining tools, plus analytical applications that may be developed using these and other tools. Analytical applications can be either dedicated applications, such as marketing automation, or part of a larger packaged application, such as SAP R/3. The desktop environment also includes desktop-to-network infrastructure used to access, retrieve, view, analyze, and manipulate data. In the Microsoft environment, this is where Plato-capable clients reside, and also where ODBC, OLE DB, and OLE DB for OLAP drivers reside.

Quality Reports for Consumers

The media for delivering reports evolve continuously from paper to terminals to PC clients to browsers to hand-held devices. Yet the goal remains the same: Give the user the most appropriate medium that current technology affords, so they have the information they need, presented in a fashion best conducive to making viable decisions in their work.

When down in the trenches building data extraction and transformation routines, it may seem to IT personnel that the point of a data warehouse is to house collected and cleansed data that has been optimized for decision support. But the ideal goal of a data warehouse is to provide quality reports. It is possible that a decision-support project—brilliantly executed in the back office—could fail because of its lack of quality in the front office. Report design and implementation must therefore be high on the project's priority list.

Yet, "quality" is a subjective construct that can be difficult to quantify and implement. With many software projects, end-user acceptance is assumed to be an important measure in judging the success of the project. With a decision-support system, end-user acceptance often focuses on its reports' content, ease of use, and flexibility of presentation. Other factors—like response time, access to appropriate data, and reliability—

may also come into play. To help ensure user acceptance, IT personnel and end-users must work together in defining data content, style of presentation, and data manipulation capabilities as well as delivery media. The complaints and praises of report consumers will focus on the reports that IT builds for them, because these reports are their only view of the system.

Quality Tools for Providers

Although IT is fully engaged in producing reports for the majority of report consumers, data analysis is largely an end-user function performed by business managers and business analysts. Such analysts produce their own reports and have their own end users to satisfy, so their concerns of quality may focus on the accuracy and usability of the query and analysis tools that IT has provided.

Concerning metadata, a query and analysis tool should both read from and write to a common metadata repository. Depending on the technical expertise of the analytic user, the tool will either shield the user from metadata or expose it completely. If possible, the query and analysis tool should integrate with common desktop products (word processors, spreadsheets, and presentation tools) as well as with any enterprise packaged applications the organization may have. Most users respond well to an attractive graphical user interface that presents functionality intuitively without much need for training.

In selecting tools—whether for IT or for analytic users—ease of use must take priority over power. If users are intimidated by the complexity of a tool, they cannot (or will not) use the tool, and IT will have to build reports and analyses to suit their needs.

Tools for the Desktop Environment

The most commonly found categories of tools for the decision-support desktop environment are listed in Table 4.1.

These categories of tools for the desktop environment are discussed in detail in the following sections of this chapter.

Table 4.1 Categories of Decision Support Tools for the Desktop Environment

TOOL CATEGORY	DESCRIPTION
Executive Information System (EIS)	Users can view reports or displays such as a Desktop Dashboard or Balanced Scorecard that are defined and run by IT personnel or knowledge workers on a regular schedule, but users do not have the ability to manipulate the report.
Desktop Reporting	Users can run reports on demand, which have been defined by IT personnel or knowledge workers.
Extended Reporting	Users can perform limited manipulation of prepared reports by performing simple slicing and dicing, pivoting, summarization, or drill down to more detail from higher levels of summarization. These types of reports are available to users running a Plato environment because someone has to set up a Plato cube with the dimensions the users require.
Managed Query	Users can run reports, with the added ability to tailor the report output by answering prompts or passing parameters, such as time interval or geographic location.
Ad Hoc Query and Analysis	Users can perform ad hoc queries of the data and then analyze the result set.
Data Mining	Users can move into the realm of advanced analysis by defining data models and running those models against databases, searching for hitherto unknown patterns in the data. Data mining is not part of the Microsoft Data Warehouse Framework and usually requires a specialized data file. Data mining tools complement OLAP analysis, but do not utilize data in OLAP cubes.
Applications	The major trend in the industry is to deploy packaged decision support applications. These applications can either be standalone—designed to solve a specific problem such as market campaign management, or they can be integrated with a packaged application such as SAP R/3 or PeopleSoft.

Executive Information Systems

The point of an executive information system (EIS) is to make data analysis as simple as possible for the high-placed business manager who requires a broad view of the key functions of the enterprise, such as finance, sales, production, and human resources. To deliver information-rich reports that are easy for a non-technical manager to interpret, however, requires a complex system and a number of personnel. The typical EIS may consist of the following software components, each with distinct personnel requirements:

Report Viewer Tool

The end user reads reports and interacts with them online with this tool. Typically, this is the only software component that the end user sees because other personnel create the reports and provide data access.

Report Development Environment

A report programmer uses this tool to design and implement the reports the end user reads. Traditionally, EISs have been complex enough to require a specially-trained report creator for this task. More recent releases, however, have increased ease of use so that some power users can create their own reports.

Database Access

IT must provide data access, which may include a data warehouse, plus manage the schedule for running reports.

EIS reports include desktop dashboards, Balanced Scorecards or the more traditional "briefing books" perspective. The former tracks key performance indicators (KPIs) such as line-of-business profit and other measures. The latter is often structured like an application, and it typically enables financial reporting and consolidation.

Benefits

The viewer tool gives executive end users a high ease of use that allows them to focus on managing the business instead of building reports and accessing data. If the reports (and any decision-support databases that may be required) are designed and implemented well, executive end users will recognize the value of decision support and will sponsor it.

Balanced Scorecard

The Balanced Scorecard (BSC) methodology, which was originally described by Norton and Kaplan in an article in the Harvard Business Review,* is an important information technology tool for many business managers. The BSC methodology analyzes the effectiveness of an organization from four perspectives. Managers define the key performance indicator (KPI) metrics they will use to measure how well the company executes within each perspective. The four perspectives, and some representative metrics, are:

1. **Financial.** Encompasses traditional financial measures such as cash flow, stock price, revenue, net income, activity-based costing, and other measures that influence the perceptions of stockholders and the financial community.
2. **Customer.** Includes measures of customer satisfaction and retention, such as service-call response time, equipment availability, price/performance, product returns, and repeat buyers.
3. **Operations.** Collects production and operating statistics for internal measures, such as order-rate fulfillment, cost per process, and production schedules.
4. **Growth.** Tracks the measures that influence the company's future growth, such as product-development cycles, investment capital, research and development, employee recruitment and retention, and improvements to business practices.

Each company uses the methodology to determine the KPIs to track within each perspective, and develops the information technology infrastructure to capture them. The power of the BSC is that it couples information systems technology to a business methodology that provides management with a short-term and long-term view of business issues.

*Kaplan, Robert, and David Norton, "The Balanced Scorecard—Measures that Drive Performance," *Harvard Business Review*, January–February 1992.

Drawbacks

An EIS keeps the IT department in the business of report creation and maintenance, a role that many are struggling to abandon. Any failure of the EIS is subject to the scrutiny of upper management because of their role as end users, which could limit their sponsorship of the current or future decision-support projects.

Desktop Reporting

Information systems of any size have numerous reports that are generated repeatedly on a recurring schedule. For example, a report on the sales figures for a certain geography may be "run" (its data refreshed with the most up-to-date data from the appropriate database), then delivered to the manager of that sales region. The report "run" may be scheduled for the end of each month or business period, and delivery may involve putting a print out on the manager's desk, sending the report in email, or copying a file that contains the report to a server or network drive. Hence, a report must be:

- **Repeatable**—Running the report hits the same data each time, although the values of that data may have changed since the last run.

- **Schedulable**—Each report runs on an established production schedule. Some users, however, may require the ability to run a report on demand whenever they need fresh data.

- **Deliverable**—Until recent years, most reports were printed and delivered on paper. Today, production reporting in many information systems has shifted to online delivery.

Most report readers receive reports that someone else created. Traditional reports (those that involve no analytic interaction) are still the domain of IT developers (either inside the organization or external consultants), who define and deploy reports according to the specifications of end users. Even so, in recent years, many IT departments have tried to get out of the time-consuming and expensive business of report definition. Some organizations have turned to user-friendly tools that enable end users—the consumers or report readers—to create, run, and distribute reports of their own design. As well as lessening the load on the IT department, this arrangement also avoids the all-too-common disconnect between user specifications and actual report implementation. Of course, IT must stay involved as the provider of the data and maintainer of the data access infrastructure.

A growing trend has been to shift the delivery of reports from paper to online media. Instead of the fat printout dropped into interoffice mail, report readers can now receive files that encapsulate the data, metadata, and visual representation of a report. A report file may be pushed to a user's hard drive, sent by way of email, copied to a server or network drive, or made available using a Web server. The user may log into a server or browse a Web site to find files that contain recently-run reports. Hence, a new category—*desktop reporting*—enables a report to be delivered to the user's computer desktop instead of the user's desk.

With desktop reporting, report readers use a report viewer (or a browser, perhaps with plug-in or a Java applet) to open and view a file that contains a report. Reading a report online has several advantages, which stem mostly from the fact that the user interacts with the data and its presentation in a way that is impossible with paper. First and foremost, the user can search a report repository for an online report. In fact, many report viewers support complex searches (with Boolean expressions) that are analogous to queries. The difference between a search and a query is that a search looks for a pre-run report, while a query creates a new, customized report. Some IT departments depend on this functionality to give end users a type of limited query that leaves operational and decision-support systems untouched. With an online report, the user can extract data (perhaps gathered as the result set of a search operation or simply copied to the Windows clipboard), and paste or import the data into other desktop applications. Report viewers provide a variety of navigational functions for traversing the report, as well as hypertext links to sections of the report, other online reports, or other applications. As with any hypertext system, the report reader can follow a personalized path through the content. To view an online report, the user must boot up a computer, but the user can also print an online report for a more traditional—but not interactive—reading experience.

In a large, networked or Web-based information system, the run, schedule, and delivery functions of production reporting are often accomplished by a report server. So-called enterprise reporting demands a server to scale up to hundreds or thousands of users. The report server usually sits on a dedicated piece of hardware and accesses databases over a network or Web infrastructure. Most report servers support security, scaling, parallel processing, and failover. The report server handles the scheduling, versioning, and push distribution of online reports. It also provides a repository of report files from which report readers can browse and pull reports. Recent versions of some report servers support the publish-and-subscribe model so an end user can select reports of interest, and the server automatically delivers them to the user's desktop. Delivery can be on demand, on a repetitive schedule—weekly or monthly, or as the result of an event such as the western region sales fell 10 percent or more this period. Actuate Software, Seagate Software, Datawatch, and SQRiBE Technologies have implemented server-based reporting engines of this type.

Extended Reporting

Many IT organizations support separate tools for reporting, ad hoc query, and analysis. To help reduce the overhead, overlapping functionality, and excessive costs associated with multiple tools, vendors have moved to deliver the three distinct functions using a single tool. This relatively new type of integrated reporting, analysis, and query (IRAQ) tool appeals to IT departments because it means fewer tools to install and less training and upgrading.

Buyers should beware because some IRAQ tools omit functionality (usually for analytic tasks) in the compromise process of shoehorning all three, tool types into a manageable client application. Java-based applet tools in particular offer limited analytic capabilities because the applet would become too large to download in an acceptable amount of time.

With IRAQ tools, users can perform limited analytic manipulation of prepared reports, by performing simple slicing and dicing, pivoting, summarization, or perhaps by drilling down into detail from higher levels of summarization. Analytic reports are by nature interactive; therefore IRAQ tools are always meant to be read online.

Managed Query

A managed query is submitted by means of a parameterized report. IT builds the report using its selected report-building tool but defines some limits of the data as variable parameters. When a user runs a parameterized report, the report prompts the user (generally with a dialog box) for values for the variable parameters, which are passed to the server. The server then runs the report, populating it with data based on the passed parameters. The values input by the user typically delimit a time interval or identify a geographic region. Hence, the user could run the report repeatedly—but with different parameters—to examine the data for various geographies and/or time periods. Some more sophisticated tools will also use the user security profile as an additional parameter, used to limit the reports and data the user can view.

A managed query gives the user something akin to query ability, without requiring the user to know a query language, data structures, or how to attach to a data source, as some ad hoc query tools do. IT personnel are usually required to write the parameterized report, but a managed query gives IT personnel control over the nature of queries hitting their databases. In some cases, it is possible to submit parameters that return large data sets, but the "runaway query" that locks up operational systems is less likely.

Benefits

By its nature, a managed query requires well-defined questions and answers; these translate into low-overhead queries, and most users understand them without training. To implement a managed query requires only the report-building tool on which the organization has chosen to standardize. Likewise, running and viewing a parameterized report requires only the standard report viewer. Most managed queries hit databases built for other decision-support purposes, without the need to create an additional dedicated data set.

Drawbacks

A managed query returns a single data set, unlike the multiple data sets encapsulated in modern online reports; the limited return set limits the amount of analysis that can be done with it. Developing a parameterized report is beyond the grasp of most users, so IT must create and maintain it. A managed query assumes that users are allowed to run a parameterized report any time and as many times as they like.

Ad Hoc Query Tools

Query tools enable end-users to interactively search databases in the storage environment layer. An "ad hoc" query allows the user to request almost any data set that can be structured from the data in the storage environment, unlike the carefully circumscribed parameters of a managed query. Users typically execute several ad hoc queries—iteratively refining the query while exploring available data—until receiving a result set that optimally expresses the measures of interest.

With some queries, the result set answers the question. For instance, an ad hoc query against an operational system might answer the question:

"How many shipping cartons of a certain size and of the type approved for international use are located in the organization's secondary warehouse but are not committed to use?" The result set contains a single integer, which is self-explanatory.

A far more complex result set would emerge from an ad hoc query such as: "Select the monthly sales totals for Western, Midwestern, and Southern regions for the second and third quarters of 1998." The user then shifts to a different collection of functionality to manipulate and analyze the result set. Once the user develops a meaningful analysis, another collection of functionality enables the user to publish the analysis. Hence, for many users, the point of ad hoc query is to collect a discrete, although complex, subset of data specifically for analysis.

Benefits

Power users can submit ad hoc queries to find and analyze almost any data they need for decision support.

Drawbacks

It is possible to submit a "query from hell" that runs for a long time and kills network bandwidth. The user may structure a query that cannot be processed in a timely fashion, or that doesn't return the results they desire. Some unfriendly query tools require knowledge of SQL, relational principles, multi-dimensional principles, or database structures.

Analysis Tools

Ad hoc query usually goes hand in hand with data analysis, and the two are often combined in the same client tool. The typical query-and-analysis tool gives end users three fundamental analytic capabilities:

1. **Visualization**—Most query and analysis tools provide numerous types of sophisticated charts and graphs to help the analyst find the view that best expresses the meaning of the data. Besides the usual business chart types (pie, bar, scatter), some vendors are incorporating compound chart types developed for statistical analysis and other scientific studies. A few tools enhance the interactive analysis experience by enabling the user to click chart parts such as a pie wedge or a bar for drill down or pivot.

2. **Drill Down**—Analysis tools show summaries on which the user can click to drill down to data of greater detail. For instance, a user viewing national sales figures could drill down to view the data for a particular state. Some tools now enable drill-through all the way to the source data, so the lineage of crucial data can be audited.

3. **Pivot**—A user viewing data in a table can rearrange and regroup the data to pivot the table. This reorders data along a dimension. For example, a user viewing a table of sales figures by geography may pivot the table to view the data grouped by product.

NOTE

Microsoft delivers a PivotTable Service with SQL Server that runs on the Windows client. Users can pivot tables using Microsoft Excel, or other applications that call the PivotTable Service, to reorganize the data view. For example, a user can view sales figures sorted by geography, then pivot the table to view the data by product. However, an Excel spreadsheet has no embedded multi-dimensional capabilities, so drilling down (or up) requires queries that fetch more data.

High-End Multi-Dimensional Analysis Tools

Multi-dimensional analysis tools support OLAP for the retrieval, visualization, and analysis of multi-dimensional data. A multi-dimensional analysis tool accesses data in either a multi-dimensional or a relational database. These high-end tools are usually integrated tightly with a particular database brand.

OLAP Tool Integrated with a Relational Database

Examples of tools that access data in a relational database include Decision Support Suite from Information Advantage, MetaCube from Informix Corporation, and SAS/EIS from SAS Institute. The relational database has been structured with logical dimensions; which provide a multi-dimensional structure for analysis as well as relational structure for SQL queries.

OLAP Tool Integrated with a Multi-Dimensional Database

Express from Oracle and GentiaDB from Gentia are examples of tight integration between an OLAP tool with a multi-dimensional database. Each product incorporates its own proprietary multi-dimensional

Multi-Dimensional APIs

Besides the multi-dimensional database brands that have been mentioned, some vendors produce multi-dimensional database engines that are "open" for use with a variety of desktop tools and development environments. Products like Essbase from Hyperion Solutions and TM1 from Applix do not have a dedicated development environment, but they support an API instead. Essbase supports the MD-API promulgated by the OLAP Council, while TM1 supports OLE DB for OLAP. These tools are often used to deploy an embedded analytic application, although they can be deployed as a generic OLAP tool.

database, but these tools are capable of extracting from other databases, as well. In each case, the tool's calculation, aggregation, and other features depend on the integrated database engine.

Whether integrated with a relational or a multi-dimensional database, the OLAP tools mentioned here include:

- **Development environment**—This is usually a collection of visually-oriented tools that may support data modeling, query definitions, charting, and user interface design for analytic reports.

- **Fourth generation language (4GL)**—The 4GL is the scripting language for the analytic reports developed with the tool.

- **Viewing environment**—The end user reads and interacts with analyses in the viewer.

- **Specialized functions**—The tool has functions such as statistical, time-series, and financial that are often dependent on the capabilities of the underlying database. Developers can also define custom functions.

- **Multi-tier support**—These product sets support multi-tier architectures for scaling and performance.

Clearly, these are high-end tool sets that require a legion of developers, knowledge workers, IT specialists, database administrators, and other personnel.

Desktop OLAP

Desktop OLAP tools are generalized to work with a variety of relational and multi-dimensional data sources. These include BrioQuery from Brio Technologies, BusinessObjects from Business Objects, PowerPlay from Cognos, and IBIS from CorVu. Most Desktop OLAP tools generate SQL and transport it to a server; after receiving the result set from the server, the tool reorganizes it to form a multi-dimensional cube called a *hyper-cube* on the client computer. Several of these vendors have extended their products recently to support server-based cubes. The local hyper-cube is suited to situations where analytic users are mobile, or in which users need ad hoc query capabilities but get little support from IT. Whether generating a local hypercube or not, the multi-dimensional view of relational data provided by the desktop OLAP tool provides the end-user with analysis in multiple dimensions, without forcing IT to purchase, install, learn, and support a multi-dimensional database management system.

The hypercube has its limitations. Only one user can manipulate and analyze the data of the hypercube, so the results are not easily shared with other knowledge workers. Hypercubes are proprietary, so they cannot be shared using analytic tools from different vendors. Furthermore, a multi-dimensional cache on a client desktop is, by definition, transient, so it needs periodic refreshing. Typically it must be completely rebuilt when data changes. Downloading a hypercube may be unacceptable for mobile users dialing into an information system because of bandwidth limitations.

Desktop OLAP tools generally have a richly visual user interface with numerous chart types, and they also have sophisticated data manipulation capabilities, such as pivot and drill down/up. The principle benefits of a desktop OLAP tool are ease of use and the ability to generate a local hypercube with limited involvement from IT personnel.

Microsoft does not provide a desktop OLAP environment as part of the SQL Server product. Microsoft SQL Server OLAP Services does have a client that can be used to manage and develop cubes which can also be used to query and analyze a SQL Server OLAP Services cube. Developers who are going to use SQL Server OLAP Services for OLAP analysis can either build a client using any language that supports the ADO or OLE DB APIs, or they can install Microsoft Excel, or install a third-party tool, such as those described in this chapter.

Data Mining

Data mining* is a still-emerging category of analysis that takes an approach somewhat different from OLAP-oriented decision support. Data mining originated in the academic world of artificial intelligence and advanced statistical analysis. A data-mining tool parses sizable amounts of data searching for patterns. It then makes connections between apparently unrelated facts to identify trends and to reveal hidden relationships. By extrapolating from a trend, the data-mining tool can even predict future directions for a trend. Deducing statistically accurate patterns, however, requires very large quantities of historic and detailed data. Data mining tools usually require transaction-level detail data, and don't benefit from summarized data. Analysis of summary data is more often done using OLAP tools.

Data mining tools are often applied to customer-centric marketing analysis. One goal might be to define the attributes of consumers who are likely to buy a certain product so that a targeted marketing campaign can be launched. Another goal might be to develop a profile for customers who are likely to commit fraud, or who are not profitable because of excessive product returns, support calls, or other problems.

A data mining tool builds a model, and uses various algorithms to analyze the model and—depending on the algorithm in use—organizes the patterns of information it discovers into a structure based on one or more of the following listed from simplest to most complex:

Clusters—As entities of similar attributes are discovered such as customers, they are grouped together in clusters. On a higher level, clusters of similar attributes may be clustered together to form a hierarchical taxonomy.

Decision trees—A data-mining tool can deduce business rules and express them as a decision tree. Such a tree might identify customers who are likely candidates for add-on products or services.

Neural nets—Very complex entities and relationships require neural nets. It is also possible to define an entity with a neural net to guide the mining operation.

---

*See Berry, Michael and Gordon Linoff, *Data Mining Techniques for Marketing, Sales and Customer Support*, (John Wiley & Sons, Inc., 1997) for an excellent introduction to data mining.

Some data mining exercises use multiple algorithms. Using clusters, a one-to-one marketer can identify the attributes of customers who have bought a certain product. The marketer would then use neural net technology (applying the data model developed with clusters) to mine prospects from a different database.

Many data mining tools have strong data visualization features that summarize data in complex graphics. An image might be:

- Three-dimensional so the user can rotate for different views.

- A compound chart that combines multiple styles of graphs to illustrate various trends.

- An "image map" that represents a cluster, decision tree, or neural net, so the user can navigate through the information.

Benefits

A data-mining tool can be an effective competitive weapon that helps target marketing and sales initiatives. Its predictive capabilities are unique in the decision-support arsenal.

Drawbacks

Data mining technology is still immature, proprietary, and it has tough learning and optimization curves. You often need specialized expertise to fully utilize a powerful data-mining tool. To ensure a statistically viable

---

Data Mining and Text Mining

Data mining analyzes structured data stored in databases. A similar technology called text mining extracts patterns from unstructured data in text documents. Similar to data-mining tools, text-mining tools depend on clusters, decision trees, and neural nets. However, a text-mining tool has the added ability to make semantic sense of the unstructured text it parses. Text mining tools are used to retrieve value from an organization's store of word processing documents, spreadsheets, presentation files, and email. These text documents contain much of an organization's "knowledge"—that is, proven solutions to recurring tasks and problems. "Knowledge management" systems often include a text-mining tool as a way of discovering and sharing solutions.

data sample, the databases the tool hits may need many gigabytes (perhaps terabytes) of historic and detail data online. There are no standards available to ensure that different types of data mining tools will work together.

Applications

One major trend in the industry is to deploy packaged decision-support applications. These applications usually fall into one of the following categories:

Analytic or Standalone applications—An application designed to solve a specific problem, such as market campaign management, customer churn, or market basket analysis.

Decision-support applications integrated with packaged applications— An analytical application integrated with a major packaged application, such as SAP R/3 or PeopleSoft.

Analytic Applications

Many end users feel that their decision-support needs are best satisfied by analytic applications specific to the industry they work in or the business function they fulfill. Instead of generic query and analysis tools, these are structured applications developed to implement a particular business function. Common functions include financial forecasting, profitability analysis, one-to-one marketing, and customer relationship management (CRM). Others serve the analysis needs of a certain industry, such as telecommunications, insurance, transportation, consumer packaged goods, or healthcare. Some analytic applications, such as customer retention analysis in banks, are specific to both function and industry.

The ideal analytic application will include an extensible data model for its industry or business task. The data model may be specific for financial forecasting or tracking common retail metrics. Note that many analytic applications are based on a data warehouse/mart or a multidimensional database. Vendors of analytic applications in industries that involve material providers or distributors often support access via an extranet so their external stakeholders can improve their operations through analysis.

An analytical application must also include logic for obtaining data from the most common, frequently used sources in the industry or function. The analytic application should access data in existing databases as well as ERP data. This logic should include functions for performing data consolidation and formatting that are routine for the industry or function. For example, the insurance industry has a variety of algorithms for analyzing risk. The data extraction and transformation software should provide support for all the major algorithms, enabling the user to simply select the most appropriate one for the specific implementation.

Finally, an analytical application will have a pre-configured set of queries and reports that are accessible through a desktop GUI. The vendor also should provide a development environment that enables tailoring, customization, and enhancements to the base-line set of reports and queries.

Benefits

Focusing on an industry or business task helps many users to be productive. The ideal analytic application will have functions specific to its industry and an industry-specific data model pre-built for true turnkey.

Drawbacks

A focused analytic application is generally not useful for generic analysis outside its focus. Some are limited by the data sources they can access. Some lack a data model, so the end-user's IT department must build it.

Decision-Support Packaged Applications for ERP

Packaged applications—especially ERP packages from Baan, PeopleSoft, or SAP—are now entrenched in industries that require enterprise-wide finance, manufacturing, purchasing, logistics, and human resources applications. But some packaged applications lack decision-support data and functions that end-users can comprehend. For example, most ERP products include a report writer that, due to its complexity or unfriendliness, requires a professional developer. Even if end-users could comprehend the report writer, the complexity of ERP schema would prevent them from finding the data they need to analyze.

One solution to this dilemma is to integrate a decision support tool with a packaged application. There are two fundamental approaches to this integration, based on the location of data that the decision support tool will access: direct access of ERP data in its native system, and access of ERP data moved to a data warehouse.

Packaged Apps Are Not Always ERP

While the most talked about packaged applications come from the enterprise resource planning vendors, not all packaged applications are ERP solutions. Thousands of independent software vendors (ISVs) provide turnkey applications that solve a specific business problem. The difference between packaged applications and ERP solutions is that ERP products are designed to integrate the major functional business units of an entire enterprise, while most packaged applications are focused on a specific business unit or industry. In this respect a packaged application is comparable to a data mart, while an ERP is like an enterprise-wide data warehouse.

Direct Access to ERP Data

With direct access, users are allowed to run queries and reports directly against the ERP transactional database. This straightforward approach meets the basic reporting needs of users and provides for limited analysis. Reporting engines, such as those from Actuate Software or SQRiBE Technologies, can access the ERP data and stage it as formatted reports on a report server. Another direct approach to ERP data is to build views into packaged application databases, perhaps using products from Business Objects, Broadquest or TopTier. Users launch queries against the views, which simplifies access to source data. This approach suffers from all the performance and navigation difficulties that led to the data warehouse movement in the first place.

Benefits

Direct accessing of packaged application data does not require significant involvement from IT, which simply configures the metadata.

Drawbacks

This approach suffers from all the major drawbacks of accessing any transaction processing system using a query and analysis tool. A user may unintentionally submit a query that slows the database server significantly, perhaps due to a multi-table join. This approach (in many cases) precludes the analysis of data from multiple sources. Many transaction-processing systems do not have adequate navigation metadata for end-users to effectively locate the data they want.

ERP Data in a Warehouse

Many organizations recognize that reporting and analysis against ERP data is too limiting for their analytic needs. Instead, they choose to build or buy a data warehouse or data mart that extracts data from the packaged application. In this way, the data is restructured for optimal responses to query and analysis tools, obviating the fear of dragging down the performance of the packaged application with queries.

There are three main approaches emerging in the marketplace.*The first is for an ISV to produce a decision support application targeted at a specific packaged application database. The vendor combines an ETML process, data model, and pre-configured queries and reports into a packaged data mart.

The second approach is for the packaged application vendor to deliver a decision support function. Some vendors build this capability themselves, while others team with a tools vendor to deliver a solution.

The third is for a company to build a decision support database that extracts data from one or more packaged applications. This approach ensures the company's decision support needs are met, but requires significantly more resources and expertise. Extracting, consolidating and transforming ERP data, plus loading it into a data warehouse, is a difficult process that requires considerable ERP and data warehousing expertise to develop. Once in place, it is a repetitive task that requires maintenance.

Users of the Desktop Environment

The long list of decision-support tool types for the desktop environment listed in the previous section of this chapter testifies to the diversity of user needs. That is, there are many categories of tools, because there are many categories of decision-support users.

*For a discussion on the integration of decision support applications and packaged applications see Craig, Robert, "Packaged Apps Meet DSS," *Database Programming & Design*, June, 1998, 11(6).

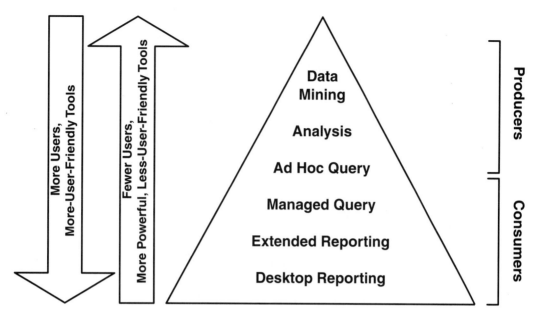

Figure 4.1   User categories correlated with tool complexity.

User Types and Tool Types

Each tool category is designed to meet the needs of a specific user type. In fact, users of the decision-support desktop environment can be categorized by the tools they use as shown in Figure 4.1.

The largest portion of users that have reporting tools (report viewers, extended report tools, and managed queries), whereas analytic users number far less by proportion and use ad hoc query and analysis tools. Generally speaking, the most numerous users have the highest ease of use, and the least numerous users have tools of the greatest complexity.

NOTE

The typical usage for an EIS runs contrary to the trends found in Figure 4.1. Often two or three users, usually at the highest level of management, have an EIS, even in a large organization. Some of these users may produce their own balanced scorecards or other analyses, but it is more likely that the analyses were developed by IT personnel for a non-technical executive consumer. Furthermore, reports from EISs typically track performance indicators that are kept confidential within the company. Thus, these are rarely shared with other internal or external consumers.

Producers and Consumers

Tool category aside, decision-support users can be partitioned roughly into two extreme categories, based on their roles as report/analysis producers or consumers.

Producers

The producer category mostly coincides with the traditional notion of *knowledge worker*—someone who uses ad hoc query-and-analysis tools to collect unique data sets and analyze them through pivot, drill down, and visualization. A knowledge worker's analyses are read—consumed—by other members of the organization, often senior management.

Knowledge workers typically have several skills honed to a sharp edge. Besides being power users of query-and-analysis tools, they are intimately acquainted with the organization's data and metadata. Many are capable of using development environments and database management utilities to gain access to an even broader range of data than may be in the data warehouse. At the highest level, some knowledge workers use data extraction and transformation tools to ensure they get the data they need for analysis.

Another important group of producers includes IT personnel who create reports for mass consumption within the organization. By extension, database administrators and others who provide data access for analysis may also be considered producers.

Consumers

The consumers or *report readers* read the reports created by knowledge workers or IT personnel. These users can run reports and managed queries. Note that consumers occasionally shift into the role of report producers, and that knowledge workers consume reports regularly.

Because consumers read documents designed by producers, consumers need a mechanism for perusing available reports, analyses, and queries as well as the ability to schedule the run and delivery of any of these. These capabilities are supported by most report servers with a Windows-Explorer-like or web-browser-based user interface.

On a percentage basis, any organization will have far more consumers than producers. However, these distinctions can be problematic because producers commonly read reports and consumers occasionally create reports. Users of the desktop environment shift roles continuously, such that there are many "shades of gray" between the black and white extremes of the producer-consumer dichotomy.

Intersection of Producers and Consumers

The numbers of knowledge workers and report readers are both growing, but the burgeoning overlap of the two reveals a more significant growth. (See Figure 4.2.) The intersection between analytic report producers and consumers is currently expanding, largely due to consumers progressively crossing into the space traditionally inhabited exclusively by the knowledge workers. Even so, the consumers-become-producers tend to make such forays only occasionally and only briefly. Most consumers return to consuming, despite temporary role shifts into producing. With more users producing reports, the volume of reports increases, so knowledge workers tend to make their usual cross into consuming territory more often than has previously occurred. User roles, already fuzzy, get fuzzier all the time.

Several factors have contributed to the upward mobility of report consumers. Ease of use has advanced significantly in recent years across all categories of tools for the desktop environment, although it is most pronounced with desktop OLAP tools. Instead of the weeks of training that an analysis tool required in the previous decade, the latest generation of

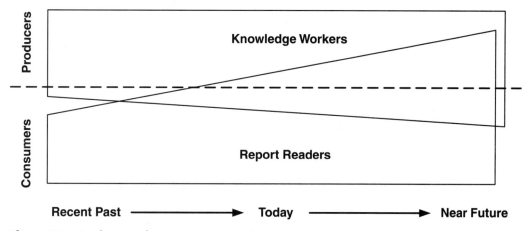

Figure 4.2   Producer and consumer intersection.

OLAP tools can accommodate the occasional analyst with minimal training.

On another front, the arrival of powerful, flexible IRAQ tools has put analytic capabilities onto the desktops of more report consumers. Functions for online analytic processing can be found in the same tool the consumer uses for running and viewing reports. Although the OLAP capabilities of an IRAQ tool are limited compared to mature query-and-analysis tools, the functionality is nonetheless present for the consumer to use. In fact, one could argue that the main function of IRAQ tools is to provide report readers with upward mobility into low-end analysis.

Other contributing factors include the trend of allowing more users to access organizational data (even external stake holders such as material providers and distributors), the desire to gain a better return on investment from the data store of an organization, and improved servers and bandwidth. Last but not least is web delivery of query-and-analysis tools; as with any software category, placing a tool in a browser greatly accelerates any tendency toward a "democratization" of the tool's use as well as any data access required by the tool.

The report readers' visits to the realm of the report producers are, to date, akin to tourism because most consumers quickly return to consuming reports. However, if certain borders are opened, many consumers may become permanent residents in the land of query and analysis. The strong trend toward data analysis in the 1990s has added value to the professions of many users; hence, the number of analysts has grown throughout the decade. Other users have been frustrated during this trend because their organizations have had neither budget nor IT expertise to implement a decision-support system.

Microsoft Corporation's SQL Server has the potential to open this border by providing an integrated platform for decision support at a price point and simplicity of technology that is suited to smaller and less sophisticated organizations. Many organizations are already implementing SQL-Server-based decision-support systems, which will provide an affordable and manageable entry point that brings many more users into the world of query and analysis.

Although an appropriate platform for the department or work group, decision support based on SQL Server has limitations concerning the number of users, data volume, and sophistication of data transformation.

So the same users who learn analysis through SQL Server technologies and tools may eventually need heftier and more feature-rich systems and tools. In this way, SQL Server provides an entry point as well as a stepping stone to larger decision support systems. In these roles, SQL Server's new integration of decision support technologies and tools promises to increase the number of analytic users (as well as the number of consumers who intermittently produce reports), while also supplying a migration path for user competence from entry level to power analyst status.

CHAPTER 5

The Data Warehouse Life Cycle

In prior chapters we covered the concept of the five environments illustrated in Figure 1.1 in Chapter 1, and we discussed the source, storage, and desktop environments in considerable detail. However, building a decision support system requires more than simply understanding the five environments and the various tools that are available or required in those environments. It also requires understanding the life cycle of the decision support system process, which brings us to the development and operational management environments. (See Figure 5.1.)

Three major life cycles comprise the decision support system process. They are:

1. Implementation
2. Management and maintenance
3. Usage

In this chapter we will discuss these three related life cycles in some detail. We will relate the issues in the life cycles to the various functions that are part of the Microsoft data warehouse framework.

We will explore these ideas by discussing a representative scenario. The scenario will discuss the process of implementing a data warehouse to

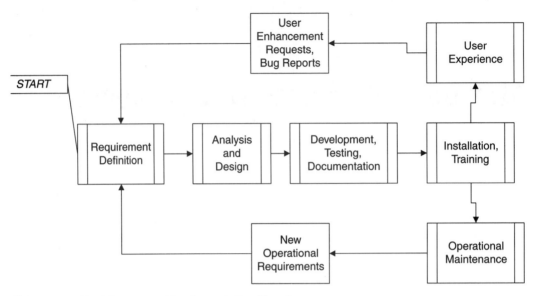

Figure 5.1 Decision support implementation life cyle.

support a CRM database, based on SQL Server 7.0, and some SQL Server OLAP Services cubes for customer-focused analysis, such as loyalty or lifetime value. Later, we will discuss adding additional sales and product data to the data warehouse, and using this data to build additional cubes for sales and product marketing analysis.

Once the databases have been implemented and deployed, the organization will need to maintain them over time. This need will result in two primary activities. The first is operational management of the databases themselves, including backup/recovery, performance analysis and management, and maintaining security, among other operational tasks.

The second primary maintenance activity involves adding additional features and functions to the application. This step is usually a result of requests from users or the operations staff for additional functionality. As users gain experience with the system, they begin to realize its full potential. This realization will result in requests for additional data and new reports and queries as users become more sophisticated and understand how they can leverage the information in the company's databases to develop a better understanding of their business. Developers also will want to change or update the software as they gain experience with the system. Because of schedule constraints, developers are often unable to add features they would like to see in the first release. Features that didn't make the cut for the first release are commonly added in the second version.

The Decision Support System Implementation Life Cycle

The decision support system implementation life cycle is a typical software development life cycle. Most companies will be able to modify their existing implementation life cycle practices to meet the needs of the decision support implementation life cycle, which is illustrated in Figure 5.1.

The other two data warehouse life-cycle components—the design and development environment, and the operations and management environment—affect all three environments described previously.

Source environment—defining and capturing data definitions from source systems; analyzing source data and defining the transformations that must be applied to the data to prepare, consolidate, cleanse, and validate it before moving it to the storage environment; establishing data mappings between source and target systems; defining the scheduling process and how operators will handle unforeseen errors.

Storage environment—For example, defining the data structures that will make up the various decision support databases; deciding whether to use a star schema, a normalized structure, or a multidimensional database; generating data definition language for relational databases, and using wizards to create multidimensional databases.

Desktop environment—For example, creating the user interface; the differences between a client/server (Windows) user interface and a web-client interface; and the state of the art of browser-based or Java-based tools to define web-client interfaces.

This chapter discusses life-cycle issues that must be addressed in these three environments. The system must be designed, implemented, deployed and managed as a unified entity. The process of designing and developing data warehouse(s)/mart(s) tends to be iterative, with tasks repeated in a spiral. The major tasks are listed in Table 5.1.

As the spiral, illustrated in Figure 5.2, cycles back to begin again with requirements, the meaning of the current circle changes. More than one interpretation is possible. Here are two different scenarios.

Table 5.1 Life Cycle Tasks

TASK	DESCRIPTION
Requirements	The organization exists for some purpose. This section will discuss how to determine the business imperatives of the organization, such as goals and objectives, critical success factors, and key performance indicators. The output of this analysis will be a document that describes the business and explains how the system can meet the needs of the business.
Planning	The planning process includes documenting the business drivers, obtaining funding and approvals, building the team, defining the project plan, and establishing realistic goals and objectives that are consistent with user and corporate expectations.
Design	The design of the end-to-end system requires a series of analysis and design steps focused on the data extraction and transformation process, database structure and design, and end-user interface design. It should include an iterative process of rapid prototyping with end-user acceptance of the design of end-user reports or query-and-analysis tools.
Development	The development phase is focused on creating and testing code for the source, storage, and desktop environments. It includes coding and testing transformations, creating and populating databases, and building the first pass of reports and queries. Development also involves testing, debugging, and quality assurance of the software developed during the development stage. It entails building operator and end-user training and documentation in the form of modules, classes, help files, and documents.
Implementation and Deployment	Implementation covers initial pilot rollout and iterative refinement based on the results of the initial pilot. The team will focus on installing or upgrading, and on testing hardware and network systems. Implementation also involves training the support or help-desk staff who will field customer calls once the software is fully implemented. At the end of this stage the warehouse is in production use by its targeted end users.

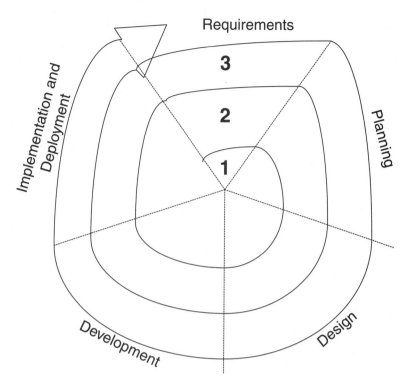

Figure 5.2   The design and development spiral.

Traditional Software Development Cycle. The first pass designs and then deploys a prototype as an alpha product to a limited body of trusted users/testers. The alpha version may have additional functionality added as a result of the test. The second pass produces a beta version, with a focus on testing and user feedback. Additional functionality is not added to the system as a result of the beta test. The third pass corrects the bugs reported during beta and deploys a production version. With each pass, the Requirements, Planning, and Design phases shrink, while the development and deployment phases remain constant or expand.

Multiple Data Marts. The first pass designs and deploys the first data mart in a series. It is important to select a mart with a relatively self-contained subject that can be achieved relatively easily. The second pass reuses work of the first pass to create a second data mart, just as the third pass produces a third mart, and so on. This model assumes that the marts share many ETML processes, a common enterprise-wide metadata definition, and perhaps some reports and analyses.

In the rest of this chapter we will discuss the implementation life cycle from the perspective of a decision support analyst/programmer who has the charter to design and develop a CRM application.

Once the basic database design has been developed, we extend the system to create a multidimensional database by means of SQL Server OLAP Services to create a multidimensional database for query and analysis. Later in the chapter we will discuss the steps needed to add additional functions to the system.

Requirements Definition

The process of collecting and defining application requirements is a complicated and difficult one, especially for many IT professionals who are more familiar and comfortable with design tools, development environments, and databases. However, a successful decision support system demands that the users be actively involved in the decision-making process, especially at the outset of the project. If the requirements definition phase is truncated or avoided, the decision support system will almost surely fail.

First Steps

Before collecting application requirements, the developer needs to establish an understanding of the business environment in which the application will be running. Although some of these points may seem obvious, it is important to collect information that has bearing on the scope, such as viability, term, and costs of the data warehouse project.

One key category of information to collect is the business environment of the organization. The designer of the application needs to understand the business of the organization and what role it plays in its particular industry. Although a great deal of detail is not always necessary, the developer should understand the industry's best practices in terms of organizational structure, marketing and product development, and information technology. The decision support database should be consistent with these practices, where appropriate, and must not work against these.

It is vital to collect the business rules that the organization uses to guide business decisions daily. Some organizations may have these rules documented, whereas others will require that you interview employees, then deduce what the rules should be. Beware that the interview process may be an enormous time sink, and that you may tread on political territories, if you try to drive the definitions of business rules. Stay focused on business rules that affect data usage and try to steer clear of others. Beware of inconsistencies; for instance, be sure to use the management-sanctioned calculation for revenue, profit, and net sales instead of the calculations of some users. Likewise, multiple departments or individuals will have synonyms for the same thing; try to establish a single term for data involved with business rules.

An important cause of decision support system failure is lack of committed executive sponsorship. Before you embark on any initiative regarding decision support system initiative, it is important to make sure that the appropriate senior management sponsor will support the project through thick and thin.

NOTE

Executive sponsorship is crucial. If you have not lined up a committed and qualified executive sponsor, then stop now and do it before proceeding any further!

The executive sponsor may be the person who initiated the project. If that is not the case, then you need to make sure someone on the senior management team is a firm believer in what you want to do. That individual must be ready and able to allocate the funds and resources needed to complete the project.

Assess the capabilities of existing personnel, based on their past experience and performance. You have to do this before the planning stage in which you determine whether the current crew will suffice, or if new hires and/or consultants will be needed. Do this for the source, storage, and desktop environments. The assessment should include database/DSS/OLAP/Tool experience, relationship between IT and users, IT backlogs and other demands on their time, and the average turnaround time of IT personnel for reports and other common projects.

WARNING

Different departments suffer from different types of pain at different times. Make sure you are addressing the right pain for the right group of users.

The first thing to do is to find a point of pain within the company that can be helped by a decision support system. This requires getting out into the field, so to speak, and talking with end-users to find out about their biggest business problems. Thus, the developer in our scenario will want to know what the role of the marketing department is and how it is oriented to address key marketing issues for the corporation, such as lead generation, campaign management, and customer retention. He or she will want to understand the relationship between marketing and other business units, such as sales, finance, procurement, manufacturing, shipping and logistics, sales and marketing, and customer service. In addition, the developer will want to understand the current state of automation in the marketing department. For example, the developer will want to know how the department manages its core business processes and what kind of information it reports to the management team.

Understanding how to provide technology solutions to business problems requires understanding the dynamics of the business problem. This is done with a combination of research and interviews.

Research

Research should be used to prepare the framework for the conversations with the users. You should try to obtain as much information as possible about the company or business unit with which you will be working, as well as the business environment in which that unit is operating. See the sidebar, "Research Topics" for a list of some of the research questions to address before you interview the users within the organization.

You should collect this data before embarking on the interview process for two reasons. The first reason is that this information will provide you with a basic understanding of the role of the business unit within the organization will acquaint you with its primary business problems. The second reason is that every profession uses a specialized language or terminology. The users will be more amenable to a conversation with IT if they believe that IT understands their unique environment and its associated business problems. IT needs to demonstrate its understanding of the business issues the users face. Understanding the professional terminology of the users is a key way to demonstrate this.

One of the most common causes of a failed decision support implementation is that the users reject the system and either refuse to use it

Research Topics

What is the history of the organization or business unit?

What is its current structure?

How many employees does it have?

Where are they located?

What is the primary purpose of the business unit in question within the enterprise?

What are the key strategic initiatives of the enterprise, and what is this unit's relationship with those initiatives?

What other important secondary purposes does it serve?

What is the nature of its relationship with other business organizations both inside and outside the enterprise?

What is its contribution to corporate revenue and costs?

In what market does the company operate?

How big is the market?

What is the company's share of that market?

Who are the other significant players in that market?

or use it only when they have no choice. In either of these scenarios, the company's management will regard the decision support system as a failure.

NOTE The business user community must be an active participant in the entire project, especially at the outset. Otherwise, the system will not meet the needs of its community, and the business will fail to meet its corporate objectives.

User Interviews

If we are collecting requirements for a CRM system, then we need to understand who needs the customer information, in which format they want to see it, and how they will use the information.

Once you have completed the preliminary research already described, you will be prepared to interview the business unit users as well as persons in related business units. The purpose of the interviews is to talk with people and find out things about their business functions and needs. Four major categories of people should be interviewed.

Senior Management Team. A decision support system, especially one that is customer oriented, can easily be mission critical. Therefore, you need to understand the expectations and measurement criteria the senior managers will use as they assess the success or failure of the project. It is particularly important to understand the issues and expectations of the CEO, CFO, VP of Marketing, CIO, and other members of the senior management team relative to the decision support system project. If their expectations are not realistic, then you may need to spend some time and effort educating them about what is feasible.

The senior management team and the major line-of-business managers may be key users of a CRM system. These users require software that is intuitive and easy to use, and which starts at a high level of functionality but enables them to move quickly and easily to much more detailed functionality. For example, a start menu could present the user with a customized "home" page that contains items of interest. From the CEO's perspective, these items are going to focus on both financial and non-financial metrics. Non-financial metrics will include data from internal functions such as marketing, shipping, production, human resources, and the sales pipeline. External information will also be useful, such as news articles or summaries on the current state of the market, press releases from competitors, SEC filings, and syndicated market feeds from third-party information providers.

The CFO, on the other hand, is going to need much more detailed information about financial performance and key performance ratios. Cash flow, cash on hand, current and projected revenue, cost accounting, accounts payable, and other financial metrics are required for the CFO to gain a clear understanding of the current and projected financial position of the company. The CFO needs a high-level picture of the company's financial position but also must be able to quickly uncover and analyze unexpected surges in costs or changes in projected revenue with a few mouse clicks. The ability to compare costs or revenues with budget forecasts is especially useful, to help the manager make a quick assessment of whether or not the company is operating to plan. If a significant discrepancy exists between budgeted and actual costs or revenues, the manager will be in a stronger position to take proactive steps either to reduce costs or reallocate budget numbers to reflect the emerging market reality.

Business Unit Manager. This individual is ultimately measured on the success or failure of the business unit and, therefore, will have a direct interest in any application systems used by the unit. The business unit may be functional (marketing) or geographical (regional sales office) in nature. Therefore, it is important to understand what expectations and issues this individual has about the decision support system project.

In addition, this individual will have personal goals and objectives beyond those of the business unit, and it is often useful to find out what they are. For example, this individual may be interested in expanding the operations of the business unit beyond its current scope (this is called empire building), and may regard the decision support system as one element in a larger strategy.

The line-of-business manager needs to start with greater detail than the CFO or CEO, but with a narrower scope. For example, while the CFO will be concerned with costs at a business unit level, the marketing manager will want reports describing the details of costs, such as lists, direct mail, and budgets. Within the scope of the CRM, this individual will probably need customer and prospect information down to the account or household level.

Information Systems Group. The third group to interview is the IS group that supports the business unit in question. This is an essential step if the decision support project team is part of a separate organization or if the core IS group is very large. You want to investigate a number of things in these interviews. For example, what kind of source systems will the decision support database need to access, what is the state of the system infrastructure (i.e., servers, network, interfaces), and what are the major production impediments that need to be considered (such as batch jobs or printing production runs)? You will also want to know about what kind of expertise your organization has, or must acquire, before deploying the system. If the IS organization is a mainframe shop you'll need to work out how you are going to install an NT-based system, using TCP/IP for connectivity, and train the production staff on its operational management.

Non-management End Users. The fourth group to interview includes other individuals who will use the system. While it may not be practical to interview all the potential users, especially in a large or geographically distributed organization, you should make an effort to identify representative or key individuals who will give you the end-user perspective.

Your questions should focus on what the users' job functions are, the things that keep them up at night, and getting them to talk about what they need to function more effectively.

WARNING

Do *not* ask users what they want the system to do! They are looking to you to determine that. *Do* ask them what they need to be more effective or efficient.

Get them to describe the current frustrations they are suffering. Try to ask questions that are open-ended, rather than asking them to select an option from a list. While open-ended questions are more difficult to codify, the responses may provide valuable insights and clues into the optimal design and behavior of the ultimate system.

Do not forget to perform an "as-is" analysis that will document the current state of the system. This means performing an inventory of existing applications and systems. You should also collect a representative set of end-user reports, which you can use to establish a baseline of the quality and caliber of information they are currently receiving.

Availability and Scalability Requirements

Several IT issues need to be addressed to define the appropriate architecture. One key issue is the location of the users who will need to access the system simultaneously. The infrastructure designer will want to know where the users are physically located, and at how many locations. This information is necessary to understand the network infrastructure that must be in place to enable the users to access the system. If users are located in different time zones, or the nature of the application is such that users will need access to the data warehouse round-the-clock, this will have a profound impact on the architecture that must be designed. On the other hand, if users only need to access the system during routine business hours in a single time zone, then availability standards can be somewhat more relaxed.

Another important architectural consideration is how many concurrent users are expected to be on the system simultaneously and whether they will be using persistent (client/server) or transient (Web browser) connections. The developer will also need to understand when peak time is and what mix of queries are expected to be running on the system during those hours. This will have important ramifications on CPU, memory and disk I/O utilization calculations. Some users will be running routine, standard reports at regular intervals (daily, weekly, or monthly), while others will be running ad hoc queries at random intervals. The mix of these activities will have a major impact on how the system should be configured.

Source Environment Requirements

The source environment represents the IT legacy that will be supplemented by the decision support database. The requirements for the source environment include obtaining information about the available data sources, the data structures within the sources, and the transformation logic that will be required to prepare the data for the data warehouse.

The designer will need to find out how many systems contain the data, where those systems are located, who manages them, and the best approach to extract data from them. Other, related requirements include the available operating systems, networks, protocols, Internet access, intranet, and client architectures.

The extraction process must usually run within a fixed production schedule in most companies. The designer will need to understand the attributes of the extraction window, which may be complicated if the company is an international concern that has a tiny window due to geography and time zone differences. The mission-critical nature of the system will also have an impact on its availability for extraction processing.

You will need to find out if there are any existing extraction routines. If there are, you will need to check their accuracy (collecting intended data), dependability (how often they crash in the middle of the night), and performance (number of hours).

If the data warehouse/mart requires historical data, be sure all of it is available. Some data may have been archived (usually on tape or optical disk). If the data has been kept in cold storage, you will need to verify that it is readable because relatively recent changes to the application that created the data may make old data unreadable. Note that each tape (or other archive medium) is a data source that needs to go through the extraction, transformation, and load process, just like any other data.

Storage Environment Requirements

Here's where you make some of the biggest decisions: for example, warehouse versus mart(s), type of marts (dependent, independent, federated), warehouse feeding dependent marts. For example, if multiple departments/organizations are involved, you may need multiple data marts to serve their diverse but specific decision support needs.

In user interviews, ask what metrics they need to know, then relate this to data that represents what they need to know. Determine the lowest level of detail data they need to do their analysis. Ask how much detail per transaction they need, and this will determine how many fields a record will have. Ask from which time period they need data; this will help determine how much historic data is required. If data reaches years back in time, it may no longer be online or could be nearline or offline. Note that great detail data may be needed only occasionally for special projects, so there is no need to collect it and keep it online every time you rebuild the data warehouse/mart.

Ask users which business dimensions they need to analyze. Couch this conversation in business, not technical, terms. Typical dimensions are time, geography, product, and customer. Determine how much detail data they need per dimension. Aggregates are combinations of metric data and business dimensions. For example, "Sales by Product by Customer" combines detail data about order amount and quantity with the customer dimension to generate an aggregate table that shows each customer's total sales. This kind of data is crucial to determining customer loyalty and lifetime value. Determine during which time periods users are interested; most common are month, quarter, year. Most users compare the current month to the previous month or the previous year's month, so they need 13 months of summary.

Will users need to update the data warehouse with the results of their analysis? "What if" analysis for budgeting or forecasting (usually for sales) is an example of an analytical application the user may want to save. A CRM solution will often result in the need to update the database as, for example, the marketing department tracks the results of a marketing campaign.

User requirements can drive the design of the data warehouse/mart. Assume that the data warehouse/mart will be multidimensional in design, unless users unanimously claim that all they want are their standard

reports (now run against the warehouse/mart instead of wł
ceded it). If users want views for slice-and-dice analysis, but dɛ
drill-down, then a multi-dimensional database may not bɛ
These views could be achieved with a denormalized databa.
in which tables are built to match the contents of standard repɔ
slice-and-dice views.

Coordinate data warehouse/mart rebuild with use of reports and
analyses. How often should the mart be rebuilt: daily, weekly, monthly,
or quarterly? The rebuild frequency depends on the timeliness requirements of the users, which is driven by the pace of change in the
marketplace.

Desktop Environment Requirements

One way to determine the requirements for a desktop tool is to collect
user requirements according to the functionality required for types of
analysis, query, and reporting:

Cross-Tabular Reports. Note that some data marts may satisfy user
needs with cross-tabs, without need for drilling capabilities. In this
case, a reporting tool that accesses denormalized database structures
is appropriate, rather than a desktop OLAP tool.

Slicing and Dicing Analysis. In this type of analysis, individual users
slice and dice data into predefined views. Each user may have unique
requirements for views, and the views may require security measures
to prevent unauthorized access to sensitive data.

Drill-Down Analysis. From a high level of data summary, users may
need to drill down into the detail data to see where the summary came
from.

Drill-Up Analysis. From a low level of detail data, users may need to
drill up to a consolidation level to see a summary.

Drill-Through Analysis. The facts in a data warehouse or mart are often
consolidated from detail data in a operational database. Some applications may require the users to retrieve and analyze detail data from
the operational database.

Once you've analyzed the types of users and the level of functionality
they require, you will want to find out which reports users must retain

with the new system. Look for reports that no one reads, and don't carry them forward into the new system. A designer should ask users what they would change. The designer needs to resist the temptation to produce voluminous 20-page reports in which no one reads anything but the total at the end. It's probably better to consider giving them aggregations in the decision support database that they can review interactively.

Planning

This phase typically focuses on producing a project plan (a written document), which includes a budget and schedule. Some corporate cultures demand a megalithic tome while others just want an outline that spells out personnel, budget, and time line. Choose the approach that is appropriate to the organization.

The Project Plan

Many organizations will produce two documents: the project requirements document (which defines the business need and lists requirements) and the project plan (resources and schedule). These should be lean-and-mean documents that clearly spell out what the project will do, in sufficient detail that no major functions are left uncovered.

Writing the project plan can be a project in and of itself. The plan will consist of two things: resources and time. While you will need to track the appropriate details, the focus should be on establishing the critical path for the project, and determining the resources required to achieve the path in the projected schedule. Beware of the temptation to create an arbitrary deadline and work backwards from the deadline to build the project plan. You should create a set of high-level functions for each environment, and then drill-down to lower levels of detail as you fill in the tasks for each level. Some aspects of the schedule can be sped up by performing them in parallel, but don't shortcut the linkages between the tasks on the critical path. For example, you can't define the source-to-target data mapping process until the target database structures have been defined.

Also, be wary of building a large, multibinder file that will have so much detail that no reader can reasonably be expected to review the document in a single sitting.

Furthermore, some engineering methods teach that "quality" is achieved when the thing built satisfies the list in the requirements document. Engineers sometimes quote the requirements document as it were a holy book handed down from on high. This leads to a reluctance to make changes due to user input during the deployment stage or QA input during the development stage. Quality certainly relates to the requirements, but user acceptance is the ultimate indicator. Be flexible in adhering to the project requirements.

The resources (e.g., people) are obviously the most important critical component for a successful project. The project plan should include a detailed list of responsibilities and list the names of the team members who have been assigned to address those responsibilities. If the in-house resources are insufficient to complete the tasks, then you will need to bring in experienced consultants to supplement the team.

The schedule is another critical planning component. It should be expressed in weeks or months, not quarters or years, and should contain a detailed project workload breakdown. The first data mart in an organization takes longer than subsequent ones, and the time to completion shortens with each one. The first usually requires a minimum of six months, the second requires a minimum of three months, and later ones may require as little as one month. This assumes that all these reuse similar templates and other stuff.

Once the schedule has been created and resources have been identified, you're in a position to create a budget. The budget can often be

Budget Politics

The budget can easily become a political football. Sometimes the budget is created before the project has been fully scoped out. *This is a classic cause of data warehouse failure!* **No budget commitments should be made by the organization until the effort required to deploy the application has been analyzed and costs allocated.**

Identifying the cost of the people can be another political problem, since it requires understanding their salary, benefits, and overhead costs. Sensitivity to these issues is important because the inadvertent release of this personal salary information can create problems if it gets into the wrong hands.

produced by the project planning tool. You create a budget by assigning costs to resources, such as people, software, and equipment.

Companies often don't have a full understanding of their people costs. These costs consist of three major elements: salary, direct overhead, and indirect overhead. Salary is relatively easy to determine because it is on file with the human resources department. Direct and indirect overhead is usually computed.

Direct overhead expenses are non-salary expenses that can be allocated to an individual employee. You can think of them as similar to variable costs in manufacturing. Direct overhead includes such as things as vacation pay, various forms of insurance (health, life, disability), payroll taxes, pension or matching 401-k payments, stock options, and holiday pay. A rough rule of thumb one author (RSC) has used in the past is to add 50 percent of a salary to account for direct overhead.

Indirect overhead charges are costs that are not directly allocated to an individual employee. You can think of indirect overhead as comparable to fixed manufacturing costs. Indirect overhead includes such things as rent, utilities, computer services, postage, depreciation, and general and administrative support staff. It is reasonable to double the combined salary and direct expenses to compute indirect overhead charges to compute the total cost of the employee. Then multiply this cost by the number of hours the employee is expected to work on the project to determine that individual's total cost. You may need to play around with these numbers a little, especially if indirect overhead data is available to factor into the equation.

Other costs for equipment, hardware, services (such as training) and software can be determined by surveying the vendors providing the

---

Computing Personnel Cost Example

Salary = $80,000/year = $40/hour (@2,000 hours/year).
Direct overhead = 40 x 1.5 = $60/hr.
Add indirect overhead = 60 x 2 = $120/hr total hourly cost.
120 x 1,000 hours (6 months) = $120,000 total cost.

(Assumes 2,000 work hours per year at 40 work hours per week, with no overtime.)

goods. The price of a contractor or consultant usually is negotiated, but most contractors will be in the range of $150 to $250 per hour, depending on experience, seniority, and the length of the project. You can usually get a better rate for a contractor if you are able to sign a long-term contract.

The executive sponsor is most likely going to be the person approving the project budget. If there is little (or no!) budget, the developer needs to work with the sponsor to scope out the amount of work required, a reasonable list of products and services, and a schedule. These can be used to define a budget that should clearly be tied to the project plan. A reasonable budget shows commitment and vice versa. Identify key milestones for determining when the next batch of budget dollars should be released.

Design

Every piece of the design must contribute toward the project's real goal: providing a demonstrable solution to a well-defined business pain. If this is not the case, then you risk losing sponsorship, and the users will reject the system.

Analysis and Design

When you have completed the requirements definition interviews you should have a clear, documented understanding of the functionality the system should exhibit. This should include information about the various data sources with which the system must connect and the major reports the system should produce. At this point in the process you should have a good idea what the user interface should look like for the various categories of end users. You should know what customization features will be required to meet their personalized data display needs.

Decision Support Architecture

One of the first analysis and design function points to select is the overall system architecture.

Microsoft has delivered a flexible, scalable architecture based on the Windows 2000 Server operating system and SQL Server. This architecture can store detail data in a star schema data model on the server, with the ability to deploy separate SQL Server OLAP Services cubes for query and analysis, as shown in Figure 5.3.

The client uses either OLE DB for OLAP or ADO to access the Pivot-Table Service. PivotTable Service, in turn, communicates with the Analysis Server, which is the server that contains the multidimensional cube. This represents a typical MOLAP option. The Analysis Server communicates with the MOLAP store using OLE DB for OLAP and retrieves data for the cube from the relational DBMS Server using OLE DB.

Two additional configuration options are available. One is to use a query-and-analysis tool directly against SQL Server. This is the ROLAP option, which combines the functional capabilities of the Analytical Server (primarily calculation and formatting) with the star schema data model. The other approach is to use SQL Server OLAP Services and select the HOLAP option, which places all the detail data on the analytic server and the detail data on the RDBMS server.

At this point you are ready to turn your attention to the core analysis and design functions within the source, storage, and desktop environments.

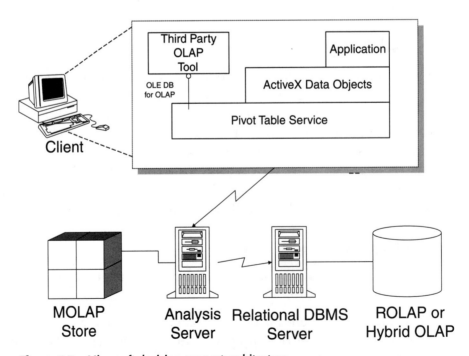

Figure 5.3 Microsoft decision support architecture.

Source Environment Design

For the source environment, you will need to inventory the source systems and define the processes that will extract the data from the source systems, prepare the data for the decision support database, and move it to the target database. DTS is the Microsoft SQL Server tool that Microsoft provides to perform these tasks once they have been defined. If DTS lacks necessary functionality, such as native access to mainframe-based IMS files, you may need to evaluate a third-party ETML tool to deliver the features you need. Alternatively, it may be sufficient to write a program to extract the mainframe data into a flat file that DTS can read by way of a mainframe-to-NT gateway or TCP/IP. The cost of ongoing maintenance of custom software should be weighed against the cost of purchasing a tool. While the initial purchase price of the tool may seem high, the life cycle cost of using the tool may be considerably lower than maintaining a complex extraction and transformation program.

There are a number of design questions you will need to ask regarding the source databases. For example, what's the quality of its data model? Do the current system staff understand it? If not, then you will need to consider how much time it will require to reconstruct the model and build your understanding of it. Has the model kept pace with changes to the organization's business rules and information needs? How easily will it map directly into a warehouse/mart? Do the databases suffer from significant data quality problems that will require a cleansing process? Are there redundancies between databases that may conflict? How can we resolve these programmatically?

Is there data in the source systems to support the analysis that end users want? Sometimes there is not, so you may need to expand the list of source systems. Some types of analysis demand third-party data for general demographics, market segmentation, or financial ratings. Also watch for non-networked or limited access systems (like spreadsheets or Access databases on a user's PC or a workgroup server) that contain valuable or even historic data collected by a team or department.

A major chore in this area is to work out the specific source-to-target data-mapping process. This entails first identifying precise data in source systems to extract, then defining how these, on a metadata level, must be transformed or consolidated before being loaded into the data warehouse/mart. Another complex chore concerns consolidating data from multiple source systems into a single target record. This process can be particularly complex if the source systems have unique, incompatible identifiers for key business objects, such as customer, product, or sales unit.

Storage Environment Design

For the storage environment, you will need to decide where to store the detail data and where to store the dimensional data, and which format to use. In our scenario, we will store customer detail in a star schema data model. SQL Server OLAP Services requires that the database storing the detail data be based on a star model. A third normal form (3NF) data model is more appropriate as a data staging platform or operational data store. It is not appropriate for end users that need to perform multidimensional query and analysis. For multidimensional analysis, we recommend using SQL Server OLAP Services to deploy an analytical database. Microsoft SQL Server OLAP Services provides you with three choices for configuring your dimensional database:

1. A star schema model in the SQL Server database (ROLAP option)
2. A multidimensional database resident on a separate server that obtains data from the SQL Server database (MOLAP option)
3. A hybrid OLAP database, with summary data resident on the OLAP server and detail data residing on the SQL Server platform (HOLAP option).

Issues to consider include user needs, the anticipated load on the system, the degree of sparseness in the data, and the need to design flexibility into the system for future growth and the later addition of new functional requirements.

The first issue in designing the storage environment is to decide which of the three options should be used. The decision often rests in the users' requirements. For our CRM application we will use a star schema for holding the detail data, and a SQL Server OLAP Services cube for analytical data. The SQL Server OLAP Services cube will contain summary data, while detail data will be stored in the fact table. This means that any queries against detail transaction data will go directly to the fact table, while queries against summary, dimensional data will go against the cube. This schema uses the HOLAP option.

Star Schema or 3NF?

Some DBAs believe you should build the detail data store using a fully normalized third normal form (3NF) data model, rather than a star schema. They believe the 3NF model reduces data redundancy, ensures referential integrity, and enables the system to support high-performance transaction processing. Also, a decision support database using a 3NF model in theory is able to answer any question. However, this normalization comes at the price of navigational complexity, which makes it relatively difficult for end users to query the database. A typical 3NF model may have hundreds or even thousands of tables, and a user will often find it challenging to figure out where to start. A typical query in a 3NF model may join a large number of tables. Most relational databases, including SQL Server, have problems managing complex, multitable joins, although the technology is improving. The 3NF model lacks data aggregation, which can make queries that summarize data run excessively (from the user's perspective) long.

We believe that star schema is the best way to create a relational dimensional database for decision support. It is a simpler model for end users to navigate. A star can substantially improve query performance by reducing the number of table joins needed to respond to a typical decision support query. Aggregate tables can be embedded in the star model to enhance performance.

The disadvantage of the star is that it consumes more space because it is a denormalized structure. It may take longer to populate and update the database. Also many DBA's are not familiar with the star, and it is easy to get confused about which data should go into the fact table and which data should go into the dimension tables. Finally, it takes more time to prepare the database because the dimensions need to be updated as new data is added to the fact table.

In some (but not all) scenarios a star schema view layered on a 3NF model will enable the database to deliver a user-friendly, summarized data view while simultaneously enabling power users to dive deeply into complex analytical questions.

A second goal is to determine the warehouse/mart's content. At this stage, you are designing the data warehouse/mart itself. Essentially, you are designing the data structures that will be stored in it. Two things can guide you:

Common data model. If you anticipate rolling out a series of federated data marts, try to create a general data model that can apply to all. Without it, you can never integrate the data marts so that queries can hit more than one. The subject of some data marts will require unique data; however, this is in addition to the common data model. The federated data mart model requires a common metadata repository that all systems and tools in the DSS can share, and which has provisions for containing data definitions that are specific to a particular data mart.

Enterprise-wide data model. The common data model, although made for storage environment systems, should be constructed with source environment systems in mind. That is, consider the ETML procedures that will build the data warehouse or mart. ETML often consists of several discrete processes because several sources are usually involved and several different ways exist to transform data. It's best to componentize these, so that each data mart subject can be put together as a unique combination of components. This way, you reuse instead of reinvent.

The storage environment design should include:

- Subject area(s)
- Dimensions
- Metrics
- Business Rules
- Source Systems

All these should comply to a common data model and therefore be applicable across several dependent or federated data marts. The storage environment design should include a plan for rolling out a series of subject-oriented marts or a series of subject areas within a warehouse. The plan must account for the shared components (metadata and ETML routines) required for each.

The data model and ETML components will evolve after deployment, as you:

- Learn by building additional data marts
- Respond to user requests for data model changes and additions
- Delete data that users never touch
- Build in more aggregations because many users are building them ad hoc

Don't Change the Subject

A data warehouse or mart covers one or more information domains or "subjects," such as human resources, accounting and finance, or marketing management. Many data marts are focused on one subject. But if a data mart is for a large organization (like a division), it may have to include several subjects. A well-organized data warehouse will address several subjects.

A focus on subjects provides a unit that is small enough to be understood by mere mortal brains and can be designed fully without weeks of torture, plus it is small enough to be developed and deployed in a controlled and predictable fashion. Even so, a subject is conceptually complete, so it gives a user something useful for analysis.

Hence, clearly defining the subject is a good goal. The first prototype of a data mart should be one subject; once it is tested, more subjects can be added to it, developed, tested, and deployed incrementally for control, predictability, and measurable results.

Selecting the first subject to implement is crucial, since it will set expectations for all future work. Pick a subject that has a high likelihood of success. Since the initial data mart success will be a measure of how it cures a business pain, look for a subject with a clearly defined pain involving a well-bounded collection of data. An obvious choice for a first subject would be sales data, because sales has high visibility. Users will use any system if it increases their commission, and most organizations will perceive a fairly immediate ROI by improving sales performance through analysis. Fuzzy subjects such as improving inventory storage processes or optimizing material procurement have a more elusive return and may be relegated to later data mart rollouts after the success of the system is demonstrated.

In our customer relationship management system scenario, the fact table will contain data about customer interactions. It will be surrounded by dimension tables that address such business subjects as time, accounts, and sales location. SQL Server OLAP Services cubes can be populated from this star and provide the primary user interface for reporting and analysis, such as profitability analysis, loyalty and risk projections, and comparisons between expected and actual results of promotional campaigns.

This architecture is scalable in that additional back-end database and front-end cubes can be added to address the load imposed by additional users or to add new analytical applications. As we will see later in this chapter, establishing a back-end SQL Server data warehouse separate from the analysis cubes gives us the flexibility to change or add additional data structures at a later time while minimizing the impact on end users. Additional applications can be added by creating new SQL Server databases or by adding OLAP cubes. A common set of DTS packages stored in the Microsoft Repository can ensure that the metadata and ETML logic is consistent across servers and databases as we extend the architecture. Using DTS and the Microsoft Repository ensures consistent transformation logic and consistent dimensions across multidimensional decision support databases. (See Figure 5.4.)

This architecture also leverages the power and flexibility of the PC architecture, by moving specialized functions, such as OLAP analysis, onto separate, relatively inexpensive, servers. This is a useful model for adding parallelism into the system design because different categories of users can access cubes on separate platforms simultaneously, without

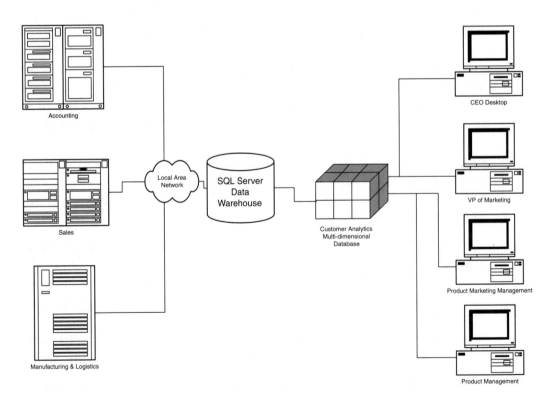

Figure 5.4 Customer reporting system architecture.

interfering with each other's performance. The drawback is that you have more machines to manage. The management task can be alleviated somewhat by the presence of Microsoft Management Console (MMC), which can be used to administer multiple systems from a single management console.

Note that the distribution of the databases is logical, meaning they can all be run on a single server and then moved to separate servers for better performance as the system load increases.

In the desktop environment, the focus is on the application functionality your users need (this will be derived from their business requirements defined during the first phase of the project) and the appropriate user interface for delivering this functionality.

Desktop Environment Design

The design of desktop applications must satisfy the users' requirements, as determined through the requirements definition, interview, and research process.

The different types of users will each have a discrete set of requirements that the applications you design and the tools you select must satisfy.

- Report readers
- Report producers
- Analysts
- Executive users

Most of the reports, queries, or analyses a user visits repetitively should be a mere mouse click or two away. Furthermore, typing is a bad thing: don't expect users to type metadata, SQL, or parameters; instead, use

Ease of Use Is Everything

A difficult user interface will be a barrier to user acceptance, which is the bar you must get over to be called successful. Ease of use is defined as the state that exists when most of the functions the user wants are readily accessible without having to traverse deep menu trees and complex dialog boxes.

English-language-labeled UI controls (check boxes, radio buttons, list boxes) that the user can select to achieve the equivalent of these.

Most users are report readers who are neither equipped nor inclined to build their own reports, analyses, queries, or analytic applications. Based on the requirements collected, IT must design reports that deliver the information these users need.

Many reports will be static in that they pose the same query each time they are run. A static report returns a set of information that needs to be read and considered without interaction such as altering the query or rotating the presentation. Some report users, however, need parameterized reports, so they have some leeway with the query. Even with managed query, don't demand that the user enter table names; that's too hard for them and opens the query to nonsense parameters or ones that could lock up the warehouse. Instead, present a user interface in which the user clicks to select the parameters; this way, a list of possible parameters prevents runaway queries and shields the users from metadata.

Most query users want to be able to compare this month's metrics to that of last month or the same month last year. Query users need a tool that performs comparisons flexibly and quickly. Obviously, most query users should never see the SQL the tool generates; however, your organization may have a few power users who need to edit the generated SQL.

Most reports contain comparisons. These should be built as multiple queries that the desktop tool or application processes to make the comparison.

Query tools must have a button the user can click to halt processing of a query. It is inevitable that even the best analysts will create killer queries that must be stopped. Queries take time, so the user's PC must be available for use with other applications while the query tool awaits a response from a server.

Visualizing data in charts and graphs is part of any decision-support activity. Any tools you choose or applications you develop should have an export mechanism so users can transfer data to their favorite desktop programs for various purposes. A good example is the need to export to spreadsheets, word processors, or presentation software.

Design Workflow

We recommend designing the desktop first, followed by storage and then source. If you start with application requirements from the users' perspective, one of the items that will fall out of that analysis is the data the applications will require. Once you've defined the application interface and data variables, you can move to determining the database structures needed to prepare and contain the data. The design of the data structures will have a major impact on how the users can navigate the data and also on the overall performance of the system.

Database design is a necessary prerequisite to determining the appropriate source systems and designing the ETML logic. You need to understand where to obtain the data, the transformation/consolidation required to prepare the data for the target, and how to define the source-to-target data mapping before you can embark on designing the ETML process.

Development, Testing, and Documentation

The development process is a complex, multi-layered process that must proceed in parallel on three fronts: source, storage, and desktop.

As a result of the logical disconnection of these three environments, the development team will need to use multiple tools to build the systems in each of the environments, while simultaneously building, working from, and refining common metadata and database design elements. This same separation, however, also ensures that multiple development tracks can proceed in parallel, which can significantly reduce the development cycle over a traditional waterfall methodology. In essence, parallel and incremental design and development enables faster deployment, with fewer errors, as long as the developers adhere to a few simple rules.

In many projects, the development stage will take relatively little time if its details were properly covered during the preceding three stages. Otherwise, development time will be burned up with backtracking in the three preceding stages.

The Development Process

While it is beyond the scope of this book to present a development methodology, we believe it is worthwhile to describe a number of practical tips and techniques for managing the process.*

TIP

Some people only feel good when they are actually writing code. Avoid the temptation to rush to the development stage, because if you cheat requirement gathering and planning, you could build something the users won't accept, which makes you scramble to rebuild it from scratch during the pilot and implementation stages. If you cheat design, you will build overly complex code that is difficult to maintain.

One of the key best practices to use during development is the incremental build process.

Incremental Builds. The first rule is to implement an incremental development process that relies on frequent building and testing. The idea is to demonstrate real progress by creating functional modules quickly.

The process is fairly straightforward, but it requires discipline to implement and maintain. Development code should be stored in a development repository, under the control of a configuration management tool. When a developer is going to work on a code module, he or she checks out the module, works on it, and checks it back into the repository. Other programmers can read the module while it is checked out, but they cannot modify it.

Then, on a regular, scheduled basis, all the software modules are returned to the development repository and compiled into a single build. The build should be done daily, if possible, but certainly at no less than weekly intervals. The build process should be performed on a dedicated system, and versions of previous builds stored, so the software is in a known, tested state at the completion of each cycle.

Incremental Testing. The second rule is to test the software after each build. The fact that a daily build compiled successfully is insufficient.

*McCarthy, Jim, *Dynamics of Software Development* (Microsoft Press, 1995), for an excellent and entertaining discussion about software development processes and procedures.

Development Failure

Two software development teams worked side by side at a large computer manufacturer. One team used an incremental build process with frequent, routine builds and bug reviews. The other team waited until a large chunk of code was "ready" and then did a build, but often did not test the software until much later. Although the second team was able to write more lines of code than the first team, the quality of the code was so poor that the product was ultimately withdrawn from the market. The product developed by the first team was successfully launched and eventually sold at a profit.

When a build fails with a fatal error, it exposes one or more bugs that can be identified, isolated, and fixed. Once bugs that cause the build to fail are fixed, the developer must turn his or her attention to functional logic bugs. These are bugs that cause the software to behave in an unexpected fashion. As the builds become more complete and multiple modules are added, the developer can move toward integration testing, which focuses on testing interfaces between modules.

The key to success in this process is to allocate time in the development schedule to write software, complete a build, and test and debug the software module before moving on to the next software module. The discipline required to uncover and fix bugs early in the process can be difficult for some IT organizations to adopt. These organizations prefer to have the software developers perform their own individual unit builds and then perform a comprehensive build at infrequent intervals before throwing it over the wall to a separate quality assurance and testing team. This approach should be avoided because the incremental build approach has been shown to allow more rapid delivery of higher quality software at lower cost.

In fact, the process of going through a regular build cycle can help a team develop a quality culture, since no one wants to be seen as responsible for causing a build to fail. A daily build also presents the opportunity for the team to review its progress and obtain timely feedback. Every day a new build completes successfully, the team can see new functionality gradually coming to life in the software. This immediate feedback can be an excellent way for a team to measure its progress towards a goal—getting the software into the hands of users.

Source Environment Development

In a decision support application project, a significant proportion of development work is dedicated to mapping data from source systems to storage systems. This assumes that mappings were defined in the design stage. Many tools automate this process, so you should seriously consider an ETML tool instead of hand coding. An ETML code could speed up a task that is the bulk of the development stage. Furthermore, an ETML tool will give you a systematic mechanism for populating and maintaining metadata. DTS Designer is the tool you use to manage the data mapping and transformation development process.

To invoke DTS Designer, start the SQL Server Enterprise Console, select the Data Transformation Packages folder, right-click the folder, and select "New Package ..." from the pop-up menu. This process is represented in Figure 5.5.

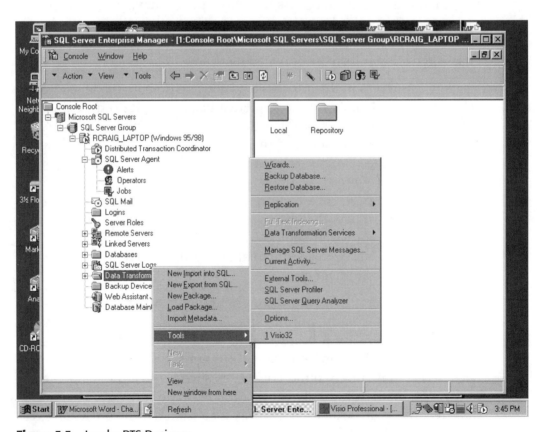

Figure 5.5 Invoke DTS Designer.

After the database and its tables have been created, the next step is to use DTS to populate the database with data.

Once you invoke DTS Designer, you can use the mouse to select and configure one or more data sources, transformation processes (which are in the form of ActiveX scripts, or SQL functions), and target databases. You link these various objects together with workflow arrows, as illustrated in Figure 5.6.

DTS also has import and export wizards that can be run from the Enterprise Manager screen. The DTS import wizard lets you select data from any ODBC-compliant data source or from either a variable or fixed-length flat file.

To run the DTS wizard, click on Tools, select Data Transformation Services, and select Import into SQL. The wizard will prompt you for a data source. Select a source from the drop-down box. Sources include all the Microsoft databases, including Excel, Access, and FoxPro; Paradox; dBase; several OLE DB providers; and text files. Once you identify the file and enter the appropriate security parameters (user name and password), you will be given the opportunity to copy the data directly into

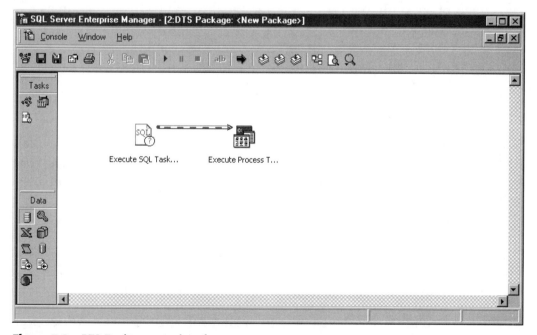

Figure 5.6 DTS Designer user interface.

the SQL Server database. The wizard is used to make a straight copy to the database and has no transformation capabilities. You will need to run the DTS Designer to do anything more complex than a copy.

Storage Environment Development

The ETML code and processes created in the development stage require testing before the deployment stage. Quality Assurance (QA) personnel will need to check for time to load, abnormally terminated extraction routines, exceptions logged for transformations, level of network traffic, accuracy of scheduling, and other details that require further development attention. In the process, QA will discover data quality issues that need attention, such as nonsense data and conflicting redundancies from the source systems.

It is a good idea to use prototypes during the development and deployment stages. As soon as possible, developers should pull together a functioning prototype for the ETML process so it can be tested for bugs and performance. You really want to do this before exposing your system to users so they don't lose confidence or overreact too soon. The development prototype should be tested by way of a real-world situation. Considering that most data warehouses or marts are built at the end of a month, period, or quarter, the prototype should be run as if it were the actual thing.

Database Development

SQL Server provides a data-modeling environment with several design wizards for both the relational and multidimensional databases.

The process of database design and development requires you to plan two key stages. The first stage is developing the core database. The core database may include an operational data store (ODS) that is separate from the analytical database. The role of an ODS is controversial, but it is typically used as a data consolidation and transformation platform that stores the transformed data in a 3NF schema. The ODS data is then available to be forwarded to analytical databases, which are either star schema or multidimensional databases. In this scenario, the core database will be SQL Server using a star schema data model.

The second stage is developing the analytical SQL Server OLAP Services cubes that will obtain data from the core database. If you plan to create a hybrid SQL Server OLAP Services cube with detail data stored in the SQL Server database and aggregate data stored in the cubes, you will need to design a star in the SQL Server database.

In our scenario, we develop a database for customer-related information. This database will contain information obtained from accounting, sales, product management, manufacturing and logistics, and customer service systems. Figure 5.7 shows a simple order processing data model for customer orders. It manages data about customers, product inventories, invoices, and accounts receivable.

This model can serve as our operational data model. Once we have defined the operational data model, we are ready to define what the analysis databases will look like. This will require defining the star schema relational DBMS tables that will contain the base data, along with the OLAP cubes for end-user query and analysis.

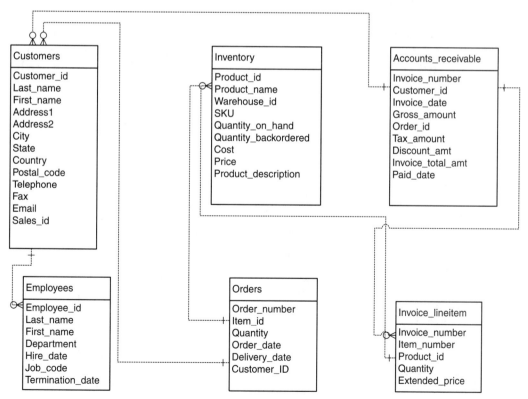

Figure 5.7 Simple order processing database schema.

The analytical database we are going to design is for CRM. A CRM application is concerned with customer lifetime value, purchase patterns, and demographic data, among other things. This additional information is seen in Figure 5.8.

Let's say we're building our CRM for a financial services institution, such as a bank. The products would be the various types of financial instruments the bank sells, such as different types of checking or savings accounts, and various categories of personal and commercial loans. The bank needs to understand who its best customers are, how profitable they are, which products are profitable, which customers are at risk of converting to another bank (so-called "customer churn"), and how to uncover and capitalize on opportunities to sell additional products. These kinds of concerns are also common in many other types of organizations, such as retail shops, insurance companies, telephone and cable TV providers, and airlines. Essentially, any company that has customers who purchase services or products has these, and similar, issues. These issues will drive the design of the database from several perspectives.

Probably the single, most important design driver is the actual data that is required. For example, if you look at the customer dimension table in Figure 5.8, you will see there is no data that will help assign the customer to a particular market segment. However, the address information can be

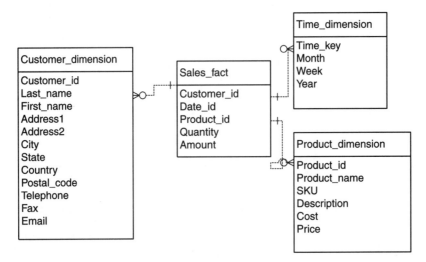

Figure 5.8 CRM star schema.

combined with data supplied by external sources, such as data consolidators and the U.S. Census Bureau. This combined data can be used to establish the customer's approximate income bracket, education level, household status (rent/own), marital status, and so on. This information can be helpful to a financial services institution because it can indicate opportunities to cross-sell or up-sell additional products. For example, if the customer has a savings account with $10,000, is currently renting, and has pre-school age children, it is likely that this person is thinking about buying a house. The company might find it worthwhile to put together a program for first-time homebuyers and pitch it to people who match that profile.

Create the Database

Once you have defined the logical layout of the database tables, you will be ready to define the database and its tables using the SQL Server Enterprise Manager tool.

The Enterprise Manager has a Create Database wizard that is used to create a SQL Server database. You start up the Create Database wizard by starting the SQL Server Enterprise Manager. (See Figure 5.9.)

From the Enterprise Manager screen, you can perform the following tasks:

1. Create a database.
2. Create views, indexes, and stored procedures.
3. Set up security.

The Enterprise Manager assumes you have already designed the database. It is the tool you use to create the database once the design has been established. The Create Database wizard steps you through the process of naming the database, selecting the device and directory where it will reside, and establishing some important baseline database parameters. For example, you specify the initial size of the database, whether it can grow as data is added to it, and its maximum size.

SQL Server requires log files to maintain the integrity of the database. The wizard gives you the opportunity to identify one or more transaction log files that will be used to maintain database integrity. (If a database transaction fails, the information in the log files is used to recover

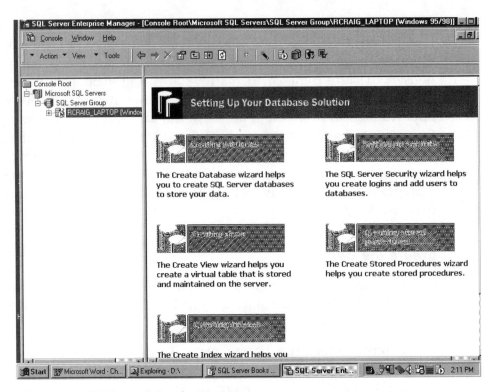

Figure 5.9 SQL Server Enterprise Manager.

the database.) You can specify whether the transaction logs can grow, and if so, what their maximal size will be. The Enterprise Manager also has wizards to define security, indexes, views, and stored procedures within the database.

Once you have created the database, the next step is to create one or more tables within the database. You do this by performing the following steps.

1. Select (double-click) the database you have defined from the list of databases in the Enterprise Manager. A sublist of folders will appear.

2. Double-click the Tables folder to open it.

3. Click the right mouse button and select "New Table..." This will bring up a dialog box with an entry for the table name.

4. Enter the table name and click "OK."

5. Enter the table column names and attributes in the Microsoft Management Console screen that is displayed, as shown in Figure 5.10.

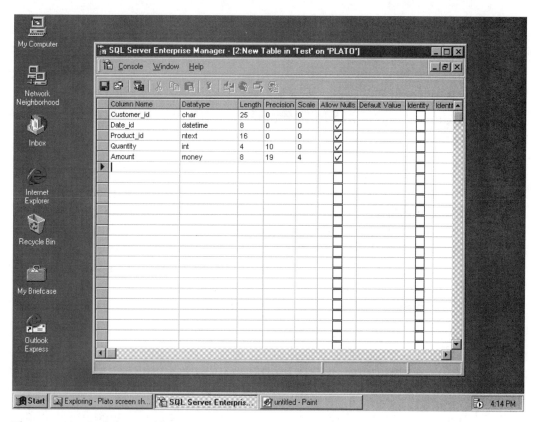

Figure 5.10   Defining a table.

You fill out the fields for each column you're defining in the table. For example, to create the columns for the table illustrated, select a line, enter the column name, its data type (default is char), maximum length, and whether to allow NULLs.

When you're done with each table, you save it (by clicking on the Save icon), exit the screen, which returns you to the Enterprise Manager, and create the next table in the database.

Since SQL Server does not provide a wizard or a graphical table definition tool, you may want to use one of the many tools on the market that lets you define one or more tables using a graphical editor and which can generate DDL to create the tables. Some of these tools enable you to define primary key/foreign key relationships between tables and can analyze the correctness of the key relationships, which can be helpful to debug the logical structure of the tables before you create them in the database.

Create a Cube

Once you have created the star schema in SQL Server and populated the tables, the next step is to define the OLAP cubes your users will use to analyze the data.

You define a cube using the Cube Creation Wizard. To start the Cube Creation Wizard, you invoke the OLAP Manager on the server. (OLAP Manager is a snap-in for MMC.) The OLAP Manager starts up a hierarchical view of the system, and from that view you select the Cubes folder. Right-click on the Cubes folder, and select New Cube. The Wizard will guide you through the process of selecting data source tables and defining the properties of the cube, including the dimensions and measures. The Wizard will offer you the choice of a MOLAP, ROLAP, or HOLAP cube storage option. It will then run the Aggregation Wizard that will define a first pass aggregation schema based on a heuristic examination of the source table metadata.

You then have the option of processing the cube. Processing the cube populates it with data. Initial processing of the cube may take a considerable amount of time, depending on the amount of data to be loaded into the cube and the amount of aggregation you define.

Later, after you put the cube into production you will need to select the most appropriate mechanism to update the cube. You have the choice either to update the cube incrementally or to rebuild the cube. If you select the update procedure, the cube will still be available to users while the incremental update is proceeding. If you choose to rebuild the cube (which you must do if you are changing the cube structure), the cube will be unavailable to users while the rebuild is processing.

Dimensions, Levels, and Measures

Cubes contain *dimensions* and *measures*. Each dimension consists of one or more *levels*. For example, typical levels for a time dimension are day, month, and year. A measure is a numerical fact stored at a specific level. A CRM cube can contain customer, product, time, and location dimensions (each dimension containing multiple levels), with measures for budget and actual values. Measures are typically derived from the fact table, whereas dimensions are derived from the dimension tables.

Desktop Development

The development of decision support applications is complicated by the varying needs of the different categories of users. A CEO, for example, wants to see a high-level EIS-style application with dials and gauges that give him or her an overall perspective on how the business is functioning. The popularity of balanced scorecard (BSC) applications is indicative of the trend toward providing summarized strategic information to senior management.

The CFO, on the other hand, needs a mix of regular (weekly, monthly, quarterly, and yearly) reports indicating the financial position of the company. These reports generally include transaction updates (general ledger postings, accounts payable, and accounts receivable status), financial statements (balanced sheet, income statement, cash flow statement), and cost figures (activity-based costing). The design of these reports and the data to support them is well understood, and is often driven by external factors, including generally accepted accounting principles, and regulatory requirements. The financial analyst also requires access to spreadsheets, and in fact, many financial analysis applications are implemented as Excel macros.

OLAP Analysis

Drill-down analysis enables the user to examine lower levels of detail data. Another way of describing drill-down is that it adds new dimensions for analysis. For example, the sales manager will want to be able to analyze product sales by geography and uncover areas where sales have slipped or aren't hitting budget targets. If he or she begins at the Western Region, the next drill-down level might be to the State level, then down to the City level, then down to the Local Neighborhood level, and finally to the Store level.

Another form of drill-down adds new dimensions to the desktop analysis, enriching the type of data available. For example, adding a time dimension can enrich an analysis of sales data by region so that the analysis can proceed by both region and time.

Pivoting is the process of reconfiguring the axis of the table or graph that is being viewed. For example, the sales manager may be evaluating sales by region, with time along the top axis and region along the left axis. By pivoting the table, the time can be brought to the left axis and product displayed along the top axis, giving the manager a very different view of the same data.

The line-of-business manager, such as the director of sales and marketing or a business unit manager, needs interactive analysis of product and sales data. This usually means delivering OLAP functionality to that individual's desktop. Two basic categories of OLAP analysis are *drill-down* and *pivot*.

The development cycle for end users must take these different requirements into consideration, and developers should recognize that taking a "one application fits all" approach will fail because some of the users will reject the system. The CEO, CFO, and other senior managers have different expectations and information needs than line-of-business managers or statistical analysts.

A better approach is to select one category of user, develop a high-quality application for those users, and then proceed to the next group, and so on. This results in several benefits. If the application for the first user community is successful, word will get around and other users will be more inclined to participate in the design-and-development cycle when it's their turn. Also, the experience gained in developing for one group of users can be useful in terms of lessons learned, when it comes time to take on the next group. Developing applications for different categories of users lets the developer focus on the needs of those users, limiting the temptation to compromise functionality. Finally, the process of building a reusable library of business objects stored in a metadata repository will allow developers to create additional applications quicker and at lower cost by leveraging code reuse wherever feasible.

Client software can be developed and deployed using a wide variety of tools from Microsoft and other companies. SQL Server includes a simple client data access capability, but this is not an application, nor is it suitable for nontechnical end users. Depending on the needs of the user communtity, most developers will deploy one of four modes of applications:

1. Microsoft Excel or other spreadsheets, possibly with macros for enhanced functionality.
2. Traditional client package, written in Visual Basic, Java, or some other language or tool that a programmer can use to create a visual user interface.
3. Web-based application, using either a browser or Java.
4. Third-party analytical tools.

Microsoft Data Access Interfaces

Microsoft has developed several interfaces that developers can use to access data in server-based databases. These include ODBC, OLE DB, OLE DB for OLAP, and ADO.

ODBC was Microsoft's first attempt at enabling universal access to data, and it was rapidly adopted as the de facto standard for accessing relational data. ODBC only works with relational databases, although some nonrelational database vendors have created ODBC front-end drives that hide the nonrelational aspect of the data from client-side tools.

If a developer is going to use ODBC, a driver must be installed on the PC using a data link library (DLL). If the client can't support an ODBC driver (such as a Web browser) then the ODBC driver must be installed on a server between the client software and the database.

OLE DB is a set of COM objects that enables access to both relational and nonrelational data providers. Nonrelational data providers include text files, spreadsheets, and nonrelational databases. OLE DB for OLAP is a subset of OLE DB that adds support for the MDX language. MDX is a query language similar to SQL that enables client software to navigate and query a multidimensional cube.

ADO is a higher-level interface to OLE DB that shields developers from needing to know the intricacies of COM interfaces.

Microsoft expects that developers will use ADO for routine business applications and OLE DB for tools, utilities, or system-level programs.

The Excel approach will be preferred for finance and analytical professionals who are very comfortable with the spreadsheet environment. These users tend to have extensive experience with spreadsheets, understand how to create macros, and have often had exposure to the limited OLAP capabilities of the earlier version of Excel. The analytical features of Excel are primarily limited to pivoting and are supported by Excel 2000 PivotTable services.

Traditional client/server packages require a developer who is familiar with the language, who knows how to build visual interfaces, and who understands how to interface the client to the data server. In the Microsoft environment, these interfaces are written using ActiveX Data Objects (ADO), OLE DB, OLE DB for OLAP, or ODBC. Microsoft's visual languages (Visual Basic, Visual C++, Visual Java, Visual Studio) all support these interfaces, and can be used to access SQL Server and

SQL Server OLAP Services data sources. SQL Server exposes SQLOLEDB, which is Microsoft's OLE DB Provider for SQL Server.

Creating an OLE DB application for SQL Server involves three steps. The steps are to open a connection with the server, execute one or more commands, and process the results.

Open Connection. The first thing the application needs to do is open a connection from the client to the server. To open the connection, the client must create a data source object. This is done by calling the `CoCreateInstance` method. The object has an interface that the client (or data consumer) uses to send authentication information to the server. Standard authentication data includes the server name, database name, user ID, and user password.

Execute Commands. After the connection is established, the client creates a session by calling the `IDBCreateSession::CreateSession` method. Commands are executed by way of the session which is also used to manage rowsets and transactions. A rowset is a collection of zero or more rows that are returned as the result of a command, usually a SELECT statement.

A transaction is an update that occurs on the server. A transaction is a special type of command, which requires specific syntax to ensure database consistency. A properly constructed transaction has four properties, known as the ACID properties, which are described in Table 5.2.

If the client wants to work directly with tables it uses the `IOpenRowset::OpenRowset` method, which includes all the rows from a single table (or index.) If the client wants to execute a command, such as a SELECT statement, it first calls the `ICommandText::Create Command` method to define the command object. Then it calls the `ICommandText::SetCommandText` method to create the command string that will be sent to the server. Finally, it invokes the Execute command to execute the command string.

Process Results. If the command string produces a rowset, the client calls the `IRowset::GetData` method to fetch the data into a buffer, one row at a time. The rowset buffer will be initialized differently depending on the language being used (Visual Basic, Visual C++, etc.) Once the rowset buffer has been initialized, an accessor is called using the `IAccessor::CreateAccessor` method to fill the buffer. The

Table 5.2 The ACID Properties of Transactions

ACID PROPERTY	DESCRIPTION
Atomic	All the changes within a transaction are treated as single unit. A transaction is started using the Open Transaction command and is terminated with either the Commit or Rollback command. A Commit command applies all the changes within the transaction to the database. A Rollback returns the database to the state it was in before the transaction began.
Consistency	A properly designed and executed transaction always leaves the database in a logically and physically consistent state.
Isolation	No process can see a change to a database until the transaction has been committed. This ensures that a second process cannot take action based on data that may disappear as the result of a transaction rollback. Isolation is usually enforced by using locks.
Durability	The system guarantees that a committed transaction is in the database and that it cannot be removed, except by another transaction.

application then processes the data, depending on its functional requirements. For example, an analysis application would load the data into an array that the user can manipulate, or it might pass the data on to a charting application by way of an OLE call.

DSS Browser Technology

The third way to enable a client to access your SQL Server application is by way of the web. This is usually done through a Web browser or via a Java application.

A browser-based application has a number of advantages. First, the user interface—the browser—is essentially free, since it can either be downloaded from the Web or is embedded in the operating system. Second, the system administration associated with a browser is reduced compared with a PC client/server application, which requires someone to physically install the software on the PC. A browser-based application doesn't need to be installed, configured, and maintained on the PC because the application logic runs on a server. This also makes it feasible to deploy an application to hundreds or thousands of desktops without creating a bloated support infrastructure.

Web-enabled applications liberate the system administrator to focus on administering the application server (performance, security, availability, and so on). And, because access to the server is usually controlled by means of a concurrent user licensing scheme, license management is simplified and overall costs are reduced.

Four technologies are currently available for building web-enabled user interfaces: HTML, Java, ADO, and browser plug-ins. Table 5.3 outlines the strengths, weaknesses and best usage for the various web-enabled technologies.

HTML

The simplest, easiest browser-based applications use HTML to manage the application interface. HTML is simple, straightforward, and works on any browser regardless of platform, and hypertext links let a user navigate by clicking on links. HTML includes support for graphics and many features associated with forms.

Table 5.3 Internet Technology Strengths and Weaknesses

	STRENGTHS	WEAKNESSES	BEST USAGE
HTML	Open standard. Works on any browser or platform. Good support for static graphics.	Static pages, not highly interactive. Dynamic HTML limits platform portability.	Static reports that involve minimal OLAP functionality, or where target platform is unknown.
Java	Platform independent. Improved security environment. Many programmers working on Java.	Interpretive language. Application download time can be significantly longer. May not work on older browsers or platforms.	Interactive OLAP client, in environment where load time is not a factor, or with diverse platforms.
ADO	Compiled, better performance. Tightly coupled to Windows environment. Well known by many programmers.	Windows-specific code excludes non-Windows platforms. Potential security breaches and DLL conflicts.	Windows-only OLAP clients, with good control of DLL environment.
Plug-in	Compiled, better performance. Tightly coupled with browser environment. Limited portability to multiple platforms.	Browser-specific. Developer must maintain versions for supported browsers. Plug-in may be large, causing network congestion if downloaded too often.	OLAP clients on multiple platforms in which network bandwidth limitations prohibit use of Java.

HTML is a text-based page markup language, not a programming language. Application requirements, such as sophisticated query and analysis capabilities with features like drag-and-drop, table pivots, and chart or graph rotation, are difficult to accomplish in HTML. Dynamic HTML, which has recently become available, adds support for VBScript, JavaScript or ActiveX controls in an HTML environment. However, the two major browser platforms from Microsoft and Netscape have incompatible implementations of dynamic HTML, which limits the portability of the application. Finally, HTML is "stateless," which means that the context of the network link between the browser and the application is not maintained between connections.

OLAP features, such as pivot and drilldown, can be simulated by generating new HTML pages, which provide the functionality the user is expecting, but at the cost of waiting for the page to be generated and downloaded to the workstation. However, the user can still navigate the set of pages on the desktop by using the familiar Back and Forward buttons. And, since the pages are standard HTML, the browser's "Print" and "Save as…" functions work as expected.

Enterprise reporting is also an excellent use of HTML. A number of reporting products provide web-enabled clients that display reports on users' browsers using HTML.

Java

With Java, a developer can create the functionality associated with a high-end client/server DSS tool, such as advanced 3D visualization, drag and drop, and drill-through. Java is available on all major client platforms, including Windows 3.x. Some developers feel that Java provides a relatively secure environment because applets are not allowed to write to hard drives or print to local printers. For some DSS applications, this can be a problem if the user wants to store a report or query result.

Java is an interpretive language and doesn't have the speed of a compiled language. Also, not every desktop is equipped with a Java-enabled browser, which reduces the ability to support all platforms. Finally, Java applets need to be downloaded from a server every time they are run. If the applet is large or the network is busy, the download time can become an issue for the user. Recent releases of Java applets can be persistent. A persistent Java applet is stored on a local hard drive, and the application can check with the applet source to see if it needs to be upgraded. However, this is the responsibility of the application developer.

ADO

ADO is Microsoft's solution for distributed Web-based applications. Both Java applets and ADO are examples of the new wave of component technologies designed to enable developers to quickly and easily build modern applications using reusable components.

ADO (which is implemented as Microsoft data link libraries or DLLs) can be automatically installed by being downloaded from a server by a browser. ADO runs only on Windows platforms, which eliminates Unix or Macintosh clients from consideration. However, the software is compiled and native to the Windows environment, enabling performance that is superior to Java, which is mostly interpreted at run-time. Microsoft has added an extension to ADO, called ADO/MD, that can be used to create ActiveX controls in Visual Basic to browse, chart, or report on data in OLAP Services from a Web page. This extension is part of Pivot-Table Services.

If the ADO DLL isn't carefully written or is downloaded from an unreliable source, it can open up security holes. Also, the possibility exists that the downloaded DLLs may overwrite existing DLLs with the same name or may conflict with older DLLs that haven't been upgraded.

Plug-ins

Plug-ins are browser-specific programs that work within the browser itself and can be installed on a local hard drive. Because each browser has its own plug-in architecture, it may be necessary to standardize on one browser if this approach is chosen. Again, depending on the platform, DLL conflicts and security breaches may occur. However, both ADO and plug-ins can detect if a more recent edition is available on the server and will automatically download and install the update without requiring any user intervention.

Web Architecture

The downside to creating a Web-based decision support application is the increased complexity of the architecture you need to deploy. In a client/server model, you need to deploy a two-tier or three-tier architecture. In a Web environment, you add additional tiers to handle the unique dynamics of Web access. (See Figure 5.11.) At a minimum, you

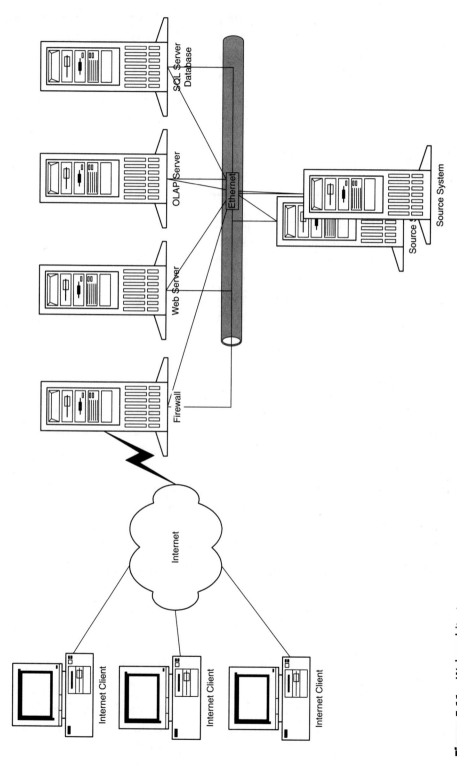

Figure 5.11 Web architecture.

will need to deploy a Web server between the browser client and the analytical database. If you are deploying your decision support application on the Internet, you will also need to configure a firewall to protect your corporate systems from external attacks.

While there are a lot of good tools on the market to help with the development of Web-based applications, you will still need to develop an understanding of the hypertext transport protocol (HTTP), and the hypertext markup language (HTML). If you intend to provide a dynamic environment for the end user, then you will also need to learn Java or the Web extensions to languages such as Visual Basic or Visual C++.

Opening a decision support application, or any application, to access by way of the Internet can create a significant load on your system and network infrastructure. Your system may be subjected to indeterminate, dynamically varying loads as users access your databases from various global locations. Since the Internet is a worldwide phenomenon, you will be subject to higher availability requirements and will have to enhance your security infrastructure.

Third-Party Tools

It's very likely that a significant percentage of your end users will require a powerful query-and-analysis tool rather than a preconfigured application. Power users, such as business analysts or statisticians, need to perform detailed, ad hoc analysis of data. In many instances, these users will want to create and manage their own arbitrarily complex SQL queries. For example, a retail grocery chain interested in market basket analysis—which attempts to find categories of products that sell with each other—may turn this task over to a business analyst or statistical specialist.

Although it is possible to write a generalized query-and-analysis tool for this category of user, it is much more viable to let them use a third-party tool. A variety of tools are on the market, and the number is growing rapidly. Leading vendors at the time this is written include Cognos, Business Objects, Brio, SAS, SPSS, Seagate Software, and many others. These companies all support the Microsoft APIs, including OLE DB, OLE DB for OLAP, and ADO.

The high-end analysis market is heavily dominated by data mining vendors. Microsoft does not provide any native data mining features in SQL Server and SQL Server OLAP Services is a multidimensional cube, not

Beware Scope Creep

A final word on successful development. It is crucial to control the scope of the project. From the beginning, the team must stay focused on the business task that the system is designed to solve. In some respects it doesn't matter what the particular business problem is. It may be streamlining operations, optimizing customer management, improving sales performance, discovering market advantage, or reducing credit card fraud. The design and development team must clearly define the task and review it regularly. This will help to eliminate "scope creep," which can be fatal to the success of the project. Ultimately, the project will be judged by whether it fulfills this business need.

The key to managing scope creep is to focus on the specific point of pain that the decision support database is designed to eliminate. If there is no real pain, the system will not be perceived as crucial, and therefore may not be supported by senior management. If it is a technology solution in search of a problem, then, in the end, it will not be perceived as successful because it doesn't cure a commonly perceived pain. The greater the suffering of the pain and the more relief the system affords, the greater the prospects the data warehouse will be perceived as a success.

a data mining engine. Therefore, if your analytical users need to perform extended analysis functions that are not supported by SQL Server or the various OLAP tools mentioned above, you should evaluate the range of data mining products.

Installation

At this point the application has been written and tested and the installation, end-user, and operations documentation has been produced. We are now ready to begin the deployment process, which entails application installation and training.

The installation process can be straightforward or incredibly complex, depending on the application configuration and the current state of your corporate infrastructure. You should consider deploying three separate environments: development and testing, training, and production. You will want a development and testing environment that will be fluid and changing dynamically, especially as you reconfigure to address bug reports or implement new releases. The production environment must be kept sacrosanct and inviolate so users don't come to feel it is too unstable or unreliable. For this reason, you will also need to deploy a separate training environment in which new users can make mistakes and play with the system without worrying about corrupting the data in the database.

Base Platform Installation

The base platforms include the servers and network. You need to identify and characterize your organization's reliability, availability, and scalability (RAS) requirements. RAS requirements are related but can be considered separately.

1. **Reliability** addresses the system's ability to deliver the quality of service and data integrity the users require.

2. **Availability** is the amount of time the system is usable by the user community. Unplanned outages, such as network, machine, or database crashes decrease availability, as do planned outages, such as database updates and backups.

3. **Scalability** refers to the ability of the system to gracefully increase its capacity to accommodate more data or larger numbers of simultaneous users.

Reliability

Reliability and availability go hand in hand. What you want is an architecture that enables the system to recover gracefully from an unplanned outage, and system software that reduces planned outages. SQL Server, for example, supports transaction processing, which ensures data reliability. When a SQL Server system reboots after a system crash, the database automatically recovers the database from the system log files. Uncommitted transactions are removed from the database, and the system is designed to guarantee that all committed transactions will be in the database.

NOTE

The ACID properties ensure that committed transactions will not disappear if the system crashes. However, the database recovery process removes any uncommitted transactions that were "in flight" at the time of the crash. Therefore transaction processing does not guarantee no loss of data, only no loss of *committed* data. Transactions that were open will need to be restarted by the user.

SQL Server also supports enhanced availability by enabling on-line backups. On-line backup means the database can be backed up while users are actively modifying it.

A Word about RAID

Availability and reliability are both substantially enhanced by using redundant array of inexpensive disk (RAID) drives. The several levels of RAID range from RAID 0 to RAID 5.

RAID 0 is also known as striping. Striping evenly distributes the data pages (or blocks) across all the drives in the array, using a round robin algorithm. For example, in a 3-disk array, block #1 goes on drive #1, block #2 goes on drive #2, block #3 goes on drive #3, block #4 goes on drive #1, and so forth.

RAID 0 speeds up performance, especially if each drive is controlled by a separate controller. However, RAID 0 leaves the entire array vulnerable to a single disk failure. If a drive crashes, the entire array becomes unusable because fully $1/N$ (N = number of disks) of the data blocks are unavailable.

RAID 1 is mirroring. Mirroring protects each drive by adding a second drive that maintains an exact copy of the primary drive. The big advantage of RAID 1 is that the data is protected from a disk failure. If a drive fails, the RAID system uses the duplicate drive. However, the cost of disks is double the cost of deploying the database on single drives. Thus, if you are implementing a database with 100 GB of data, you will need 200 GB of disk. (Remember that the amount of space required by the database is not just the amount of data being loaded. You also need to configure sufficient capacity to hold system tables, indexes, aggregate tables, and temp table space, plus additional capacity for planned growth.)

RAID 1 protects the database against the physical corruption or loss of a disk, not against logical data corruption. If the database becomes corrupted because of a CPU crash, operator error, or software bug, both the primary and mirror drives are corrupted.

RAID 1 exacts a small performance penalty in that the data must be updated on two drives simultaneously. This penalty is greater if you deploy a software RAID configuration. A RAID 1 array will not provide any data parallelism beyond that implemented by the database itself.

However, if a data hot spot exists, a RAID-1 array may respond faster to read requests, which can help alleviate the I/O overload on that disk.

RAID 0+1 combines RAID 0 and RAID 1 to provide a high degree of availability and performance, but at the cost of doubling the number of required drives.

RAID 3 and **RAID 4** are parity schemes that distribute parity information in different ways. However, they are less sophisticated than RAID 5 and are not widely used.

RAID 5 is based on the concept of a stripe set with parity. Data integrity is protected by striping parity data across the entire array. The RAID-5 parity data can be used to reconstruct the data if a drive fails. The storage overhead of a RAID-5 system is approximately equal to $1/N$, where N is the total number of drives. This can be compared with 100 percent storage overhead for a RAID-1 (mirroring) system, so the savings can be considerable in the number of disks that must be deployed. However, if a RAID 5 drive fails, the system performance will be diminished while the data is being reconstructed using the parity data.

Most sites implement either RAID 0+1 (striping plus mirroring), or RAID 5 (parity checking). RAID 0+1 costs a lot more but doesn't have the performance loss that RAID 5 suffers from when a drive fails.

When you are configuring a RAID array, you should consider whether to implement software RAID or hardware RAID. Although hardware RAID is usually more expensive than software RAID (which comes with the Windows 2000 Server operating system), it consumes fewer CPU cycles and delivers better performance (especially for write operations), greater scalability, and better availability. Most hardware RAID products support hot spares and hot swapping. A hot spare is a disk that the RAID array can use to rebuild a failed disk. This is particularly useful in an unattended, lights-out environment. Hot swapping is a feature that enables the system administrator to replace disks without bringing the array down. Both are desirable features for a mission-critical application.

NOTE

Just because you have a RAID array doesn't mean you shouldn't back up your data. Site disasters, such as fire, flood, earthquake, or other problems such as electrical failure or operator error can damage a RAID array beyond repair. Some RAID configurations cannot recover gracefully from a multidisk failure. Therefore, you should still perform routine full and incremental data backups and store the backup tapes in a secure, off-site location.

Microsoft Clusters

One other availability option for Microsoft systems is clusters. A cluster is a set of two or more separate machines that share a common system image and disk drives. (See Figure 5.12.)

Clusters are primarily used to enhance availability rather than scalability. Clusters enhance availability by ensuring that another machine is available to provide services to desktop clients if a cluster node goes down.

Some cluster products can enhance scalability by allowing two or more nodes to simultaneously read and write to a database. This requires coordination and messaging software that prevents two nodes from updating the same record at the same time. Microsoft clustering does not support a distributed lock manager to enable cross-cluster coordination of database updates. Therefore SQL Server works in a cluster in an active/passive configuration. One member of the cluster acts as the active database server to all the clients, while the other cluster member either stands by or is used for some other purpose, such as an email server. Clients access the cluster by connecting to a virtual cluster member, which has a name and IP address separate from the other members of the cluster. In the event of a primary node failure, Microsoft Cluster

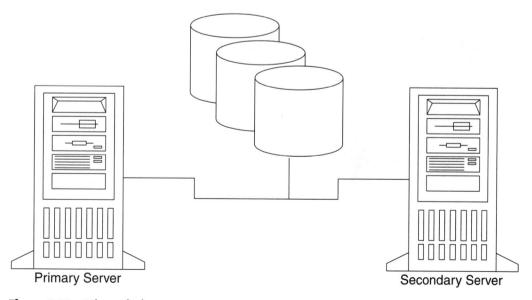

Primary Server   Secondary Server

Figure 5.12   Microsoft cluster.

Services (MSCS) and SQL Server can restart the database on the surviving member. Open, uncommitted transactions are rolled back to ensure database consistency. Clients with an open database must reconnect before they can continue processing.

Clusters can improve performance though load balancing. Load balancing software intercepts requests for data or services, assesses the load on the server machines, and distributes the work to the system with the lightest load. Microsoft supports this capability through the Windows NT Load Balancing Service (WLBS) software, which is available from a third-party software company.

WLBS creates a front-end cluster that can accept incoming data requests and send them to a back-end data server. (See Figure 5.13.) The software can automatically reconfigure itself if a node fails. Note that the WLBS cluster does not enable a site to share a database across two or more cluster

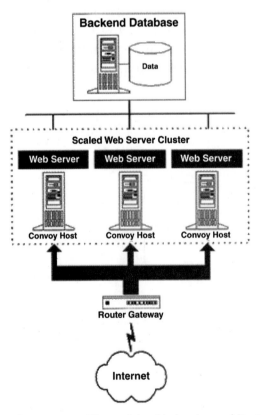

Figure 5.13 Microsoft load balancing architecture.

nodes; however, it does enable you to deploy application software on multiple nodes that share a single data source.

Platform Considerations

Since clustering cannot be used for scalability, you will need to identify the appropriate server platform to support the volume of data and the expected peak number of concurrent users.

When you are configuring data volume, you need to consider the total amount of data that is going to be stored, not just the detail data. In addition, you need to configure sufficient disk capacity to allow for future growth of the data. While it is difficult to provide a method for calculating the total amount of disk capacity that needs to be configured, some rule-of-thumb calculations can be helpful.

For relational data, compute the size of the average row in each table and then multiply the row size by the anticipated number of rows to arrive at the raw data capacity. Do this calculation for each table, and sum the total. For example, if you are deploying the simple CRM star schema illustrated in Figure 5.8 you can compute the following data volumes.

This simple schema can reasonably be expected to occupy 267 MB of data, which is a relatively small decision support database. We then add system table space, index space, aggregate table space, and temp table space to this number. A reasonable multiplication factor is between 3× and 5×. Thus, the database can be sized at between 800 MB and 1,335 MB, not including RAID capacity.

Platform Architecture

The next consideration is the hardware platform. If you expect more than a few dozen concurrent users, you should consider a symmetric

Table 5.4 Data Volume Estimate

TABLE	ROW SIZE (BYTES)	NUMBER OF ROWS	SIZE (KB)
Sales_fact	40	1,000,000	40,000
Customer_dimension	230	100,000	225,000
Time_dimension	75	1,000	75
Product_dimension	112	10,000	1,094
		Total	266,169

multiprocessing (SMP) engine. Microsoft's Windows 2000 Server (formerly known as Windows NT 5.0 Server), supports SMP systems.

SMP machines have a practical limit to the number of processors they can support. This limit arises because SMP machines are based on a shared-memory architecture. All the processors in an SMP machine are attached to the system backplane and share the available memory in the machine. Also, each CPU has its own on-board memory cache, which is used to store recently changed data that may be required by the CPU. The system must ensure that the contents of main memory and the CPU caches are consistent. This interprocessor coordination can be done in a number of ways, but they all carry varying degrees of overhead.

As additional CPUs are added to the system, the messages that must move between the CPUs to ensure memory and cache coherence consume increasing amounts of system bus bandwidth, causing wait states and using more CPU cycles. Thus, as illustrated in Figure 5.14, each additional CPU does not contribute 100 percent of its potential processing

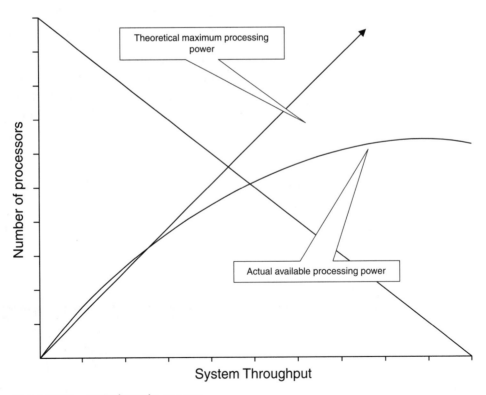

Figure 5.14 SMP throughput curve.

power to the machine, and, at a certain point, adding more CPUs does not result in the ability to perform additional work. In fact, at a certain point, increasing the number of CPUs can cause so much overhead that total system throughput actually decreases.

The current maximal number of Intel CPUs supported by Windows 2000 is approximately 8 CPUs, although some Microsoft/Intel business partners, such as Compaq, have deployed systems with more processors.

The biggest single factor affecting the scalability of the SMP architecture is the workload pattern because it is only when data must be shared simultaneously by multiple CPUs that interprocessor coordination becomes a significant issue. Unfortunately, there is no quick, easy way to predict the workload pattern of your specific application without running a benchmark test that can reasonably reproduce the pattern you will see once you go into production. This is one reason to roll out the decision support application to a small, select group of users as a pilot project. In a pilot environment, you can assess the workload on the system with a small, defined number of users and make performance adjustments based on reasonably hard statistics.

Other processor architectures that can deliver scalability, primarily massively parallel processor (MPP) and nonuniform memory architecture (NUMA), are available from several hardware vendors. However, Microsoft's operating systems and databases do not currently support these architectures.

Network Infrastructure

Once you have selected the appropriate platform, you need to turn your attention to your network infrastructure. This is especially true if you intend to deploy an application that will be available on the Internet.

Networks need to be fast and reliable. This means deploying high-speed routers and redundant components. You may need to upgrade your routers to support the volume of data access you expect. You may also want to consider deploying redundant network interface cards (NICs) connected to dual-path networks. This will ensure that if one network goes down, the system can use the alternate network. Alternatively, the dual networks can be used for different purposes.

You may consider upgrading the network from a bus topology to a switch topology. In a bus topology, all the computers on the network are connected to the same backbone, typically an Ethernet. Since only one packet can be on the network at a time, Ethernet relies on collision detection to find out whether the network is occupied. Once the Ethernet reaches approximately 65 percent utilization, collisions result in a reduction in overall throughput. A switched network, illustrated in Figure 5.15, on the other hand, provides each machine with its own dedicated Ethernet segment.

The switch is typically connected to a high-speed backbone, which could be based on a non-bus topology, such as asynchronous transfer mode (ATM). An alternative is to deploy fast Ethernet, by upgrading from 10-MB to 100-MB adapters. Gigabyte speed Ethernet will also be available on the market by the year 2000 and beyond.

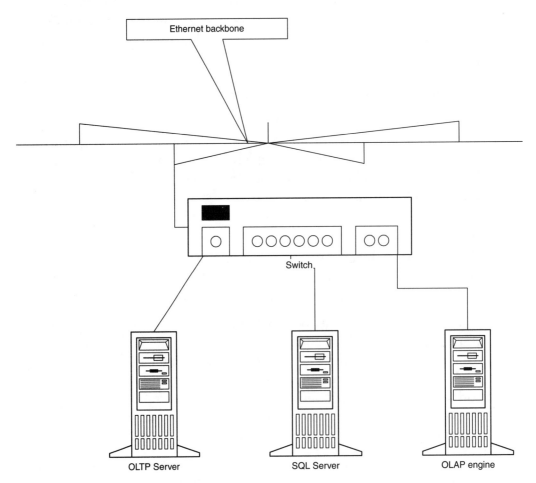

Figure 5.15 Switched Ethernet topology.

File Placement

SQL Server supports partitioning into filegroups. A filegroup consists of one or more files which can be individually placed on specific drives. For example, files data1.ndf, data2.ndf, and data3.ndf can be placed on three drives and linked together as a filegroup called Data. As data is added to the filegroup, it is evenly distributed between the three files, using the same concept as a RAID 1 stripe set. The difference is that the striping is done within the files, by SQL Server, rather than at the disk level by the operating system. SQL Server also enables secondary files to be added to a filegroup. This allows the site manager to expand the database if a single SQL Server data file exceeds the limits imposed by the operating system or if new disk drives are added to the configuration.

A performance advantage is gained by configuring the database using a filegroup rather than as a single file on a RAID array. SQL Server automatically recognizes that multiple files exist in a filegroup and runs multiple threads (one for each file) for user queries. If, on the other hand, the table is stored as a single file placed on a multidisk stripe set, SQL Server cannot run parallel query threads against the file.

Index files can also be placed on separate drives by creating the index in a separate filegroup. If an index file is on a drive with its own controller that is separate from the database files, more queries can be run against the database before the drive controllers become saturated.

Log files should also be placed on drives that are separate from the database drives for maximal throughput and reliability. If the disk holding the database crashes, the log file will still be intact and can be used to recover the database. The process is to install a new disk, restore the database from the latest set of full and incremental backup tapes, and then apply the log files that have been updated since the most recent backup.

It's also a good idea to put the database files on disks that are separate from the disk holding the system image and swap files.

Training

Before you can deploy the system, you must be prepared to provide training. Three categories of personnel will require training: developers, operations personnel, and end users. Ideally, you have had representatives from all three groups as members of the development team from the beginning, so that their needs are addressed before the software is actually ready for deployment.

Developer Training

Developers will require training at the outset of the project. Given the complex, multistage nature of the data warehouse process, it is advisable to divide your development staff into subteams and focus each team on one of the five environments. You should also designate a project leader and a lead architect. The project leader will be the person responsible for the overall success of the project. It is probably best to use someone who is technically savvy but also close to the business users to function in this role. The lead architect, on the other hand, should be one of the more technically sophisticated people on the team. This individual should be able to see the entire decision support application from an overall architectural perspective and should be able to define the interfaces between the various layers.

Application developers will focus on one of three areas. The first is the desktop environment, where they will need to work with the development tools that have been selected to produce the desktop application. The development tools may be Visual Basic or Visual C++, or they may be more sophisticated query-and-analysis tools. Since OLE DB is the native API for SQL Server, the developers will need to be familiar with the specifications and usage of these APIs as well as with the development and deployment of COM objects. If the application is going to use the OLE DB for OLAP APIs, the developers must also be trained in the syntax and grammar of the MDX language. These developers will obviously need to be fully trained in the use of these tools and in how to manage a development environment, especially where multiple developers may need to share access to the software.

The second category of application developers is focused on the database. These individuals will be concerned with the physical and logical modeling and layout of the database. They will need to have a deep understanding of relational and multidimensional technology. They will also require expertise in data modeling tools, database security, and query processing.

The third group of developers will be concerned with managing the data extraction and transformation process. These developers will need to understand the structure of the source data, the most appropriate method for extracting that data, and how to prepare that data prior to loading it into the decision support database. The data preparation phase will require using DTS in the Microsoft environment, or a third-party tool if it is determined that the system requires functionality that is not available with DTS. Because DTS is a COM-based package, the developers will need an in-depth understanding of how to develop and manage COM objects.

In most instances, it will be more cost-effective to hire outside training for the development team rather than develop the training expertise in-house. The exception would be a case in which the organization is large enough that it already has a dedicated training organization.

Operations Training

The core operational person is the DBA. This individual will be concerned with the daily care and feeding of the database. The DBA must be completely familiar with the features, capabilities, and limitations of the SQL Server database and its associated technology. This person should be fully trained on the backup, recovery, and statistical collection utilities as well as on how to manage the end-user query environment. For example, the SQL Server DBA needs to understand how hints and views work to ensure that queries work the way users expect them to. The DBA is also responsible for maintaining indexes, aggregate tables, and database reorganization and partitioning to ensure the best possible performance.

Other operational personnel who will require training on the system include the daily operations staff. These individuals will be responsible for running scheduled batch and print jobs as well as maintaining user accounts. They will need to be fully trained on the daily operations of a production system based on the Windows 2000 platform. You will also need a network administrator who will manage the network domains and track utilization and security of the network. This person will need to be brought up to date on the network requirements created by deploying the decision support application.

End-User Training

Considering that there are going to be several categories of end users that will use the decision support system, you will need to develop and deliver a range of training. The biggest problem you will face is actually getting people to attend a series of training courses. Our recommendation is to offer a computer-based training program, which should include a tutorial on how to use the system you have designed and deployed. This tutorial should not be a generic decision support course but should use examples based on the actual application the users will encounter. It will be helpful if access to the on-line tutorial is an option on the Help menu.

You should plan to introduce three types of training for the users. The introduction course should be designed to acquaint the user with the fundamental concepts of decision support and multidimensional databases. This should probably be about one day in length and should be a prerequisite for additional training courses. The second level of training should be directed at those end users who are going to run a managed query environment and who will not ordinarily be running ad hoc queries. You may want to define a special section of this course oriented at the senior management team, as well. The third training program should be oriented toward the needs of business analysts and other power users, who will be expected to use a query and analysis tool rather than a preconfigured application.

These courses need to teach the following common set of core competencies:

1. The concepts of multidimensional data views.
2. How to navigate the decision support database.
3. The location, functions, frequency, and parameters of reports.
4. How to print or export data to desktop applications.

Operational Management

Once the application has been written, debugged, and documented and a pilot test run has been completed, you are ready to deploy the operational application. When you turn the system over to the operations staff, they will begin running the system, which entails a number of activities that are different from development. These activities include security management, performance analysis, and reliability management.

When you deploy a system, you need to adopt a production mind-set, which is very different from a development mind-set. A development mind-set encourages change and experimentation. A production mind-set must be extremely careful about implementing untested or poorly designed changes into a working system. Although a system must be architected for change, the actual production process must be clearly defined and documented. The production management structure must encourage a sense of ownership on the part of the product team members. The career evaluations process should include metrics that measure how well the team members execute their respective functions.

The management team is responsible for defining clear policies and procedures that will ensure the system runs smoothly. Some of the issues that need to be considered include:

Change management. Change management established a process to implement changes to the system without introducing bugs or system instability. Changes can include adding new software functions, changing database structures, or enhancing the base platforms by, for example, adding new peripherals or memory. A process should be put in place for testing and certifying suggested changes. Users should be notified of changes that will affect system downtime so they can plan accordingly. Management should define who has the final authority to sanction and schedule changes.

Security. Security includes the process of defining user accounts and data access privileges. Users may be assigned individual accounts or may be assigned a role based on their business functions. The security process should also have a method for tracking unauthorized attempts to enter the system. The security system should be closely linked with human resources so accounts can be quickly disabled when users leave the company.

Performance analysis. The system will need to be closely monitored to ensure that CPU, memory, I/O bandwidth, and network resources are not saturated. Routine reports should analyze query response time, peak CPU utilization, and disk I/O rates. Disk reports should also identify disk queues, which can indicate the disk is not able to respond to the request load. Memory utilization should be assessed from the perspective of both the operating system and database. SQL Server has the ability to allocate all available memory, but the system administrator can indicate both minimal and maximal values for memory allocation by the database.

Capacity planning. The system will be stressed by three forms of growth. The first is the load introduced by additional users. Second, as the users become familiar with the system, they will submit more queries, which will also be increasingly complex. The third is the addition of more data. SQL Server gives the DBA the ability either to limit the size of data and/or log files or allow them to expand dynamically. The DBA must have the ability to monitor database growth along with performance statistics and use this analysis to project the need for additional resources. This will enable the site manager to plan to deploy additional capacity before it is needed.

Storage management. Data must be backed up to secure, offline media, and the tapes must be sent to a remote site. The site manager must implement a tape management system that will validate that the correct backup tape has been mounted and reject any incorrect tapes. If the database must be recovered, the recovery process must be synchronized with the database log files to ensure that all completed transactions are rolled forward. The tape management system must provide a mechanism for initializing and labeling new tapes. A log system should track files that have been backed up and verify the current location of the backup tapes. Management must establish a policy for how long backup tapes are kept in storage and how often a full backup is performed. Most sites do a complete backup once a week and take an incremental backup once a day.

Disaster recovery. Disaster recovery is closely linked with backup and recovery procedures, except that disaster recovery assumes that the entire computer system is unavailable because of a catastrophe, such as fire, flood, earthquake, or environmental contamination. A disaster recovery scenario will be necessary for any system that the business depends on for its daily functioning.

End-user support services. Users will require help from a help desk that can assist them with routine maintenance problems, such as when a printer is offline. The help desk can also provide a point of contact for reporting system and program errors. A problem-tracking system should be implemented that uses a prioritization scheme for tracking problem reports. Many sites institute a level of bug priorities ranging from 1 to 5. A Priority-1 bug is a major bug that makes it impossible for the user to perform a key business function. A Priority-5 bug, by contrast, indicates the user has a relatively minor problem, or one for which a work-around is available. It could also represent an enhancement request or minor documentation error. Some bugs can be addressed by using a workaround, some will require the installation of a patch, and others will require new software development or re-engineering the application.

Escalation procedures should be defined so that high priority bugs are addressed proactively, with a clear path to escalate the problem to the appropriate management. A typical escalation procedure moves the problem resolution responsibility from call center operator (who has generic software skills) to a call center software support specialist who is an expert in the application, to product engineering. Some organizations create a Web site that the users can use for reporting and tracking problem reports. The Web site can also provide limited training as well as a frequently asked question (FAQ) file.

The Life Cycle of Decision Support System Usage

Software is a living thing that changes and evolves over time. Designers and developers must be cognizant of this fact as they go through the process of implementing any software application. The software will be used by both end users and operations staff, who will respond with additional requests for new functionality. In addition, developers often want to add additional capabilities to the software. These capabilities may either be features that couldn't be added to the first release of the software, or they may be additional features that were deliberately withheld for later releases because the developers wanted to gain more experience with the software. Developers may also want to take advantage of new features and functions that come with development tools, databases, operating systems, or platforms.

Operational Experience

Operational staff will usually look for additional utility functions that will simplify or increase the reliability of their functions. Improved backup procedures, new database configuration and reallocation utilities, or more robust scheduling software can all help improve the ability of the operations to maintain the RAS attributes of the application at an optimal level. Operators will also respond with bug fix requests as a result of runtime errors, such as a DTS process that doesn't properly handle an unexpected data value.

The operational staff is also responsible for the runtime performance of the data warehouse. This means they must collect information about CPU, I/O, and data and network utilization and analyze this data to uncover current or future bottlenecks. The operational DBA will be interested in understanding how users are using the data. He or she must know which tables are being accessed and which indexes and aggregate tables are being utilized. Table utilization statistics can be especially useful to help determine whether or not to deploy additional indexes or aggregate tables. SQL Server provides the DBA with a host of statistics that will help to identify potential areas for performance improvement. The SQL Server Profiler can be run to analyze database performance and uncover slow queries. Certain SQL queries that are executed frequently may run faster if they are compiled into a stored procedure. The Profiler can be used to turn on statistics collection for later analysis of important information, such as query profiles, execution time, and logical and physical I/O.

The system administrator and DBA work together to develop additional performance enhancements that may be gained by making system-level changes. Adding memory may relieve excess swapping or disk I/O, or the team may decide that the best way to improve performance for the database is to move it to a stripe set. SQL Server uses checkpoints to flush the database cache to disk. You can use the Performance Monitor utility to monitor disk I/O rates. If you see that certain disks are hitting 100 percent utilization, you may want to consider modifying the SQL Server recovery interval option to increase the amount of time between checkpoints. (Increasing the recovery interval time will increase the time required to recover the database after a crash.)

Users' Experience

The first thing the users will want is more data, functionality, flexibility, and choices. In the second iteration of our scenario, for example, we can deploy an additional SQL Server database containing consolidated customer information, as portrayed in Figure 5.16.

This consolidated data will be stored in a database that is logically separate from the consolidated accounting information database we described

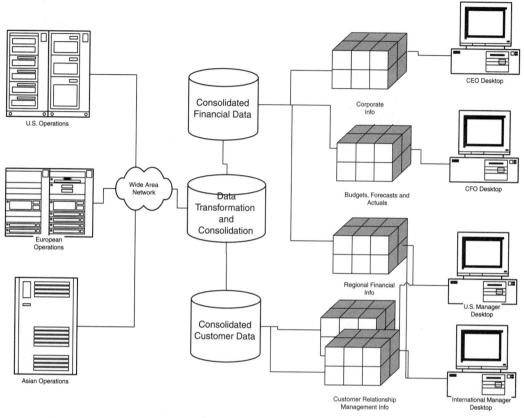

Figure 5.16   Extended information architecture.

earlier. Designing a logical separation of these databases enables the flexibility to deploy them on either the same or separate servers. The new customer information database is then used to provide summary data to one or more regional customer management SQL Server OLAP Services cubes, which are accessed by the regional managers.

Users may also come up with ideas to improve the visualization of data or enhance their ability to analyze the data. Simple questions that start with "why can't I …" can provide developers with insight into how users think, and what information they need to be more effective and productive.

The development team needs to establish a process for capturing these insights and adding them to a next version wish list along with bug reports and operational enhancement requests. Once the first iteration of the software has been in production for a reasonable time (at least four to six weeks), the team will start receiving these additional requests, which can be blended with their own product enhancement plans, to come up with a list of additional development projects. When the team is ready to begin planning for the next release, the list can be prioritized based on business needs, projected development time, and available resources, and the process starts all over again.

PART TWO

Building a Microsoft-Based Decision Support System

The previous section provided a comprehensive overview of the techniques necessary for building a data warehouse, building advanced analysis applications, and maintaining the various environments in which the data is stored and manipulated. In this section, the Microsoft tools and technologies used to build end-to-end applications are discussed in greater detail. To facilitate these discussions, we describe how to use these tools in the context of a customer relationship management (CRM) application.

Design Process and Tools

I n any development project, the design phase is the most critical phase. Microsoft has provided various tools and suites for the development community that facilitates this process. In addition, a number of emerging technologies are quickly becoming the de facto standard in their respective areas. This chapter is organized into sections, each of which corresponds to one of the three core environments discussed in Part One—Source, Storage, and Desktop. Within each section, we discuss the key enabling design and development technologies available from Microsoft.

In Chapter 1, we introduced the Microsoft Data Warehousing Framework. This framework and its surrounding tools were designed with end-user applications in mind. All of the tools have a common look and feel and can share metadata. Let's examine in detail the various tools available and the concepts behind them.

Source Environment

The design process begins with the source environment. Within this environment the developer is concerned with design issues primarily having to do with the data extraction and transformation process, and the metadata of the target DBMS.

Microsoft Repository

A main focus of the Microsoft Data Warehousing Framework is Microsoft Repository. Each system has many parts developed by many people using a wide variety of tools. A major challenge to developing, deploying, and maintaining these systems is tracking where all the pieces are maintained and the effect a change will have on the other components. With the Microsoft Repository, which is based on the industry standard Open Information Model (OIM), application project managers can effectively manage the chaos inherent in software development.

The Open Information Model is an evolving standard for representing metadata. OIM was developed by Microsoft and 20 other vendors, has been reviewed by more than 300 vendors, and will be merged with the Meta Data Coalition's Meta Data Interface Standard (MDIS). This new standard is an industry-supported, technology- and product-independent method for other industry standards such as Java, COM, and SQL to integrate with decision support systems, including data warehouses and data marts.

Microsoft Repository uses the Universal Modeling Language (UML) to represent the metadata inside a SQL Server 7 database. UML is a language originally developed by Rational Software (www.rational.com/uml) which is used to support the product and technology independent of OIM. OIM contains multiple sub-models, each specific to a particular type of metadata being represented. For example, Microsoft English Query is represented by the Semantic Information Model (SIM). When a query is created, the export tool can copy the metadata and relationships into the repository for relationship mapping and reference.

Each of the OIM sub-models is powerful in its own right, but the real value is seen when you view their interoperation. For example, SQL Server OLAP Services helps decision-makers understand their business. OLAP databases are maintained separately from the data warehouse and operational systems to allow queries to be analyzed faster than would be possible by accessing the information by way of a production system. This is because much of the summary and calculation required to analyze the data is performed when the OLAP cube is created.

When a user views data in the OLAP database, they may obtain an unexpected answer that leads them to ask related questions that cannot be answered using data in the OLAP database. Such questions may include, "Where did this data come from and how was it modified for the

data warehouse?" or, "When was the data in the OLAP cube last updated?" The Microsoft Repository contains the data that can answer
questions about the origins and lineage of data stored either in the data
warehouse or the OLAP cube. Using Repository, this user can see the
key information of the OLAP cube, the tables from the SQL Server database used to create the cube, and the Data Transformation Services
(DTS) package which gathers data from a company's various enterprise
transactional systems.

NOTE

One thing to remember about the Microsoft Repository and OIM is that they are not
code repositories, but rather a place to store detailed metadata about objects and
interfaces. Tools such as those in Visual Studio 6, which are described later, can take
this metadata and build usable objects and classes.

Included with the Microsoft Repository Software Development Kit
(SDK) are two add-ins , the English Query add-in and SQL Server OLAP
Services add-in. The English Query add-in allows for export of definitions and structures from the English Query applications. The SQL
Server OLAP Services add-in places OLAP cube metadata into the repository for modeling and tracking purposes. The add-ins allow developers to take pre-existing or older applications and convert them for use
with newer technologies and tools. By using these tools, a complete
design and analysis of running applications can be created with a relatively modest investment of resources.

COM, ODBC, and OLE DB

Microsoft defines the component object model (COM) as a binary
object interoperability standard for sharing application functions between applications. COM is designed to be a distributed architecture,
which has been extended to provide application functions between
computers, as well.

COM attempts to solve the problem of object reuse by allowing separate
developers to maintain and enhance objects that can interact with each
other at run-time by way of published interfaces and properties. Since
two or more COM objects interact through published interfaces, the internal workings of an object are hidden and can be modified as needed.

Constructing applications from objects has been important to the development community. The object-oriented approach improves both the

quality and reusability of application software. Once a developer has created and thoroughly debugged a COM object, that object can be used by developers writing other applications. COM has become a top choice for development because of its capabilities to provide the following:

- Allows for true code reuse on an enterprise scale. It allows developers to spend more time thinking about business-rule development instead of backbone architecture.

- Enables the usage of multi-vendor, multi-language development tools.

- Large, pre-installed base of users; COM is a key enabling technology in the Windows family of operating systems.

- Interoperability with multiple tools, which allows companies to leverage their current technology investment and enhance ROI.

OLE DB, Microsoft's newest programming interface for accessing any type of data source, is compatible with, and utilizes, the COM architecture. OLE DB is designed to access data in both relational and non-relational data sources. Potential OLE DB data sources include relational databases from Microsoft and other vendors, OLAP databases, text files, custom business objects, and even legacy data. OLE DB is not designed to replace ODBC, but rather to provide a bridge from relational database access, which ODBC was explicitly designed to handle, to non-relational, non-conventional data sources such as OLAP, ISAM, text files, etc. OLE DB has an ODBC driver for interfacing with the numerous drivers already present in the marketplace.

There are three types of OLE DB interfaces:

1. *OLE DB data providers*, which expose data from the source
2. *OLE DB data consumers*, which request and accept data from providers
3. *OLE DB services*, which process the data and manage data movement from provider to consumer

Each OLE DB provider is built to understand the destination's data format and can be built by any number of vendors. The OLE DB provider exposes a common interface that can be accessed by any OLE DB consumer. The OLE DB SDK was designed to allow software developers the ability to provide consistent and streamlined data interfaces in a timely manner. In addition, this openness allows organizations to reuse their existing technology investment with newer technology and applications.

Microsoft provides two OLE DB interfaces as part of SQL Server 7. Microsoft OLE DB Provider for SQL Server, also known as SQLOLEDB, is Microsoft's OLE DB provider for SQL Server 7. Tools that query SQL Server directly do so through the SQLOLEDB API. Valid queries that are compatible with SQL-92 or Transact SQL are passed through to the SQL Server engine. Invalid queries generate an error message that is returned to the requesting client. The other OLE DB interface is Microsoft OLE DB Provider for ODBC. This interface is a wrapper designed to provide backwards compatibility with older applications that use ODBC to access SQL Server data.

Microsoft SQL Server OLAP Services uses *PivotTable Services* as an OLE DB for OLAP provider that interfaces with client applications requesting OLAP data. This interface uses the MDX language. Figure 6.1 illustrates the relationships between these various APIs. An application running on the desktop uses either COM or DCOM (Microsoft's distributed COM object model) to call a business process object. The business object can be on the desktop or another computer. The business object uses ActiveX Data Objects (ADO) to retrieve data from a source database. OLE DB is the API that ADO uses to perform this function.

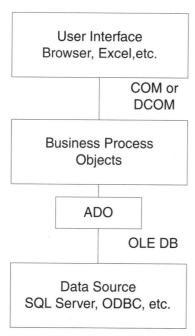

Figure 6.1   3-tier application architecture with OLE DB.

OLE DB for OLAP and MDX

OLE DB is defined as the logical data access method to access both relational and non-relational data. For example, OLAP databases are significantly different from relational databases. The biggest difference between OLAP and relational databases is that OLAP data is stored using a hierarchical structure. Microsoft realized that because of these differences, conventional SQL commands could not be used to access OLAP data, therefore a new query language was developed. This language is called *Multi Dimensional Extensions (MDX)*, and it is part of the OLE DB for OLAP specification. MDX is a query language that is aware of OLAP data structures and can extract data from them. It is similar to SQL in structure and adds functions that allow a client application to select specific intersections or aggregations of data within an OLAP cube. When querying data from an OLAP cube, instead of selecting column and table names from a table, you select dimension members and measures. Many of the more popular client applications offered on the market generate MDX code directly, rather than requiring the user to write MDX. For example, if an OLAP cube has a Time-of-Day dimension and contains the following hierarchy:

```
Time of Day
    Shift 1
        Midnight to 4AM
        4AM to 8AM
    Shift 2
        8AM to Noon
        Noon to 4PM
    Shift 3
        4PM to 8PM
        8PM to Midnight;
```

In SQL, you would use the following command to select a total number of calls received by each Time-of-Day value:

```
Select      sum(calls)
from        call_center_table
group by    time_of_day_text
```

The exact same MDX query against an OLAP cube would appear as:

```
Select      {[Time Of Day].members} on rows,
            {Measures.[Call Volume]} on columns
from        call_center_cube
```

You'll notice MDX allows you to specify which items appear as columns and rows, providing flexibility to easily pivot data items from one axis to another. The power of this is shown when multiple dimensions and measures are queried at the same time.

OLE DB for OLAP was built to issue MDX commands to OLAP cubes. Each application that calls the OLE DB for OLAP interface issues standard function calls to retrieve data. The interface is responsible for issuing MDX commands, retrieving the data, and presenting it to the application for presentation to the user.

As discussed in Chapter 3, OLE DB for OLAP is supported by a large number of vendors, and we believe it will quickly become the industry standard for OLAP data sources.

ActiveX Data Objects

ActiveX Data Objects (ADO) are designed to be a data request object layered between business objects and OLE DB as shown in Figure 6.2. ADO is a language-neutral, application-level interface for developers designed to provide high-performance access to data. This interface supports multiple enterprise architectures including multi-tier, client/server, and

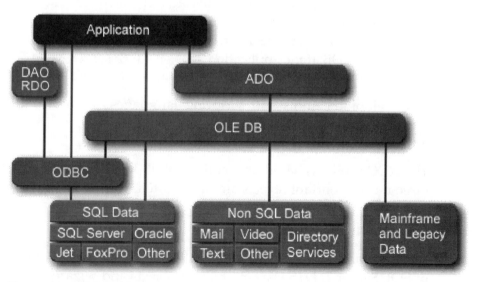

Figure 6.2 ADO architecture.

(Source: Microsoft Corp.)

Table 6.1 Important ADO Objects

ADO OBJECT	FUNCTIONS
Connection	Opens and manages a connection between a client workstation and an OLE DB provider.
Command	Sends data manipulation commands such as SQL and MDX data retrieval and update commands to OLE DB providers. For example, a stored procedure can be executed by way of the command object.
Recordset	OLE DB returns data to the client as a set of rows. The recordset object is used to display and manipulate the retrieved result set. The recordset object can add, delete, and scroll through the data.

Web-based applications. ADO is layered on and integrated with OLE DB, which is a server-side interface.

ADO was designed to replace the previous generation of data access methods including Data Access Objects (DAO) and Remote Data Objects (RDO). These first-generation methods were not designed to access the various types of data available today, and therefore the need for a new access method was born.

Applications use ADO to access OLE DB data providers. ADO can be called from an application by using COM automation techniques available in many application development tools, including Visual Studio 6. OLE DB and the corresponding ADO interfaces are included when the Microsoft Data Access Components (MDAC) are installed. MDAC needs to be installed first on each workstation that will have an application that utilizes ADO or OLE DB. If the application runs on a web server, MDAC must be installed on the web server and made aware of the ADO interfaces.

In development tools and scripting languages, a simple call to the `CreateConnection` method allows applications to utilize ADO and have the interface automatically select the correct OLE DB driver.

The ADO model is based on a collection of programmable objects. The three most important objects are highlighted in Table 6.1.

Data Transformation Services

Microsoft added *Data Transformation Services (DTS)* as part of the release of SQL Server 7. DTS is a set of COM objects and wizards designed to automate the movement of data between OLE DB-compatible databases. So far in this chapter we've discussed the various tools that allow access to data. DTS leverages these technologies to capture and execute the processes required to move data from any OLE DB data provider to any OLE DB data consumer.

In the simplest form, DTS allows a user to move data from one data source to a target. Because DTS uses OLE DB, the data source or target can be a relational or OLAP database, a file such as an Excel spreadsheet, or an ODBC-compliant data source. The DTS Import and Export Wizards allow a relatively non-technical user to quickly define the source and destination for data movement. These DTS wizards allow you to individually define how each data object is moved from source to destination.

Sophisticated developers can use *DTS Designer* to create more complex transformations than are possible using the Wizards. Since DTS is based on COM, it supports ActiveX scripting functions in any supported scripting language, such as Visual Basic Scripting Edition, Jscript, or PerlScript. These scripting functions can be used to create custom transformations to scrub, consolidate, and reformat data. Using these tools, developers can create complex data movement programs that can call OLE methods or COM objects for data validation and transformation. External methods or objects can either be internally developed modules, or they can be interfaces to commercial ETML tools from independent software vendors. This enables companies to reuse data validation and transformation functions that may have been created for other purposes, or to leverage the investment software vendors have made in specialized transformation functions.

The DTS engine was designed to allow developers to directly execute SQL queries to manage data in the database, by performing a pass-through of the query into the database. This provides a level of flexibility by ensuring that SQL statements, stored procedures, and other database objects are reusable.

DTS documents and records the process and origins of the data processed by each DTS package. This provides an audit trail of the origins of the data; the transformations made to the data, and the destination of the data.

As described above, many development tools can access the repository and use objects in other applications. This reinforces the write-once, use-many principle behind object repositories and code reuse. Microsoft SQL Server provides an integrated system scheduler, that can be used to schedule and execute packages, or these packages can be executed in response to system events.

DTS Packages

As already discussed a DTS package is a storage container for a set of transformation steps, including the execution audit trail for the package. Each package can contain one or more steps to extract, move, transform, and validate data in a specific sequence. Using the built-in wizards, DTS Package Designer, or provided APIs, DTS packages can be pre-built and saved as structured files. These files can then be used to execute the transformation as originally developed. A DTS package can be stored in Microsoft Repository, the SQL Server 7 database, or as a file. Storing packages in the Microsoft Repository works just the same as structured files, except they cannot be transported as conveniently. Microsoft DTS does allow a package to be retrieved from the Repository and saved as a file at any point in time.

One advantage to using the Repository to store a DTS package is that Microsoft Repository has the ability to create a unique DTS package identifier for each package, along with a unique version identifier for each package version. Since DTS package versions can be stored in the repository, modifications can be tracked, along with metadata about the databases that are referenced in the package. This metadata includes primary and foreign keys, column data (such as type, length), along with index data. Naturally, you can import SQL Server 7 metadata into Microsoft Repository; however, the DTS Designer allows you to import the same metadata for *any* data sources and targets referred to by the package, provided the source or target is a valid OLE DB provider.

Each task in a DTS package defines a process to be executed using data from an OLE DB data source. Tasks are controlled by step objects, which are designed to coordinate and execute tasks in a specific sequence or dependent on a set of external conditions. DTS packages can have one or more steps, which allows tasks to be executed in a parallel or serial manner.

One key task in the DTS Designer is the Transform Data task. The Transform Data task is the primary mechanism for moving data from one task to another. Other tasks implement the data transformation process. A transformation task can do any of the following:

- Perform a simple bulk copy from a source column to a target column
- Run an ActiveX script
- Execute a SQL command

- Launch a process which runs an executable program
- Perform a data-driven lookup and replace such as replace state name with an abbreviation

When a task is defined, a set of conditions is established. These conditions must be met before a step can execute the task. The conditions can be the successful execution of prior tasks, the existence of specific files in the operating system, or the return value from a program or function call.

The DTS Package Designer provides a graphical method to define complex transformations. The built-in wizards are restricted in their scope to only one source and one destination, but the designer allows any number of sources, destinations, and data transformation steps. Utilizing a visual environment, a user can define step relationships, scripts that transform data, and destinations for the data accessed.

To define a package using the designer, simply drag one or more data objects and one or more task objects from the toolbars on the right and then use the displayed wizards to define the execution step and environment. This process is illustrated in Figure 6.3. The Package Designer

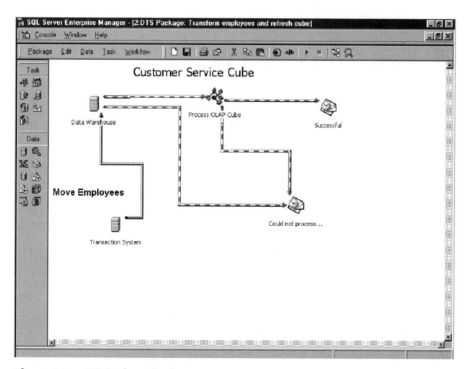

Figure 6.3   DTS Package Designer.

user interface provides a rich set of icons that illustrate the various processes available within the DTS environment. In this illustration, we see a multi-step process that moves employee data from a transactional system, such as a human resources application, to a data warehouse and then to an OLAP cube. At the end of the process an email message is generated. The content of the message depends on whether the job stream succeeded or encountered an error.

Storage Environment

To effectively design and develop Data Warehouses to meet business needs, the core components need to be robust. With the introduction of Microsoft SQL Server 7, not only has Microsoft risen to the challenge, but they have also made the administration of database even easier. As the product evolved from its predecessor, there was a need to provide companies with the ability to analyze the volumes of data being collected in data warehouses. SQL Server OLAP Services addresses the analysis needs of corporations while providing a flexible tool set to expand and extend OLAP development and administration out of the IT department.

Microsoft SQL Server 7

Microsoft has worked hard to provide SQL Server 7 with the ability to support enterprise data warehouses and data marts. Along with OLE DB and DTS, a number of wizards and tools have been developed to allow administrators more time to analyze the data they're administrating versus investing their time just maintaining system reliability and performance. Some other scalability and deployment improvements to SQL Server 7 are:

- Support for terabyte-sized databases.
- Single code base for enterprise, departmental, and desktop users. Allows system administrators the flexibility to administrate one set of database tools and data access services.
- Improved Distributed Transaction Coordinator to share query-processing workload across multiple CPUs and servers.
- System monitoring tools to provide usage-based optimization suggestions for new indices and clustering techniques.

- Replication tools that provide remote users with methods to merge and copy data quickly and easily while maintaining system integrity and reliability.

When a user who has used prior versions of SQL Server first starts SQL Server Enterprise Manager, the first things the user immediately notices is the user interface look and feel. Microsoft Management Console (MMC) is the common interface between applications and the administrator that supports them in SQL Server 7. This new approach gives ISVs and corporate developers a consistent interface and common starting point when developing customized front-end management tools. MMC provides the ability to add snap-ins for flexibility. Each snap-in is built using COM and ActiveX objects, either pre-built or those which can be developed specifically for an application.

Let's examine the MMC categories available to an administrator to properly understand the capabilities of Microsoft SQL Server. Then we'll look at some of the external tools also available.

Databases

One of the largest changes from prior versions of SQL Server is the change from device-based database storage to file-based storage. SQL Server 7 databases are stored in filegroups. Each filegroup consists of one or more database files along with its related transaction log files. This approach provides a cleaner method of database storage and backups by allowing disk administration to determine the best way to store the data. Choices can include file systems such as RAID, offline storage, or slower access devices like CD-ROM, Optical Disk, and so on.

NOTE

A SQL Server 7 database on a CD-ROM or optical disk is a read-only database. It can't be updated and it cannot grow or shrink. However, system files are stored on read-write media. This is necessary to perform management functions such as adding users, and to provide a location for transaction logs.

The filegroup systems allow for easy database management and recovery by allowing administrators to place the data and log on two different disk volumes. Placing database files and logs on separate disk volumes also helps enhance performance, by reducing I/O contention.

A database consists of a primary filegroup and zero or more user-defined filegroups. The primary filegroup contains the system tables, including the system catalog.

TIP

If the primary filegroup gets full, the system cannot add additional entries to the system catalog. Make sure the primary filegroup is allowed to expand automatically and that disk space is sufficient to accommodate its growth.

Another considerations when creating a database in a filegroup is to use a second filegroup to contain the user data, leaving the primary filegroup to contain the system tables. The second filegroup can be designated as the *default* filegroup.

TIP

If the database files are allowed to expand, they can become fragmented, especially if other files are located on the same disks. Fragmentation results in poorer performance. When you define your database files, make them as big as possible so they consume a contiguous range of disk blocks.

Existing Database

A user can see the various objects stored in the database when viewing the list of existing databases. To see the design of an object, simply select the desired item and select Design from the Action menu. For table objects, a window will be displayed listing each field, its data type, and other information necessary to design and build a table correctly. Indices and keys are stored as additional data inside this window. To see these items, select the Table and Index Properties icon from the toolbar.

In the past, an extensive set of SQL scripts or stored procedures was required to determine how much actual space a database was consuming. Microsoft has provided new windows to display this information graphically. The General and Space-Allocated windows display overall database statistics, such as currently allocated and used space for data, allocated and used space for transaction logs, last full and incremental backup date, and other key information necessary for proper maintenance of the database. The General window also provides shortcuts for common tasks performed in a specific database.

To determine individual index and table statistics, select the Table & Indexes window on the screen. This window shows a breakdown of allocated and used space for each table, and index and key in the database, grouped by table. This window is useful to determine if a specific table or index is growing excessively or consumes a large portion of your database's total space.

Creating a New Database

SQL Server provides a property window the DBA can use for the initial creation of a new database. In this window, the DBA can specify the initial size and location of the data and log files and set the basic properties for the database. After initially creating the database, the administrator should view the properties for this database and ensure that the database options and permissions are set properly. The most common options are selected by default, but some of the others might need to be set depending on your environment.

Once the database has been established, you can create new objects by using the appropriate action items and wizards. All of these wizards and utilities can be accessed from the Action menu or the second mouse button menu. Objects include tables, stored procedures, indexes, views, and triggers.

Creating a Table

When the database has been created, the developer is ready to create one or more tables within the database.

When you are designing a database, you need to consider which tables to create and which columns to create within a table. As we described in Chapter 5, the process of designing the database can be extremely complex. It involves several steps that need to be taken by all designers. The first step is to define the various business objects that are going to be in the database. In the case of a customer-relationship management database, these objects include customers, transactions, products, sales locations, and order status, among others.

The second step is to model these objects and their interactions. Modeling is the process of defining the logical relationships between the various objects in the database, and it defines the business rules that govern the behavior of the objects. One benefit of modeling is that it can help ensure that you have defined a complete set of objects; that is, no important objects are missing. Modeling is also useful to define the relationships between the objects. For example, the modeling process will establish the business rule that a customer must have an address, or that an order cannot be shipped if the system has determined that customer has an outstanding unpaid invoice that is more than 120 days old.

Database Diagrammer

One of the features of SQL Server 7 is the Database Diagrammer, a tool that is used to graphically represent the relationships between tables stored in a specific database.

The Database Diagrammer displays database and object relationships in a graphical environment. This tool allows developers to identify data relationships and referential integrity between fields. A database can have multiple diagrams, which allows each specific business relationship to be defined with the least possible confusion. Developers and administrators can use these diagrams to rapidly design and implement business objects and determine where data originated and which objects consume the data.

To utilize the modeler, select the Database Diagram option from the database overview window. The Diagram Wizard displays a list of all table and view definitions from the catalog and offers to include related tables and automatically build links between common field names in each table. To create additional diagrams, select the New Database Diagram option from the Action Menu. If there are diagrams defined for a database, a list will be shown in the right window pane and you can then select the desired diagram to view.

As an alternative, you may choose to use a third-party tool, such as Visio or ERwin, to perform this function. While a good database designer can define a sophisticated, complete model using a whiteboard or paper and pencil, the advantage of a tool is that it can generate the data definition language (DDL) code that SQL Server 7 needs to define the table and the attributes of its columns.

You create a table by opening the SQL Server Management Server window, select the appropriate database from the database tree in the left-hand panel, right-click Tables, and select New Table... This opens up a dialog box in which you enter the table name and create the column(s). New tables can also be defined with the Transact-SQL language using the CREATE TABLE command.

When you define the columns in a table, you need to determine the attributes and constraints of the column. For example, if the column represents a customer, then you want to ensure that each customer has a unique identifier, otherwise you risk mixing or duplicating customer records. What data type is the column? SQL Server 7 supports a wide variety of data types, which may be either fixed or variable length. Data types include character (`char`, `varchar`, `text`), numbers (`int`, `smallint`, `tinyint`, `decimal`, `float`, `real`), currency (`money`, `smallmoney`), date and time (`datetime`, `smalldatetime`), and special values (`bit`, `timestamp`, `global ID`).

A constraint is a restriction on the data that is acceptable to the DBMS. If a constraint is defined for a column and the data element violates the constraint, SQL Server 7 will not add the data and will return an error to the application. Constraints include minimum, maximum, or default values. The designer will need to determine if the column can contain a `null` value or if it must contain data. For example, the developer may decide that customer name and address field must contain data, whereas the email address field can be `null`. If a field must be non-null, a constraint is defined to this effect. Constraints can also be used to validate the value of a field. For example, an expression such as (CHECK cust_num >0 and <99999) can be used to verify that the customer number is within a valid range as defined by a business rule.

In Chapter 5, we described the process of designing a database and covered the issues you need to address when you are defining a star schema, with its fact table/dimensional structure. The key concern is to distinguish the data that comprise the fact table from the dimensional data that go into the dimension tables. SQL Server 7 requires that a star schema must be the source for a SQL Server OLAP Services cube. This requires you evaluate the primary key/foreign key relationships between the fact table and the various dimension tables. The primary key of the dimension table is usually a unique, system-generated key. It should not be a natural key, because the changing nature of dimensions may cause a natural key to become inconvenient to use at some later point in time. An artificial key is preferable for a dimensional table, since it has no relationship with the data that make up the row. The primary key of the fact table is a composite key, which is made up of the various dimension keys that relate to the facts being stored in the fact table. This composite key structure ensures that you can locate a row in the fact table from any related dimension table.

Data Transformation Services

DTS is the set of COM objects that are used to extract, transform and move data between source production systems and target databases. DTS allows users to move data from one OLE DB data source to another. There is a very close relationship between DTS and the Microsoft Repository.

Microsoft Repository

The Microsoft Repository stores metadata about each step in the DTS package and allows a user or administrator to determine the flow of information between these data sources. Microsoft has provided a repository search tool for these DTS packages. Using this tool can help a developer determine the correct flow and data lineage between sources, and therefore easily model similar business processes or design new front-end applications based on the data.

Each table can have fields automatically added, which provides an indicator of which DTS package inserted the data and when. To search for data flow, you can view packages that use a specific table by selecting the Package link next to the table name on the Browse window of the Repository. Other options for finding data and its source include searching by lineage identifier. To perform this action, find the lineage identifier on a specific data row and enter it on the search screen; the Repository will search the metadata and provide all packages that provided or used the data.

Package Designer

Under the Data Transformation Services folder in the Enterprise Manager are the Repository and Local Packages categories, which contain links to each of the packages defined for this server. To invoke the package designer to review or modify an existing package, simply select the desired package. Microsoft SQL Server will start the designer applet and load the package. To review the data transformation or OLE DB data source for each icon shown, double click on the icon and the item's properties will be displayed.

To create a new package, select New Package… from the Action menu. This opens an empty package and allows a user to build a complete package from the ground up. Local packages are stored on a specific computer's hard disk, while Repository packages are stored in the database itself.

The Package Designer also allows a user to print a package's definition in graphical form with specific details listed about each step in the package. This allows a company to provide the package definition as part of a project's documentation.

Tools

In keeping with its philosophy of making products that are easy to use, Microsoft has provided a wide ranging set of developer and administrative utilities with SQL Server. These tools are designed to facilitate the process of creating and managing SQL Server applications.

SQL Server Query Analyzer

One of the areas in which Microsoft has invested heavily to improve SQL Server 7 is the Query Optimizer. Much of this work becomes visible to the user through the Query Analyzer, which is a new and improved utility for evaluating the execution plan and estimated cost of a query. The Query Analyzer provides a set of integration and improved tools, including a graphical Execution Plan display. This new tool allows developers and DBAs to see how a query will execute, providing costs and execution sequences for each statement. Costs include CPU and I/O utilization as well as estimated number of rows to be returned, along with the average row size.

When viewing the graphical execution plan, you can move the mouse pointer over a specific graphic to reveal details for the specific execution step, including the action being performed, the number of rows being returned or affected, the step's execution time, and relative time to the total batch's execution time. By moving the mouse over an arrow between execution steps, you can see how many rows and the size of each row are passed from step to step. This view also allows for the computation of statistics or the addition of new indexes to the tables being referenced.

Another new feature is the ability for Query Analyzer to suggest indexes or performance improvements based on a SQL statement or SQL batch. To access this function, select Perform Index Analysis from the Query menu. Query Analyzer will execute the statements and provide suggestions to make to the database.

Overall there are few additions to the Query Analyzer application, but these few provide a new level of administration and design tools previously requiring years of database administration experience to effectively implement.

SQL Server Profiler

Another new tool in SQL Server 7 provides the ability to trace the events that occur in a database or on a server. SQL Server Profiler (see Figure 6.4) is a highly-customizable application that enables administrators to capture information about very specific events that occur in the database, or events happening in the database in general. SQL Server 7 provides a wide range of events that can be captured and analyzed by the system administrator. A few specific event classes include:

- Lock events
- Error and warning events
- SQL Operators events—insert, delete, update, and select

A good example for capturing database events is if a user complains that the Customer Service application is slow from 8 AM to 9 AM every day. An administrator can capture a trace file for the database during this time and determine what events are occurring that could impact performance during this time.

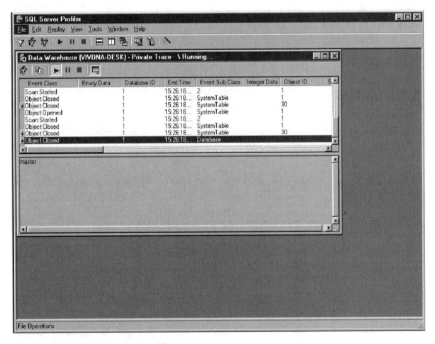

Figure 6.4 SQL Server Profiler.

Once the events are captured, the administrator can use the capture file for further analysis like Index Tuning Wizard, or can replay specific statements in the database. This replay feature allows administrators to make changes to a database and, at a later point in time, determine if these changes have an impact on a set of statements. Administrators can also make a few changes, run through the trace file, and then make other changes as necessary. This provides an educated approach to tuning that is more effective than using a hit-or-miss technique.

To create trace files, start the Profiler application and select New Trace from the File menu. The new trace wizard will begin and prompt for key information. The General tab displays properties for where to store the trace and what to call the trace file. The Events tab allows a user to specify which events to trace in the file, such as Select statements, connections, or object open and close. Data Columns allows for customized trace files by displaying specific columns in the trace; these columns include User, Connection, Database, and CPU. Finally the Filters tab enables a specific trace to be captured. Almost any item available can be filtered on, including User, Database, Server, and IO thresholds.

Index Tuning Wizard

As we discussed previously, once the events are captured, they can be saved to be replayed at a later point in time or can be passed to the Index Tuning Wizard for analysis and tuning suggestions. SQL Server Query Analyzer also allows the user to launch the Index Tuning Wizard to analyze a specific SQL statement.

Once the Tuning Wizard is started, you can specify the database and tables and how the analysis is to be performed on the database. The wizard will examine the trace file and the database and analyze how users are utilizing the data. When the analysis is complete, the Tuning Wizard displays a set of suggested improvements to apply to the database and tables. These suggestions can be implemented immediately, scheduled for later execution, or saved to a script file for further analysis and testing.

WARNING

One thing to always keep in mind when using the Index Tuning Wizard is to watch out for an excessive number of tuning suggestions being made to the user. If the Tuning Wizard suggests adding a large number of indexes to the database, this could indicate a design issue with the database.

It is possible the system environment has changed in some way, and the Index Wizard is reacting to the change. For example, the user's behavior may have changed, or a new application may have been added. In either event, the initial design of the database may not be sufficient to meet the needs of the changed environment, and design changes may be required to improve performance.

NOTE

Each index added to a table requires additional space to store the index. An index also requires more processing time to update the index during insert, delete, and update operations. You will need to factor this additional time into the data loading process. Some sites speed up the load time by dropping the index before a large update and then rebuilding it after the data load is complete.

SQL Server Agent Service

Database administrators can benefit significantly from automation of routine tasks, such as database backups. Many administration tasks can be automated using the SQL Server Agent service to create jobs and alerts to perform these tasks. Tasks can be single server or can be multi-server for help administering an enterprise environment. The components of agent service items are *jobs*, *operators*, and *alerts*.

Jobs define an administrative task once so it can be executed one or more times and monitored for success or failure each time it executes. Jobs can be executed on the local server or on multiple servers; on a schedule; as a response to an alert. A job can consist of one or more job steps. A job step can be an executable program, batch command, SQL statement, or ActiveX script. A SQL statement can include executing a stored procedure on the server.

Operators are responsible for the maintenance and upkeep of one or more servers. An operator is usually a specific individual who is responsible for managing the system. One or more operators can be defined for a single SQL Server instance. The operators can be notified of specific events by way of e-mail, pager, or network messages of specific events.

An alert is defined as a SQL Server event and a specific response. Usually, an administrator or operator cannot control when an event happens, but alerts allow for them to be notified when an event of interest occurs and enables them to define a response to the event. Alert responses can include notifying an operator, forwarding the event to another server, or returning an error condition to an application.

A comprehensive system for administering servers can be implemented using jobs, operators, and alerts, which allows administrators to concentrate on administrating the data instead of just ensuring the server is running.

The SQL Server Agent Service is not designed to be an enterprise-wide production-scheduling tool. It is intended to automate the administration and execution of specific SQL Server tasks. In many instances, these tasks will need to be coordinated with other administrative tasks, which are outside the scope of SQL Server. Many third-party tools on the market are designed to provide enterprise-level or multi-platform scheduling functionality.

SQL Server Taskpad

The Enterprise Manager provides a new feature called Taskpad for each server listed. The Taskpad is a set of pages that provide casual administrators or novice users with an easy navigation method for common administration tasks. The user can select a task and either the specific wizard or tool will be started or an additional Taskpad page will be displayed. The high-level Taskpad groupings are:

- Administrate Server
- Backup Databases
- Import/Export Data
- Administrate Database
- Help

All of the items listed, as well as the subtasks, can also be performed by using the various menus and commands.

The Taskpad is a set of HTML pages stored in resource files. This allows Taskpad navigation using the standard forward and back buttons of MMC, similar to any Web browser.

Microsoft SQL Server OLAP Services

OLAP has increased in popularity over the past few years. Today's users are increasingly demanding the ability to analyze the data being gathered in the data warehouse. To fill this need, Microsoft SQL Server OLAP Services was developed and integrated into the SQL Server product. OLAP Services cubes can be stored using one of three methods: HOLAP, MOLAP, or ROLAP.

Microsoft SQL Server OLAP Services is a key component to the Microsoft Data Warehousing Framework. It provides functions for applications to access multidimensional data and perform complex analysis upon it. Included with OLAP Services is an engine called *PivotTable Services*, which allows users to retrieve and display data with easy navigation controls.

Data Sources

The source of the data needs to be defined before beginning the design and development of any OLAP cube. In the SQL Server 7 environment, data for an OLAP cube comes from a SQL Server 7 relational DBMS, which stores the data in a star schema. SQL Server 7 further categorizes the data as either local to a cube or shared across multiple cubes in a single database. Shared data sources can be included in multiple cubes or used to create shared dimensions (see the following section titled Dimensions). Each cube must have one or more data sources defined from either the local or shared data sources.

Data sources are accessed using OLE DB that, as discussed previously, can be any relational or non-relational data source. The most common data sources are usually relational databases and text files because they are columnar in format, which provides a structured environment for data building.

Fact Tables

A *fact table* is a single table in a data warehouse and usually contains transaction-level detail data on a business function or process. It contains numeric values, which become measures by which to perform analysis. It also contains links to each of the dimensions present in an OLAP cube.

When a cube is first defined, the Cube Wizard automatically asks the user to identify a fact table. Multiple fact tables can be used in a single cube by implementing partitioning; however, each of the fact tables used must have the exact same structure. Fact tables do not always need to be tables. One effective way of combining data from multiple sources or tables is to create a view that correlates the data, while still maintaining data integrity. When creating views, always remember that the view is really a SQL statement that must be executed each time the view is accessed. This feature can cause performance degradation and should be used with caution.

Dimensions

There are three types of dimensions in a Microsoft SQL Server OLAP Services database: *shared*, *local*, and *virtual*. A shared dimension is defined in the OLAP database and can be included in multiple cubes. A local dimension is defined in a specific OLAP cube and can only be referenced in that cube. A virtual dimension is defined based on a property of a level in a given physical dimension. These properties are called *member properties*. A member property can be something like color, which is not typically stored in a dimensional table. By creating a virtual dimension based on the member property of color, the designer can enable users to analyze product sales by color, along with other measures, such as store location.

Both shared and local dimensions are stored as intersections in the cube, while virtual dimensions are referenced and linked to the dimension values.

Every non-virtual dimension must be defined as part of a hierarchy. This hierarchy represents a logical grouping that usually represents the reporting levels inside an enterprise or department. A few examples of dimensions in a Customer Relationship cube are Customer, Received Via, and Time of Day. Building dimensions requires a thorough knowledge of business processes and application usage. Here are examples of the hierarchies already listed:

```
Customer Dimension
     Region of the World
          Corporation Name
               Site Location


Received Via Dimension
     Electronic
          Web
          E-Mail
          Logged Internally
     Phone
          Toll Free Number
          Transferred from Sales
```

```
Time Dimension
     Year
          Quarter
               Month
                    Day
                         Shift
```

NOTE

In the time dimension, we typically don't add a week level. This is because of the inconsistent relationship between weeks and months. Most months don't begin or end cleanly on a week. One way to deal with this problem is to create other, artificial time periods. For example, some organizations use a calendar with 13 business periods of 4 weeks each, rather than months. Retailers define their calendars on seasonal spending patterns such as Spring, Christmas, Easter, Fourth of July.

When defining a dimension, always remember that fact tables should be linked to dimensions at their lowest level of granularity. This enables the OLAP cube to consolidate and report measurements at each level of the hierarchy.

Each dimension has two key properties: the *Member Key* and the *Member Name*. Member keys correlate to indexes in databases. These identify the scope and links to a specific member in the cube. When defining keys, if all the keys in a specific dimension are unique across the entire dimension, then data can be loaded at the lowest level only. If a dimension has a non-unique key, then the keys must be uniquely defined within their parent's context. For example, a Time dimension may have months, which are unique for a given year, but which are not unique for the entire time dimension—every year has the same months. The key can be any valid SQL expression that extracts data from any tables identified in the dimension editor.

Member names are the visible values for dimension members. These can also be any valid SQL statement executed against the identified dimension tables. When defining member names, a one-to-one correspondence to the member keys must exist. For example, in an employee dimension, no more than one employee number should map to a specific employee's name for a specific department. If you attempt to define a many-to-one mapping, possible corruption in your cube may occur, and users may obtain unexpected or invalid results.

Virtual dimensions are unique in their ability to provide additional descriptive categories for dimension members. A virtual dimension also provides another way to group the data. In the FoodMart example cube provided by Microsoft, there is a Store dimension, which is part of a hierarchy of Country, State, and Store. A virtual dimension is defined at the Store level, called Store Size in Square Feet. This virtual dimension allows for a further breakdown of stores in a Country, State, or at the all Stores level. If instead of analyzing data for all stores in California, we could write a report to compare stores of equivalent sizes, with no additional overhead to the cube or query, this would provide users with an unheralded level of flexibility in their data.

Measures

Each cube contains a set of *measures*, which are the data being analyzed. These measures are quantitative numeric values consolidated at each level of the dimensions included in the cube. In most enterprises, measures are derived from the key performance indicators (KPIs) that executives use to manage departments, divisions and corporate results. KPIs allow users to focus in on what is important to them and therefore what is important to the enterprise. They also provide a mechanism that enables comparison across functional areas.

The Cube Wizard requires at least one measure to be identified when identifying the fact table during the cube creation process, and it lists all numeric fields it locates in the fact table.

NOTE
A list of employee ID numbers would not be used as a measure, but would better serve as the lowest level of an Employee Dimension.

Once the measures are identified, various options are available within the Cube Editor for formatting the display of a measure, identifying the data type of a measure, and other properties. One important property which is useful is the Internal flag in the advanced properties window. This flag defines a measure as an internal-only measure, which can be used in calculated measures, but is not available to general users of the cube. This option enables developers to include data consolidations and other information necessary to generate meaningful KPIs, but not display the individual details required to obtain the end result.

Another key property of measures is the aggregation function, which provides different methods for creating the dimension intersection value. Allowable aggregation types are SUM, COUNT, MAX, and MIN. Each function operates as you would expect on a dimensional level. For example, if a measure is defined with an aggregation function of MAX, and the data browser displays a Customer dimension by Region of the World, the measure would display the MAX value for each of the regions listed.

One final note about measures is that the source column can be defined as a SQL statement deriving data from the fact table. This feature provides an additional level of flexibility. However, remember when using SQL statements as part of a measure, that additional processing time and resources are required to resolve the data being processed.

Calculated Members

A calculated member is dynamically calculated when retrieving the data from the cube. A highly powerful addition to measures, calculated members allow for complex calculations to be defined using a built-in function library or registered external libraries. These calculated members are not stored in the cube (thereby not increasing the size or complexity of the cube), but provide an enhanced ability to see information across multiple dimensions.

Calculated members can become the children of any dimension's levels, or they can be children of the measures dimension. Depending on the scope of the calculation and its need to apply to the entire cube, this can prove to be important when performing corporate data analysis.

An example of when you would use a calculated member is in comparing the contribution of a single member to its parent. If a calculated measure is created in the Customer dimension, as discussed previously, we can compute and display a Site's (child) profit contribution to the Corporation (parent). This would involve dividing the Profit measure's value for the current child by the Profit measure's value for the Parent.

Virtual Cubes

A virtual cube is a combination of one or more cubes linked by common dimensions. We have already examined shared dimensions and how they can be used in multiple cubes. Virtual cubes take advantage of these shared dimensions to link unrelated information. A virtual cube requires no additional storage space and allows cubes defined with different storage methods (ROLAP versus MOLAP) to be linked to each other.

One reason to build a virtual cube is to analyze cross-functional impacts from one division or department to another. For example, a virtual cube called Marketing Sales Ratios could be created from a cube analyzing Marketing Campaigns and a cube analyzing Customer Sales. These two cubes can be combined by the common dimensions Region, Product, and Time to provide an analysis on how Marketing campaigns affect sales orders and shipments.

When developing virtual cubes, any shared or virtual dimensions listed in both cubes can be included in the virtual cube, and any measures derived from the fact table can also be included.

NOTE

Calculated Members cannot be included in a virtual cube.

Partitions

Partitions are almost the opposite of virtual cubes in that they represent logical divisions of data broken down by dimension member values or data source. A cube partition can be placed on a separate storage device or server and can have different data sources. For example, you may want to archive and purge data from your active data warehouse on a rolling three-year basis for performance reasons but still be able to perform analysis on older data to establish long-term trends. Using a partition, a user can specify the same fact table, a fact table from a different data source, or a different table from the same source. You can place the older data on a slower, less-powerful server and place the current data on the new hardware platform, or you can store the data on a slow media such as optical disk or CD-ROM. This allows your enterprise to maintain good performance for analysis of current data while still providing the flexibility to query and analyze older data.

By utilizing different storage methods and number or aggregations, a minimal data storage size can be established, or a balance between size and performance can be reached.

Data slicing in partitions is accomplished by filtering the data in each partition by dimension-member value. When querying against cubes with multiple data slices, the OLAP engine interprets the consumer's request and retrieves the data from the correct partition. The OLAP engine can also determine when data is required from more than one partition and will execute the proper queries and combine the data into a single data set for the consumer.

Microsoft provides a Partition Wizard to help the database developer create a partition. A partition can be created using a data slice, a separate fact table, or the same fact table. If you create the partition using the data slice approach, the Partition Wizard attempts to generate a filter, such as a range of values, to select the data that goes into the partition. Be aware that in this case the `MemberKeyColumn` and `MemberKeyName` of the level's properties must refer to the same column in the source fact table.

If you create a partition using separate fact tables, the structure of the fact tables that make up the partitions must be exactly the same. This structure is useful if you want to divide the partitions based on data by year, for example.

Finally, if you create multiple partitions using the same fact table, the different partitions can contain data from specific dimensional hierarchies. It is important to ensure that the data items in the partitions are not used more than once; otherwise, it is possible to obtain spurious results such as double-counts when you combine data from multiple partitions for analysis.

Replication

Corporations are constantly struggling with the mission-critical operations that are becoming increasingly global and mobile. To help tackle this problem, SQL Server 7 provides replication services to distribute data across an enterprise reliably and quickly. Replication affords an opportunity to provide users with relatively recent data without requiring them to be connected to the same database at the same time. Choosing a replication method requires planning and thought regarding the resolution of data conflicts and update options.

The following two important issues should be considered when implementing data replication:

1. Update latency

2. Site independence

Update latency refers to the interval that is acceptable between the time an update in a source database is replicated to a target. A continuum exists, ranging from immediate, synchronized updates—which require a two-phase commit—to relaxed, delayed updates. SQL Server 7 supports three major categories of replication.

Transactional Replication

The first is *transactional replication*, which stores updates in a distribution database. The distribution database functions like a queue, and updates are transmitted to the subscriber database where they are applied. Transactional replication can utilize the two-phase commit protocol for immediate updates; however, this should be reserved for the exceptional case in which update latency must be zero and network reliability is high. Transaction replication stores the actual transactions, which occurred in the source database—INSERT, UPDATE, DELETE statements. The transactions are then "played" back to the target database, and the data is updated. This is a much quicker method of data update but provides no data validation to ensure that the target database has not been modified since the remote's last refresh.

Snapshot Replication

The second category of replication is *snapshot replication,* which periodically copies a snapshot of the entire replication dataset to the subscriber database. Since snapshot replication actually copies the data source from one location to another, it enables a remote site to be completely disconnected from the master site while still providing remote users with good performance. Snapshot replication requires fewer CPU resources on the source because there is no need to constantly monitor all transactions, but it may consume significant network bandwidth when the dataset is replicated. Also, this category is not suitable when the application requirements call for bi-directional replication. Merge replication is used when two or more databases need to share updates on a bi-directional basis.

Merge Replication

Merge replication takes all data in a remote database and attempts to make changes to the local data that has been modified in the remote database. If the local data has been changed since the remote's last refresh, the merge replication shows the data conflict and allows a user or administrator to resolve the conflict. While this provides a consistency checking process, it also requires manual intervention. On data sources that change often on both sides, this can prove to be a time-consuming task. Merge replication is more complex than the other two schemes but is useful for truly distributed operations in which remote sites must interact autonomously with their databases.

Desktop Environment

The desktop environment is where all the hard work invested in building the storage and source environments starts to pay off. By designing and developing a comprehensive and complete data warehouse architecture, you can leverage emerging technologies, standards, and components to deploy reporting and data-analysis tools by plugging in the various pieces and pointing them at the data warehouse. Most of the database-related tools available from Microsoft, and independent query and analysis tools vendors, understand the nature of data warehousing and how to access data using various interfaces.

Many third-party tools are developed to provide functionality that is not available from Microsoft. Before you take on the development and maintenance responsibilities associated with creating an internally developed application to browse and report on the data stored in the data warehouse or OLAP cubes, you should evaluate the technologies and tools already available. It's highly likely that are some of them have been deployed within your company.

PivotTable Service

The new PivotTable Service, which is installed with the OLAP client or with Office 2000, is an OLE DB provider. This provider interacts between any applications that understand OLE DB, and OLAP or relational data sources, such as OLAP Services, SQL Server, and Oracle. In addition, it provides the ability to buffer data from the source and create "offline" files for data browsing and analysis while disconnected from the source.

Since the PivotTable service interacts with OLAP and relational data sources, it is optimized for MDX expressions and SQL queries. In addition, it provides some new functionality for creating and updating the offline files.

This new provider can be used with a number of the tools to be described, including Visual Studio, Office 2000, Active Server Pages, and many others. By creating this service, just like any OLE DB or ODBC driver, the source and application can be modified and updated to reflect changes in development trends, but the OLE DB interface remains a constant entry point for data retrieval.

Microsoft Office

Probably the single most popular desktop application suite is Microsoft Office. A key to the popularity of Microsoft Office is the high degree of integration Microsoft has traditionally provided between the components that make up Office. With the release of SQL Server 7, this level of desktop integration has been extended to the database and OLAP cubes, as well.

Excel 97

While Excel 97 does not natively support OLE DB and OLE DB for OLAP, many vendors are developing add-ins to interface with these data access methods. For more information see the section titled Third-Party Tools. Power users who need to see the specific numbers and want to create their own charts based on the data usually use Excel's data analysis capabilities. For native support of OLE DB data sources in Excel, Office 2000 provides a whole new set of tools and wizards.

SQL Server 7 provides an updated ODBC driver, which allows applications that are not OLE DB-aware to still use ODBC for data access. Since Pivot Table and MS Query for Office 97 can use ODBC drivers, these tools can still access data stored in the data warehouse and perform advanced analysis against it. As discussed in an earlier section, ODBC is limited to relational database access and therefore cannot access Microsoft SQL Server OLAP Services cubes.

Office 2000

Office 2000* provides an entire suite of tools enabled for OLE DB data sources. Each of the applications—Word, Excel, PowerPoint, Access, Outlook, and so on—can use ActiveX components, COM objects, and OLE DB providers. By including the PivotTable service and developing an updated version of the classic PivotTable and PivotChart wizards, Microsoft has made it even easier to access data with a consistent look-and-feel across the enterprise.

Excel 2000 and MS Query have wizards that will assist you in connecting to the data warehouse or OLAP cube and allow you to format and choose which data to display. In the other Office tools, a user can simply insert the Pivot Table or Pivot Chart ActiveX controls, then choose the control's properties to specify the data source and connection options. Once the connection has been established, dimensions, measures, and columns can be dragged from the field list into the Pivot Table or Pivot Chart and formatted for display.

Publishing to HTML

With the release of Office 97, Microsoft introduced the concept of saving worksheets and documents as HTML files. Office 2000 continues this functionality, but adds a new and powerful feature, called Interactivity. The Interactivity feature allows browser users who are viewing worksheets, documents, and presentations to interact with these items as if they were using the native applications. This enables Excel to create Pivot Table and Pivot Chart worksheets, which can be accessed with all the functionality of Excel by a user with a Web browser.

Saving a file without Interactivity allows browser users to view a static page, which must be refreshed manually by the document owner, by starting the native application and opening the file, then re-saving it. With Interactivity enabled, users are able to perform dynamic data analysis, such as adding new page filters or changing the dimensions of table columns, displayed in the Pivot Table. The user can then save the changed document to the local workstation for future use, or if the correct file permissions can be obtained, save it across the network connection. The same principles apply to the Pivot Chart object with regard to changing axis definitions, filters, and legend information.

*In beta at the time this book was written.

Web Pages

The Web has become a very popular medium for delivering applications to users. Microsoft has created an entire infrastructure for creating, deploying and managing web-based applications. These infrastructure elements include development tools and run-time platforms that all interact with Internet Explorer, which is Microsoft's Web browser. These elements are interoperable with SQL Server, enabling developers to create Web applications that use SQL Server data.

Active Server Pages

Active Server Pages (ASP) running on Internet Information Server (IIS) enables companies to build powerful internet/intranet applications using development tools that are already in use across the enterprise. JScript, JavaScript, or Visual Basic Scripting (VBScript) allows Web pages to become dynamic data warehouse-driven consumers. Installing OLE DB on the same server running IIS, enables all of the features and options available to n-tier application development tools to become available to the ASP page.

ASP page development can be accomplished using a number of development tools available in the market today. Microsoft's tools include Visual Studio and Visual InterDev, which provide a graphical environment to create and test Intranet/Internet ASP pages.

Dynamic analysis can be performed by the user through ASP pages, while allowing the site administrator to maintain control over security and data retrieval templates. Using the same ActiveX controls, Pivot Table and Pivot Chart, as available to Office users, enables Microsoft to deliver on its goal for a consistent look and feel on either a traditional client/server desktop or a Web browser.

HTML Page Subscriptions

SQL Server 7 includes an HTML publish-and-subscribe function in the database engine. A subscription enables HTML pages to be created or refreshed whenever a trigger occurs in the identified data source. A trigger can be a data update, a scheduled time, a DTS transaction, or any number of events and responses available to the SQL Server engine and SQL Server Agent.

The published HTML page can contain filtered data directly from a table, the results of a SQL statement, or the output from a stored procedure. This flexibility allows a single data extraction vehicle to be developed and used in multiple reporting environments, always ensuring the data will be in the same format, with the same columns, and according to the design of the data warehouse.

However, the subscription functionality does not provide the ability to derive data from sources outside the SQL Server databases. It also does not provide for error monitoring without viewing each page generation command individually.

Visual Studio 6

The latest version of Microsoft Visual Studio provides a comprehensive development environment to support the development of enterprise applications. The development environment for each of the tools has been updated and looks almost identical, similar to Office's level of look-and-feel. Also included are additional objects, tools, and functions that allow applications to be built for managing, updating, and analyzing data warehouses. To understand some of the new functionality behind these tools, let's take a quick look at the features each one provides.

Visual C++

The most common use for Visual C++ is to develop Dynamic Link Libraries, COM objects, ActiveX components and client/server applications. The language provides a robust set of functionality to create core architecture components for object-oriented development. C++ was designed to be a high-performance language with access to operating system level function calls and APIs. Visual C++ is intimately linked with the Window family of operating systems and provides a high degree of flexibility for developers. If application performance and scalability are critical components to a project, then development in Visual C++ is a must.

Visual Basic

Visual Basic (VB) is one of the most popular programming languages for application and component development as well as Rapid Application

Development (RAD) and application prototyping. VB provides a set of wizards and pre-built templates that allow developers to focus on building business rules instead of architecture components.

Visual Basic contains updated tools for managing, developing and accessing data stored in any data source. These tools help build applications which are aware of the intricacies of the database but that do not come with the overhead usually associated with building database applications. Visual Basic applications development allows developers to leverage their skill with other Microsoft development tools such as Visual Basic for Applications, which is used in Microsoft Office, or Visual Basic Scripting Edition (VBScript), which can be used with Active Server Pages as discussed previously.

Visual J++

Visual J++ provides an environment to develop cross-platform and thin-client applications in a graphical environment. Visual J++ leverages the component-oriented development present in the other Visual Studio tools, which enables the development of Java-based Windows and IIS-based applications. Visual J++ enables developers to create portable Java applets or Dynamic HTML programs for use with other platforms or Web-browser technologies.

Visual InterDev

Visual InterDev is an Internet- and Intranet-development environment. One of the most important features of Visual InterDev is the ability to create multi-platform database applications that are run on a Web browser. Visual InterDev creates Active Server Pages that can include VBScript or JScript commands. This enables the development of Web applications that can run on multiple platforms and Web browsers.

Visual SourceSafe

SourceSafe is a source code version control system, which manages revisions to application code and components. Visual SourceSafe is integrated into the Visual Studio environment. The development languages that are part of Visual Studio can insert or retrieve code and objects stored by Visual SourceSafe.

Modifications, fixes, and enhancements will need to be made once the initial development of an application is completed. SourceSafe is a version control system that allows developers to work off the same version of the source while ensuring that no other developers are working on the same item simultaneously. Additionally, if a developer needs to go back to the previous version of the code to work on it, SourceSafe can easily retrieve the version for the developer.

Visual Modeler

The Visual Modeling tool allows developers to create components quickly and easily in any one of the Visual Studio tools, based on the Universal Modeling Language definition stored in the Repository. This tool reinforces the ability to create enterprise applications in multiple languages and the principle of write-once, reuse multiple times.

Microsoft Repository

Microsoft Repository is where developers store metadata about objects. Each component and object created in the Visual Studio tools can be stored in the Repository for reuse by other tools. Using the UML, the information is stored in one of the models as defined by the OIM.

Component Manager

The Visual Component Manager provides an interface for reading and writing UML definitions in the Microsoft Repository. It supports the ability to catalog the components discussed in this chapter, such as COM objects, ActiveX components, ASP pages, and others.

Visual Studio Analyzer

Visual Studio Analyzer provides a peek into running Visual Studio applications, which enables developers to analyze n-tier and distributed applications. It provides a graphical flow from one object or component to another, including the events that occur in that object. Developers can now see how the execution sequence happens, which allows for processing refinements and performance tuning that is done for specific reasons and with a flow.

Microsoft English Query

English Query is the latest addition to the data warehousing tool set available today. English Query enables a user to retrieve information from the data warehouse using English-like sentences and statements. An English Query user does not need to know the table relationships and columns needed to retrieve the data.

A knowledge repository is created which maps columns and relationships to tables and columns in the data warehouse. The repository is called a domain and is stored in the English Query engine and applications. A development tool that maps tables, fields, and joins to grammatical structures such as nouns, verbs, and adjectives, is used to create the English Query domains. English Query contains an application that allows the development of these domains in a graphical environment.

When the mapping has been completed, a developer creates a Visual Basic or Active Server Page application, which accepts a user's English syntax query. The query is then passed to the English Query application, which uses the domain information to translate the query into a SQL statement. That SQL statement is then run against the database, and the results are passed from the database to an HTML page, which is then displayed to the user.

Third-Party Tools

When Microsoft SQL Server 7 was launched at Comdex/Fall 1998, 300 vendors and 1200 products already supported the SQL Server 7 product and its components. When deciding to implement a data warehouse, always remind yourself that someone else probably has had a similar problem and has either solved it or is working on solving it.

In the previous sections, we described a few technologies that are available as third-party tools and technologies. For COM object development and ActiveX component, a number of web sites and commercial development firms with pre-built objects can be tailored to your specific environment. In addition, a number of firms specialize in this type of software development.

Summary

The design process requires different sets of activities in the source, storage and desktop environments. In this chapter we covered some of the major design capabilities provided by Microsoft with the release of SQL Server 7, focusing mostly on the extraction and data transformation processes, as well as the creation and deployment of the SQL Server 7 database and its related SQL Server OLAP Services cubes. Finally, we closed with a review of the various design and development tools provided by Microsoft.

CHAPTER 7

Development

In the previous chapter, we discussed the various tools and technologies available to develop effective data warehouses and decision support systems. In this chapter, we will build on that framework and understanding to describe the development process used to assemble the pieces into a viable system. Throughout this chapter, we will examine in detail the various wizards in each area and identify when it's appropriate to use each one.

SQL Server 7

Looking at the core of any data warehouse, anyone can see that mastering the key concepts of the relational database engine is one of the most important items to address first. To properly understand how multiple diverse enterprise transactional systems can be built into a single data storage entity, let's review how transactional systems are built.

Transactional systems are designed to focus on one particular business function of an enterprise, such as order processing, customer service, or accounting. Companies typically select multiple systems or multiple modules of a single system (in the case of an enterprise resource planning application, such as SAP R/3) to service the needs of the corporation as a whole. Each module or system focuses on a set of business rules and processes to service the needs of a department or division. While implementing these systems, a set of data requirements are identified early on in the process. This set of requirements is used to establish a framework for users to enter and retrieve data from the applications. Database administrators and application developers see this process in a very different light. When designing systems to support business processes, a number of details need to be reviewed and decisions on how to implement the design need to be made.

During the design and development process, a database schema and its layout need to be identified. As discussed in Section I, the two basic schema types used for decision support are the Star and Snowflake models. Another key feature to consider is developing an audit trail for each piece of data, which allows end users and the administrator to determine how, when, and by whom the data was inserted and how, when, and by whom the data was last updated. At the same time, details about each item to be stored in the database need to be established. Developers typically identify these as attributes of the data key.

By now you're asking, "What does this have to do with my data warehouse?" If you understand the concepts of an audit trail, data attributes, and a database schema, the development of a comprehensive data warehouse is made much easier.

Building Business Data

During the design of the decision support database, decisions on which data to store and how and where to store it were made. Now we actually need to build the environment that fulfills all of these requirements. The two most common SQL Server tools for building these objects are Enterprise Manager and SQL Query Analyzer, each of which provides advantages when creating database objects.

Once the design has been reviewed, developers can see how to create the basic structures inside the database. These are usually built as a set of tables, each set representing a unique business need. One of the most important features of a data warehouse is the ability to combine seemingly disparate data from the various transactional systems. For example, a list of customers from the Customer Service system could be combined with the customer list from the Sales system, providing a consolidated and complete customer list. This allows the data warehouse to classify one master table for a particular type of information and then effectively use it further in the analysis application.

Something to remember when developing data warehouse objects is to combine data where it makes sense, but not to "overcombine" data to reduce the number of objects in the warehouse. Combining data from multiple sources that have no reason to be combined causes complications later, as development and analysis resources spend time trying to make sense of the data relationships. This usually results in an increased number of interfaces and applications that need to be developed just to support the data.

Using SQL Server 7 Enterprise Manager, a set of objects can be created to support these design and implementation decisions. Let's begin by creating a database, a table, and an index for that table. We review the various wizards available and use them to perform these functions.

Creating the Data Warehouse

Database

To create a database, start Enterprise Manager and expand the list of servers. Select the server that will physically store your data warehouse. Immediately, the right, window pane displays the SQL Server Taskpad (see Figure 7.1). As discussed in Chapter 6, the Taskpad contains a set of shortcuts to common administrative tasks. Using these shortcuts eliminates the need to remember where administration tasks are stored in the various menus.

To create a new database, click on the icon "Set Up Your Database Solution." This takes you to another taskpad page, which contains an icon labeled "Create a Database." Click on this icon and the Create Database wizard starts. By filling in the appropriate values and using the "Next" button, the wizard creates a database and transaction log for use. Once the database has been created, a set of user IDs should be created, or NT authentication should be enabled for database access. By using the "Create a Login" icon, either or both of these two security methods can be used to control which users can see the data.

Tables

Once a database and user IDs have been established, we can begin to build tables and other objects in the data warehouse. First, let's build the

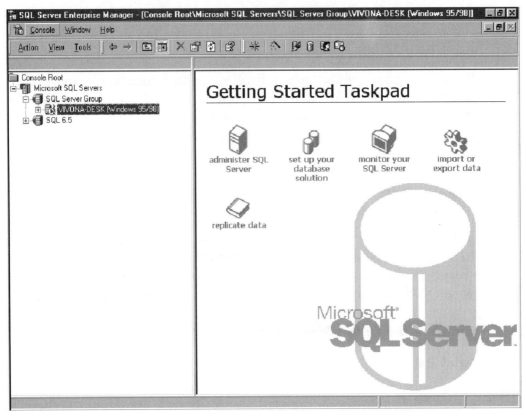

Figure 7.1 SQL Server Enterprise Manager Taskpad.

main data storage table by selecting the database just created and expanding the list of folders associated with this database. When you highlight the database, the right window of Enterprise Manager displays statistics about the database and objects it contains. Three windows are available. "General" displays information about backups, maintenance plans, and metadata about the database (see Figure 7.2). In addition, the General window has a set of shortcuts to the various wizards that allow an administrator to maintain the database. The "Tables & Indexes" page displays a list of tables and their associated indexes and shows how much space each object consumes along with the number of rows in each table. Finally the "Space Allocated" page displays the amount of space allocated for the Table and Transaction log. It also displays used versus free space for each.

To create a table, select the Tables folder and then select Action/New Table. This starts the table designer, which prompts you for a name for

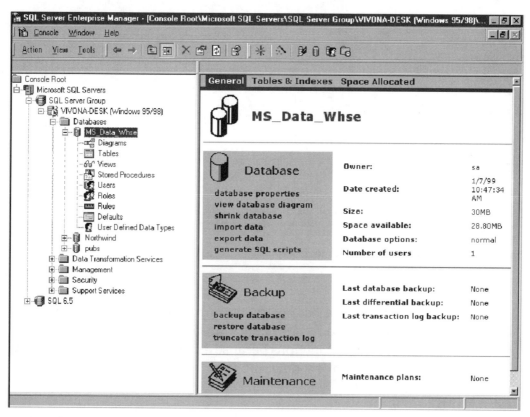

Figure 7.2 Data warehouse database with properties window.

the new table. Enter a table name and click on the OK button. You can now begin building the table's columns and datatypes. Once you have entered the table's columns and properties, save the table. In Figure 7.3, the Customer table has been created and the Customer ID field has been identified as the primary key since this provides the link to the other data warehouse tables that record customers. Other activities that can be performed in the table designer either during the initial design of the table or after the table has been saved are:

- Creating indexes and triggers
- Displaying access permissions
- Displaying other object dependencies between this table and other tables
- Creating a SQL script that can be used to build the table in SQL Query Analyzer.

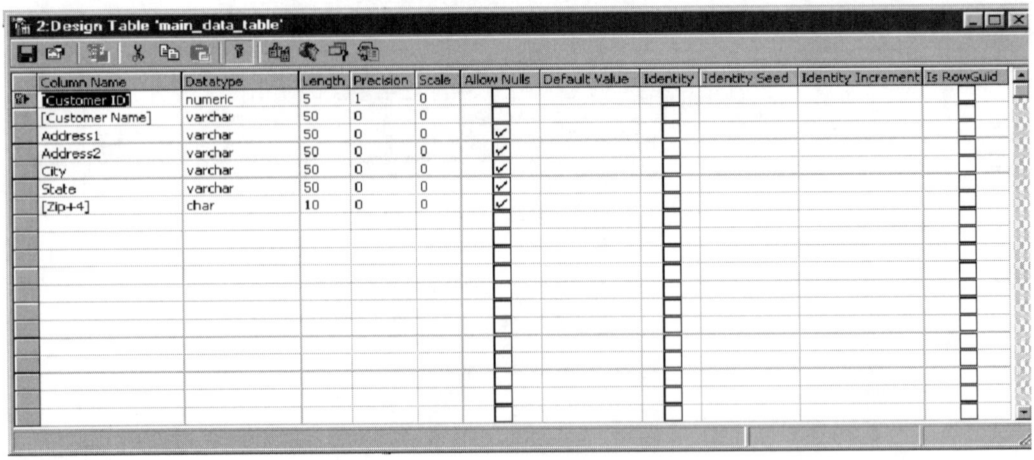

Figure 7.3 Table designer for Customer table.

Since this database is a data warehouse, you would not ordinarily use triggers to perform processing. Data Transformation Services should be used to perform these functions because a trigger can decrease performance and potentially affect data integrity.

Indexes

Once the table has been created and saved, you need to decide which columns should have an index so that performance may be optimized for queries, reports and analytical applications. In most cases, the indexes used in the transactional systems are not applicable for the data warehouse. When designing these indexes, an analysis of how the data is used and its relationship with other data needs to be performed. For example, in a transactional system, the Customer table is indexed by Customer Name to facilitate searching of individual customers, but in reporting and analysis, people usually search for information that applies to multiple customers, such as location (State or Zip Code), or recent activity (Invoices). These fields would represent better candidates for indexing.

Two index attributes should be considered: clustering and uniqueness. Clustered indexes force the table to be sorted in the order of the indexed column. This can provide a faster method for data access by enabling SQL Server to use a binary search to retrieve data in sorted order. But clustered indexes come with a price in terms of index size and table manipulation speed. When a row in the database is created, deleted, or updated and the index is affected, the system needs to process the index and insert the data in the correct location. This can cause a reshuffling of the index and data in the table because the index requires the data in the table to be stored in sorted order. Clustered indexes are also larger than other types of indexes because of the way SQL Server stores data pages with links to other data pages. In addition, only one clustered index is allowed per table. Again, this is because the clustered index enforces a sort order on the table rows, based on the value of a single column.

NOTE

While a table can have only one clustered index, it can support as many as 256 non-clustered indexes.

Unique indexes identify a column or group of columns as a key, which can allow a user to ensure that one, and only one, row is selected at a time. If a user attempts to insert another row using the same key, the database returns an error and the data is not placed in the table. A unique index is created using a primary key to ensure the data's referential integrity.

To create an index, select the "Table and Index Properties" icon from the toolbar, then select the Indexes/Key tab from the window. All currently defined indexes and keys are displayed along with the type and columns that make up the index or key (see Figure 7.4). To create an index, click on the "New" button and fill in the appropriate values. When you are ready, close the window and save the table, and the indexes and keys will be created.

Database Diagrammer

Database diagrams allow a database administrator or application developer to graphically explore the relationships between database objects without examining all of the details about the tables, keys, and indexes. Providing a graphical representation of this relationship (see Figure 7.5) allows documentation to be maintained and easily accessible and also permits updates whenever changes are made.

Additionally, objects displayed in the diagram can be modified by selecting menu items with the right mouse button (see Figure 7.6).

The Database Diagram wizard can automatically build portions of the diagram based on primary and foreign keys as defined for each table. You can also include the related tables automatically by selecting the

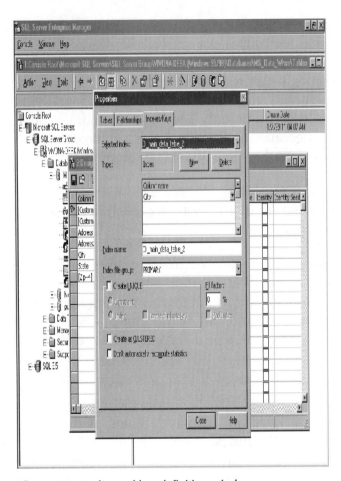

Figure 7.4   Index and key definition window.

option when determining which tables to include in the diagram. This ensures that all referential links are maintained in the database and the diagram.

The Database Diagrammer can also include text annotations for making special notes to development teams and administrators to notify them of special conditions or external requirements on the data. These diagrams can be printed and used to provide documentation to end users and developers for use in other applications or report development.

Views

A view is a virtual table that consists of a SQL statement that is executed whenever the view is accessed. Users access views in the same manner

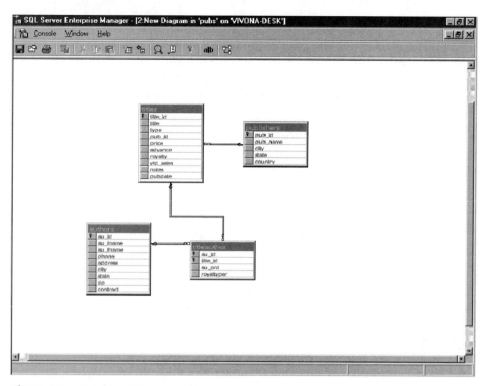

Figure 7.5 Database Diagrammer.

Figure 7.6 Right mouse button menu.

as tables. Typically views are built to make end-user reporting and application development easier when reading complex relationship information from many tables. Since views are SQL statements, a database administrator can develop and tune these statements for performance and allow anyone to access the data, ensuring the hardware is not consumed by a poorly defined query. A view is also a useful method of limiting access to confidential data because a user security profile can be associated with a view.

The View Wizard allows the selection of one or more tables, a number of columns, and a WHERE clause to match tables and restrict data, and it produces a single view from this information. Before the view is created, the user has the ability to review the SQL statement being built and make edits before actually building the view. To create a new view, select "Create a View" from the Setup Taskpad or select "New View" from the Views folder's right mouse button menu.

Security

Information is the most valuable asset your company has, and not everyone should have access to that asset. SQL Server 7 provides two methods of security—NT Authentication and SQL Server security. Each object in the database has its own set of permissions, which can be restricted according to user or group. Additionally, a user or group can be assigned a database role, which consists of a set of prepackaged access permissions and functionality. To assign users or groups access to an object, you can either select the user or group in the Users folder for a database or you can individually select each object and assign permissions to it.

Performance Tuning

Speed is a primary concern in any application or report being used in a production environment. When the data warehouse is being used on a regular basis, the SQL Server Profiler should be used to identify other indexes that could be created to achieve faster performance. The profiler should gather data for a period of time that represents a normal amount of usage, including batch updates and reporting. To start the profiler, select "SQL Server Profiler" from the Tools menu of Enterprise Manager (see Figure 7.7), or start the SQL Server profiler from the SQL Server 7

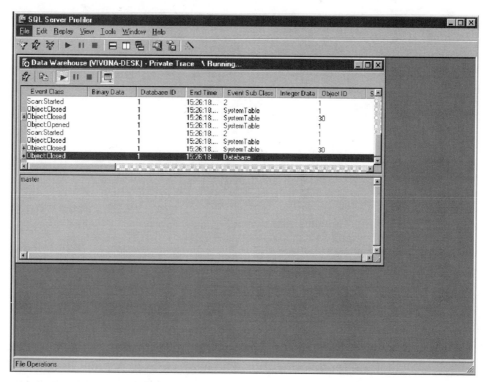

Figure 7.7   SQL Server Profiler.

program group. Establish a filter that captures all events for the data warehouse. You can request the profiler to focus on specific users, poorly performing queries, or other items by selecting the Wizard from the Tools menu. Once you have identified the items to capture, allow the system to gather data for a reasonable period.

After the events and data have been captured, the file can then be used with the Index Tuning Wizard for analysis and suggestions. Start the Index Tuning wizard by selecting "Index Tuning Wizard" from the Tools menu. After identifying the database and server to analyze, select the file or table name that has captured the recent trace data. The wizard will then analyze the trace file and the data in the tables to provide suggestions and indexes to create (see Figure 7.8). Once the analysis is complete, the wizard displays the suggestions and allows you to execute them now, schedule them for later execution or save the changes to a file for use with other tools.

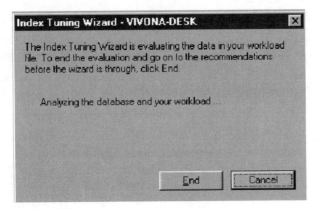

Figure 7.8 Index Tuning wizard.

SQL Server 7 OLAP Services

As soon as the data warehouse has been established and data gathering begins, users typically begin to ask for reporting and analysis of that data. One method for meeting this need is to use SQL Server OLAP Services. By building cubes that represent departmental functions and then combining these cubes to create cross-functional analysis cubes, a wide range of questions and needs can be addressed. In Section I, we discussed each of the components necessary for the successful design and deployment of an OLAP cube. In this section we describe the process of building a cube.

Fact Tables

Each SQL Server OLAP Services cube must have a single fact table that provides the measurement information. Each row in the fact table needs to identify a member from each dimension defined in the cube. When deciding which table to use as the fact table, a common question arises: Should I use one of the data warehouse tables or create a separate entity from which to drive the OLAP analysis. This question is usually decided by the amount of disk space available, the degree of logical data separation in the database, and other administrative issues present in the installation. For most analysis applications, using the data warehouse table is a good idea because the transformation and load processes update these tables directly, and indexes are built with reporting in mind.

An alternative to directly using the warehouse fact table is using another table that is a subset or copy of the original data. This data can be gathered and computed by using an additional DTS package or package step. If this method is used, remember to reimplement the indexes originally identified in the warehouse, or design and deploy new ones that apply to the OLAP analysis usage.

Dimensions

Dimensions describe and create reporting hierarchies for the data represented in the fact table. Two types of dimensions exist in SQL Server 7: *time* and *standard*. Time dimensions are those which represent a calendar or clock hierarchy to the data. For example, a Time dimension based upon the calendar may have the following members listed:

```
1998
    Quarter 1
        January
        Februray
        March
    Quarter 2
        April
        May
        June
```

By using the built-in time hierarchies, advanced time-based measures can be built using MDX expressions in the cube. Additionally, the implementation of complex balance-oriented analysis can be performed. For example, a measurement that represents the inbound call volume for a specific phone number in the current period could be implemented by using the `PeriodToDate` MDX function. These measures always contain a running sum of the call volume regardless of what the actual date is. You would not have to add additional days or months to the calculation to have the volume correctly reflected in the OLAP cube.

Balance-oriented transactions allow for a relative time period to be used when calculating the current balance value. For example, your checking account balance for Quarter 1 is not the sum of the ending balances from January, February, and March; rather, it is the balance from March. By using the `ClosingPeriod` function, the correct values can be reflected for all hierarchies in the dimension. These types of measures are called semi-additive measures.

SQL Server OLAP Services also has the ability to perform current-period versus previous-period analysis and other complex time-oriented calculations and comparisons. For more information, review the SQL Server OLAP Services on-line help system.

Standard dimensions are used for all nontime-oriented dimensions being created. These dimensions can include Products, Customers, Status, and so on, and have no practical limits on their contents. Additionally, if the time-dimension hierarchies do not meet the business needs of your organization, a pseudotime dimension can be built from data, but the predefined complex time analysis functions already described no longer work.

When building dimensions, you can select either a single table or a snowflake data layout when identifying the data source. If a single table is selected, all of the dimension hierarchy levels must come from the selected table. Snowflake dimensions allow for the combination of several tables and fields, thereby creating a pseudo-SQL statement from which the dimension levels and members can be created. Dimensions can be created as local dimensions or shared dimensions. As already described, shared dimensions can be used in multiple cubes and virtual cubes, whereas local dimensions can only be used in the cube in which they were originally defined.

One other consideration when building dimensions is that all dimensions must be defined as balanced; for example, one node on the hierarchy cannot have more levels than another node. Graphically balanced and unbalanced hierarchies can be represented as:

```
Status
    Open
        New
        Researching
    Closed
```

Example 1 Unbalanced hierarchy.

```
Status
    Open
    New
    Researching
Closed
    Closed
```

Example 2 Balanced hierarchy.

In Example 1, the closed node does not have any children while the Open node does. This results in an unbalanced or jagged hierarchy. Since all data from the fact table is mapped and loaded at the lowest level for each dimension, all facts with a status of closed could never be loaded. In Example 2, this problem has been resolved by duplicating the closed level on both the lowest and roll-up levels.

When deciding how to balance hierarchies, take into account the data being loaded. In Example 2, duplicating the closed member did not introduce any significant overhead or additional aggregations to store in the OLAP cube. The following example of a typical customer dimension necessitates a different decision to be made on which data to duplicate or eliminate.

```
CustomerLocation
    England
        London
            Customer 1
            Customer 2
        Berkshire
            Customer 3
            Customer 4
    United States
        Georgia
            Atlanta
                Customer 99
                Customer 100
```

Since the United States (and some other countries) inject another geographic identifier between Country and Customer, a decision needs to be made about eliminating a level for only certain countries or regions, or duplicating a certain amount of data. If the decision is made to duplicate data for countries without states, which data to duplicate becomes a critical decision. Duplicating the cities of London and Berkshire in the following fashion

```
CustomerLocation
    England
        London
            London
                Customer 1
                Customer 2
        Berkshire
            Berkshire
                Customer 3
                Customer 4
```

```
United States
    Georgia
        Atlanta
            Customer 99
            Customer 100
```

would cause a significant expansion of the OLAP cube. If there were three other dimensions in the cube with 10 hierarchy members each, the total number of intersections or aggregations would increase by 2000 ($10 \times 10 \times 10 \times 2$), versus 100 if the country of England were duplicated instead. By carefully designing the data to duplicate and create balanced hierarchies, a compromise between performance, database size, and report functionality can be achieved.

Creating a Cube

To see how the facts and dimensions fit together and to provide a working example of the OLAP cube, let's build one using OLAP Manager (see Figure 7.9). Begin by starting the OLAP Manager MMC Snap-In and

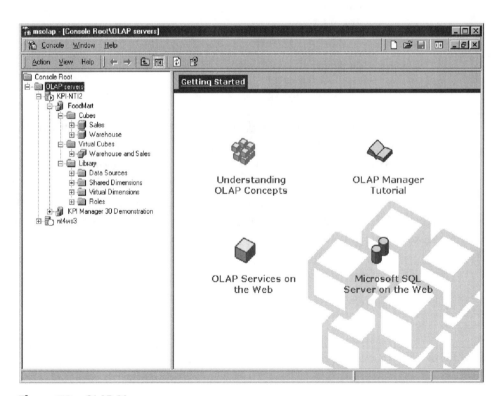

Figure 7.9   OLAP Manager.

opening up the registered server which represents the computer you're using. Displayed below the server name is a list of databases that have been previously created. Microsoft provides an example database named FoodMart to help with the tutorial and demonstrations available in OLAP Manager. Create a new Database by selecting "New Database" from the Action menu, and a new folder will be created.

Name the database, Data Warehouse Example and press Enter. Open the database just created, and three additional folders are displayed: Cubes, Virtual Cubes, and Library. To start, open the Library folder and an additional set of folders is displayed. Click on the Data Source folder and select "New Data Source" from the Action Menu. This starts the Data Source wizard, which helps build an OLE DB connection for data warehouse access.

A dialog box appears with a list of the OLE DB providers that are installed on your computer. Select the "Microsoft OLE DB Provider for SQL Server," and click on the Next button. Fill in the fields displayed on the Connect tab—each of these provides necessary information for connecting and validating access to the data source. Before saving the connection string, click on the "Test Connection" button (see Figure 7.10), which attempts to open a connection to the database and validate that it can be reached. If the Wizard connects to the database, a success message appears.

Once a data source has been created, shared dimensions can be created. In the Library folder, highlight the Shared Dimensions folders and select "New Dimension" from the Action menu. A submenu appears. Select "Wizard" from this menu. The Dimension Wizard begins by asking if this dimension is created from single table or a snowflake design. Based on the dimension tables established in the data warehouse, select the appropriate option. Each of the data sources previously defined will be listed along with the tables in each of these sources. Select the appropriate table or tables and click on the "Next" button. If the correct data source is not listed, you can create a new data source by selecting the "New Data Source" button displayed below the list of available tables.

The next screen allows the type of dimension to be defined. As already discussed, you can select a standard or time dimension. If Time is selected, one column must contain a date field and be identified as the data driver for the time period analysis functions and dimension members. Select the "Next" button, and the Dimension Level window is displayed.

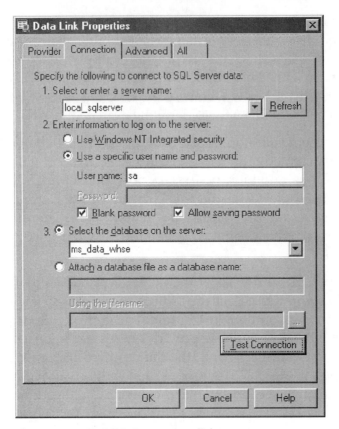

Figure 7.10 OLE DB Connection dialog.

This window is where you define the dimensional hierarchy. By selecting columns from the left side and copying them to the right side, a data
hierarchy is built.

NOTE

In the previously discussed Customer dimension, OLAP Manager would require
that there be more cities than countries. If more countries were detected, the
system would provide a message offering to reorder the dimension levels based
on the number of members available. You can override this reordering, but care
should be taken to ensure the reordering is being performed for the correct reasons.

When building dimensions, the same column cannot be selected for
two different levels because the field is removed from the list of available fields. Using a field in multiple dimension levels and combining

multiple fields together to create a single field is the next topic covered. When the hierarchy levels have been established, select the "Next" button, and the Dimension Wizard allows you to preview the hierarchy and its members (see Figure 7.11). If the hierarchy has been built as expected, type in a dimension name and select the "Finish" button. The dimension will be saved and the Dimension Editor will be started.

The Dimension Editor (see Figure 7.12) is designed to allow a developer to configure individual options for each of the levels in the hierarchy or to reconfigure to populate the data in the dimension. A number of properties can be manipulated to provide a complete and comprehensive dimension for each of the levels listed.

Begin by viewing the properties for the dimension as a whole. On the Basic Properties tab, the description for the dimension can be modified. This description is displayed when you view the metadata for the dimension, and it is used in multiple places by OLAP Manager. The Advanced tab has three properties: "All Level," "All Caption," and "Type."

The "All Level" property enables or disables the dimension to contain a total rollup level that is not present in the data. This level provides a

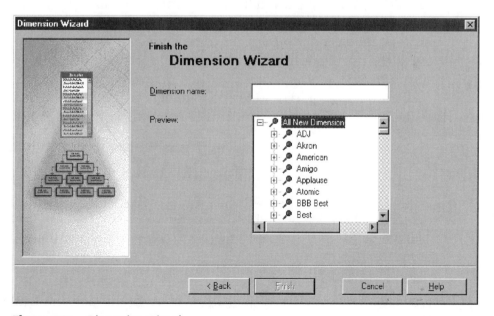

Figure 7.11 Dimension Wizard.

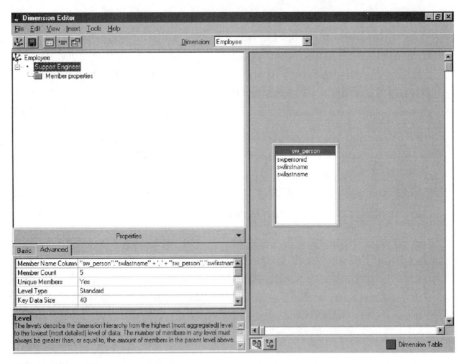

Figure 7.12 Dimension Editor.

"Totals" member to exist in the dimension for easier reporting and data breakdown. Without this level in the data, each of the top-level values for this dimension would need to be added together to compute the overall aggregations for a set of measures. For example, if a time dimension is created in which years are the top level, and "All Levels" is not enabled, a user would need to add together the measure values for each of the individual years (1996, 1997, 1998, etc.) to report "All of Time" measurements.

The "All Caption" property allows for a customized label for the "All Levels" rollup inserted into the hierarchy by enabling the "All Levels" property. By default this label is "All" combined with the dimension name; for example, the Status dimension would have an All Caption of "All Status." Depending on the terms used in a database, this label may or may not be appropriate.

Finally, the Type property is the same standard and time dimension types available when creating the dimension through the Dimension Wizard.

Each of the dimension levels listed has its own set of properties. To review the dimension level properties, select a dimension level and then select the "Basic Properties" tab. This tab contains three important pieces of information: "Name," "Description," and "Key column."

The Name is the level's proper name, which is displayed in data retrieval tools to help users select appropriate data based on logical hierarchy levels. For example, for the "Time" dimension, the first level may be called "Years," the next "Quarters," and so on. The Description property for the level will be displayed when viewing the metadata about a dimension and its levels, or it can act as a definition, which can be seen in most of the end-user reporting tools.

The final basic property, "Member Key Column," and the first advanced property, "Member Name Column," need to be discussed together. Member Keys and Member Names do not necessarily need to be the same data. The Member Key allows for a unique identification in a level of the dimension and can be used for sorting purposes. The Member Name column is the value displayed to the user when viewing a specific member in the dimension. Usually these two fields are used in conjunction to provide a system identification for a member and then display a formatted value to the end user. Additionally, both fields can be retrieved using a valid SQL statement. The Member Key is usually a single column in the dimension table, whereas the Member Name is the result of a SQL statement to make the displayed value user-friendly. For example, if we were building a dimension of Employees with a three-tier hierarchy of Division - Department - Employee, we might want to have the employee members displayed as a formatted value of 'Last Name, First Name' even though these values are stored in two separate fields. By building the Member Name field with the following syntax, the values will be displayed in that format.

```
Employee.last_name + ', ' + employee.first_name
```

An alternative would be to display the employee names as "First Name Last Name". In most situations, this would cause the name to be sorted by first name. This is where the Member Key versus Member Name becomes useful, since the Member Key can be set to the "Last Name, First Name" format, whereas the Member Name can be "First Name Last Name." By using the advanced property "Order By Key," the data can be identified as sorted by the Member Key or the Member Name. Developers can use these fields to build a customizable and user-friendly dimension. Many of the dimensions can be built by using the Wizard and properties available in the wizards. Regardless of whether the dimension are shared dimensions or local dimensions, the Wizard and Editor work exactly the same and accept the same types of data and values.

Once you've created all of the dimensions necessary to create an effective reporting environment, you can begin creating a cube. Select the Cubes folders using OLAP Manager under the database you want to use to populate the cube, and select "New Cube" from the Action menu. A submenu appears; select "Wizard" from this menu. The Cube Wizard is started and begins by asking for a fact table. Similar to dimensions, a list of tables available for each defined data source is displayed. If the data source that contains the fact table is not shown, you can define a new data source by selecting the "New Data Source" button.

Once you have selected a fact table, a list of numeric fields is displayed. These fields represent the columns that can be used to create measures. Select the fields that will be present in the cube for measurements from the list. Next, the wizard will ask which dimensions to include in the cube and display a list of shared and local dimensions. If you want a dimension that is not listed, you can create a new one by selecting the "New Dimension" button on the window, which will start the Dimension Wizard. After you have selected the desired dimensions, the system will create the cube and attempt to automatically identify the links between each of the dimensions and the fact table. If a dimension cannot be linked, OLAP Manager will display a message box stating which dimension tables it had problems with. The Cube Wizard will ask you to provide a name for the cube and then save the cube design in the repository.

The Cube Editor will then display the cube and its design. Additional dimensions can be added, new measures can be identified and the cube structure can be modified using the Table Layout window in the Cube Editor. You can link fields from any table to any table, even between dimension tables, where the columns are of the same data type. This allows for the cube builder to take advantage of foreign keys and indexes previously created in the database. To ensure the cube design matches expectations, the Cube Editor can generate sample data for previewing what the cube will look like. This feature is very helpful for testing measures and how the dimensions will work with each other to create aggregations.

The Cube Editor can display a number of properties for each of the object types. In this section, we'll focus on the Measure properties. Each of the measures has a set of properties, which control how the value is displayed, if it is displayed, and how the data is calculated.

The Aggregate Function property controls how the source data is consolidated for each of the members in the hierarchies. Sum, Count, Min, and Max are the four available functions to calculate data. These functions provide the largest flexibility when processing data, depending on how the data is structured and how the information is being loaded. The Data Type and Display Format options on the Advanced tab control how the data is displayed to the user. OLAP Manager attempts to make a guess at the data type and format based on a sampling of the data performed when initially creating the cube. The number of decimals, percentages, and other formatting can be performed by selecting the appropriate value from the list or by typing in a custom format. For example, to display a value with a percent sign and two decimal places, you would enter `#.00 %` in the Display Format field. One thing to remember is that not all query tools use these formats. Others may require an additional function to be called to determine the format from the cube.

The Is Internal property is designed to allow for a measure to be included in a cube for use in other calculations, but it is not displayed to the end user. For example, a measure may add a column of elapsed time to be used in calculating an average elapsed time, but the aggregated elapsed time is not an appropriate or relevant item to display in reports. This feature allows the measure to be hidden from view where it cannot be selected in any of the reporting tools.

Calculated Members are an advanced method for computing measures that are not natively stored in the fact table. For example, the developer may want to create an "Average Elapsed Time" measure for support calls. This measure given is calculated by dividing the total elapsed time by the number of calls received. To create a calculated member, select the folder and select "Calculated Member" from the Insert menu. The Member Builder will start and display all dimension and measures in the cube, as well as the functions available for creating complex calculations. By using MDX expressions, a calculated member can represent a value at any given intersection in the cube, or can be a simple averaging calculation. To create a specific value for an intersection, simply drag the dimension or dimension members and the appropriate measures into the expression builder and define the calculation logic. The calculation logic can include conditional calculations such as `If - then - else`, or use any of the functions listed in the Function Window. For example, to calculate the Percent calls which were closed by using a knowledge database, the following calculation could be created:

```
If ([Measures].[Linked To Resolutions] > 0, [Measures].[Linked To
Resolutions] / [Measures].[New Case Volume], NULL)
```

This measurement will perform the calculation of Linked to Resolutions divided by New Case Volume only if there is a value in the Linked to Resolutions field, otherwise it will return a blank value. Like many other tools, if a calculation is performed it will be performed for every intersection as specified. If this formula did not check for "Linked to Resolutions" to contain a value and if either field is empty, the calculation returns an error and displays a division error indicator in the data. Similar to measures, the format and display properties for the calculated measure can be controlled through the Basic and Advanced properties.

Storage

Once the cube has been designed, the cube metadata needs to be saved to the repository and the cube needs to be processed so users can access the cube (see Figure 7.13). Before processing the cube though, a cube storage type needs to be selected. In Chapter 3, we discussed the various storage methods and advantages of each. The OLAP Manager Storage

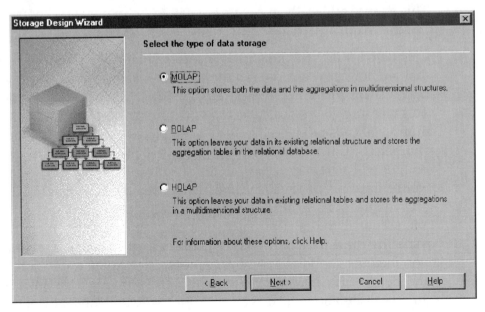

Figure 7.13 Cube Design Wizard.

Wizard allows you to select one of these storage methods and design how aggregations are stored. Select the appropriate method from the window and proceed to the next screen.

The next window allows you to specify the number of aggregations that will be calculated in the cube. As previously discussed, pre-calculating aggregations allow the cube to provide information faster and with less processing overhead. The Aggregation Wizard displays three options for determining how many aggregations to store in the cube: "Storage-based," "Performance," and "Custom." Always remember more aggregations mean more storage is used, but also means faster query performance.

If your system has limited space, enter the maximum size the cube can be and the Design Wizard will calculate how many aggregations it can store in the given space. Alternatively, you can specify the percent of performance improvement desired regardless of disk space used. To calculate every possible aggregation available in the cube, set the aggregation performance percent to 100 and allow the system to generate the aggregations. Once the system determines how many aggregations and how big the cube will be, this information will be displayed along with a graph estimating performance versus size.

When determining how many aggregations to calculate, a common misperception is that the percent performance increase is the same as the percent of total aggregations. This is not the case in OLAP Manager. The performance increase is a calculation based upon the maximal and minimal query time desired for a given set of queries. To compute the percent performance gain, calculate the maximal and minimal time to perform queries on a non-optimized cube and use the following calculation

```
100 * (Max Query - Target Query) / (Max Query - Min Query)
```

For example, if an un-optimized query takes 30 seconds, and the best possible query time is 5 seconds, you specify an 80 percent performance target to achieve a 10-second response time. OLAP Manager will then determine how many aggregations are required to achieve the desired performance increase.

Once the aggregation storage is designed, you can either continue processing the cube or can go back and redesign the aggregations. To populate the cube with data, SQL Server OLAP Services must process it. To process the cube, select "Next" from the aggregation window and highlight the "Process Now" option. Once you select "Finish" from the Storage Wizard, OLAP manager will save the appropriate information to the repository and proceed to process the cube as specified (see Figure 7.14).

While the cube is being processed, a status window will be displayed, listing each step being performed. In the event of an error, the window will display a "Stop" icon on the step, and once processing has been completed, allow you to select the step and determine what caused the error and what return codes were provided. Processing the cube may take considerable time if a large volume of data is to be loaded or there are many aggregates to define. Once the processing is complete, your cube is ready for access by the users.

NOTE
Users are not allowed to access the cube while it is being processed for the first time because results may be inconsistent if a user analyzes a dimension that is incomplete.

Security

Just like access to your data warehouse should be guarded, controlling access to the OLAP cubes should be a priority. OLAP Manager has two

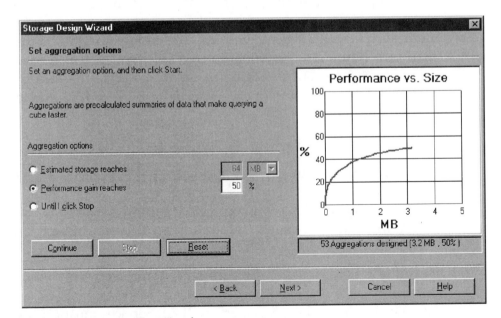

Figure 7.14 Aggregation Wizard.

levels of data access in a cube: Read and Read/Write. Security is managed by creating roles in each of the OLAP cubes, or the Library for a set of cubes, and adding users to each of the roles as appropriate.

A user can exist in more than one role. For example, a user may have Read access to one cube in a database, but have Read/Write access to another. Once at least one role is established, any user without specific access permissions to the cube cannot read the cube; for example, if a user is not listed in a role, the user cannot access the data.

To create a new role, select "Manage Roles" from the Role folder in either the Library or a specific cube. Select the "New Role" button and name the role. You can then add users or groups from the desired domains to the role and grant Read or Read/Write permission to the Role.

Optimization

Once the cube has been used for a while, users may notice that certain queries or intersections of data take longer that other queries. Microsoft has provided an integrated optimizer for determining if the cube should be modified to include some aggregations and not others. Four performance areas can be analyzed:

1. All queries between two dates
2. Frequently run queries
3. Queries that ran longer than "x" seconds
4. Queries for a specific user

OLAP Manager can analyze these queries to determine if more aggregations or a different mix of aggregations should be created to help performance for specific users or common queries. Once OLAP Manager has analyzed the queries and determined that changes are necessary, it will allow you to reprocess the cube. Remember that the cube will be unavailable to the users while it is being restructured and new data is being added. This utility can help resolve consistent performance problems with queries and determine how users are using the system.

Data Transformation Services

When you create a data warehouse or prepare data for use in OLAP cubes, you need a consistent and dependable method for moving data from one location to another. Microsoft created Data Transformation

Services (DTS) and related tools to meet this data movement need. Additionally, DTS can help administrators and users track data sources and transformation logic, as well as provide a graphical flow of the data flow from start to finish.

Multiple methods can be used when building transformations to move data successfully from a data source to a target. Table-to-table copies, single table transformations or complex scripts, or SQL and ActiveX programs can be developed and deployed. We're going to illustrate the process of building a DTS package that moves employee data from a transactional system into the data warehouse, then executes an OLAP cube process to incrementally add new members and data rows into the cube, based on the example PUBS database supplied by Microsoft. If the employee data transformation fails, a mail message will be sent to the operators and processing will end.

Begin by selecting "New Package" from the Action menu in Enterprise Manager. Enterprise Manager will create a new blank package and open the Package Designer. The first step is to define the data sources. To create a data source, highlight the "OLE DB Provider for SQL Server" icon and click it. The OLE DB Connection Designer will start and ask for connection information, such as server name and database. Select the PUBS database from SQL Server as the source. Create a second connection that points to the data warehouse. Now highlight both connections and select "Add Transform" from the Workflow menu. This creates a data transformation indicator between the two data sources. To edit the transformation, double click on the indicator and the transformation properties will be displayed. On the source table, select the Employee table from the PUBS database. On the destination tab, since we don't currently have an employee table defined, select the "Create New" button. A SQL statement for creating the table will be displayed. To generate the table, click on the OK button. This will create a new table that is an identical copy of the Employee Table. On the transformation tab, a graphical map of how the data will be moved from one table to the other is displayed. To have a field from one table moved to another, highlight the source field and drag it to the destination field. A source field can be moved into more than one destination field.

Next, add a mail message step to the package by selecting the "Send Mail" icon. Fill in the appropriate mail recipient information and a short mail message. Highlight the data warehouse data source and the mail message step and select "On Failure" from the Workflow menu.

A red-dashed line is drawn between these two items, indicating a process flow when a failure occurs (see Figure 7.15). Create a new Active Script Task and enter in the following code:

```
Function Main()
Dim oServer as Object
Const PROCESS_FULL = 1
set oServer = CreateObject("DSO.Server")
oServer.Connect = "local"
oServer.MDStores("MyCubeDatabase").Cubes("MyCube").Process _
PROCESS_FULL
Main = DTSTaskExecResult_Success
End Function
```

Now highlight the Active Script Task and the data warehouse data source and select "On Success" from the Workflow menu. This creates a link between the Warehouse Active Script, which causes execution to happen only when all of the transformations and tasks against the data warehouse have completed successfully.

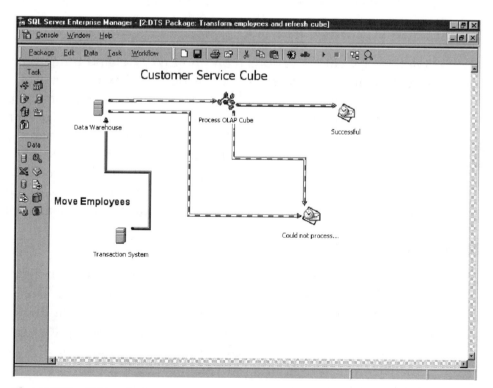

Figure 7.15 DTS package.

Once the package has been completed, additional text and labels can be inserted to help document the process and data flow. You can also print the diagram for use in documentation and presentations. To save the package to the repository, select "Save" from the Package menu. Ensure that the SQL Server repository is selected in the Source field. Once the package is saved, the repository will have control over maintaining multiple versions and documenting the package and determining where and when the package was last run.

Replication

One of the primary design goals of SQL Server 7 was to make replication easier to define, manage, and use. Microsoft addressed this goal through a combination of wizards and sophisticated design and monitoring tools. SQL Server Enterprise Manager introduces several new wizards to simplify the installation and maintenance of replication. You can use SQL Server Enterprise Manager to set up a complete replication environment spanning as many servers as necessary across your enterprise from any server or workstation that has SQL Server installed.

Replication Wizards

SQL Server includes various replication wizards and numerous dialog boxes to simplify the steps necessary to build and manage replication. The Push and Pull wizards assist in the development of subscriptions from one server to another. The Conflict Viewer reviews recent conflict resolutions and allows the resolutions to be configured. The Create and Configure wizards allow for a new publication to be created and enable control over how the publication is managed and scheduled. Once you have used the wizards to initially configure replication or create publications and articles, you can change most of the initial settings through dialog boxes.

Replication Monitor

Use Replication Monitor to view the status of replication agents and troubleshoot potential problems at the distribution server. The Replication Monitor acts as a component of a server only when the server is enabled for distribution and the user belongs to the System Administrator SQL Server role. The SQL Server Agent scheduling service must be active on each replication server. Each replication instance is scheduled through this service.

Replication Monitor is used to view available replication objects and scheduling information as well as monitoring real-time replications occurring on the server. The monitor can also be set to fire off alerts as a result of replication events. If a replication event occurs, SQL Server Agent can respond according to pre-established event responses. This is accomplished by allowing SQL Server Agent to monitor the Window NT event log. If a logged event occurs which is a defined item, the Agent responds automatically, either by executing a task that you have defined or by notifying an operator.

To assist in troubleshooting, Replication Monitor graphically monitors each of the replication agents: Snapshot, Log Reader, Distribution, and Merge. To display the four agents, select a server, and then click "Replication Monitor." To see the detailed activity and the task history for that agent, expand one of the agent nodes.

To create a new publication, select Replication | Create and Manage Publications from the Tools menu. This will start the Create Publication wizard. Next select the data warehouse database as the source. When the Publication Wizard starts, allow the current server to act as the Distributor. Next, select the type of replication. Each type of replication has benefits. You need to select the appropriate type of replication for your environment, as described in Chapter 6. For this example we'll select Snapshot. If real-time updating is desired, select "Allow Immediate Update Subscriptions" in the next window. For off-line publications, select "No" for this option. Since the replication system has all the functionality of SQL Server, the destination of the publication does not need to be another SQL Server. Any OLE DB or ODBC-compliant database can be a replication destination. For now, select SQL Server from the list (see Figure 7.16).

The next window will display a list of tables and allow you to select which ones will be published to the remote server. After selecting the appropriate tables, the next window will allow you to filter data to be published. For example, if a certain site only needs data for a specific country, filter the data being pushed to that site to reduce network traffic and improve replication performance. Once the replication has been established, the schedule needs to be created. The wizard will display a schedule window that can be changed according to your company's needs.

Now that the publication has been established, Enterprise Manager creates the publication and establishes the replication schedule. To

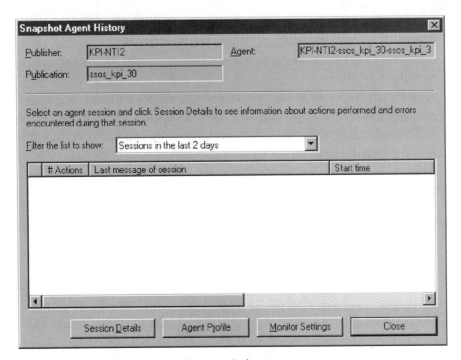

Figure 7.16   Replication agent history window.

monitor the replication and its schedule, select the correct Distributor from the Replication Monitor folder then select the corresponding publication or agent as previously described.

Microsoft Repository

Throughout this chapter, we have repeatedly mentioned the repository and its ability to store objects and track data during the transformation life cycle. When each package or UML object is saved in the repository, a unique version and object is assigned to each. Each version of a single package is tracked and maintained separately. This allows a developer or administrator to determine if recent changes have affected data integrity and then determine if an older version of the package should be placed back into production.

You can use the repository to review a prior version by selecting the version of the package. The package can then be saved as another package or can replace the current version.

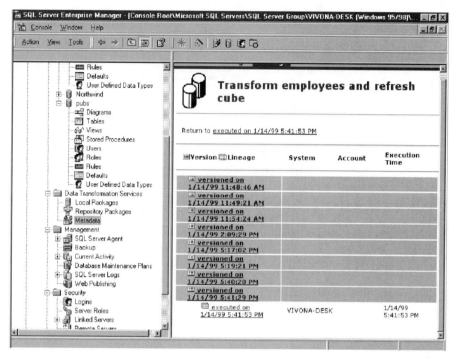

Figure 7.17 DTS package history.

In Figure 7.17, a data lineage record is listed below the last package version. This information allows developers to track data movement from one location to another by assigning a unique package execution identifier to each row processed by the transformation package. This identifier can be used to locate how the data was placed into the table. By viewing a specific row in the database and selecting the Long or Short Lineage identifier, a user can search for the package and package version that inserted or updated the data in the table (see Figure 7.18). Once the identifier is entered, click on the Search link, and the package that inserted the data will be displayed.

Accessing Data with OLE DB

Once the data warehouse and OLAP cubes have been built, the next task to accomplish is enabling data access for end-users. Although many tools are being developed or are available, they all share a common data access method: OLE DB. Deploying and using OLE DB is an integral

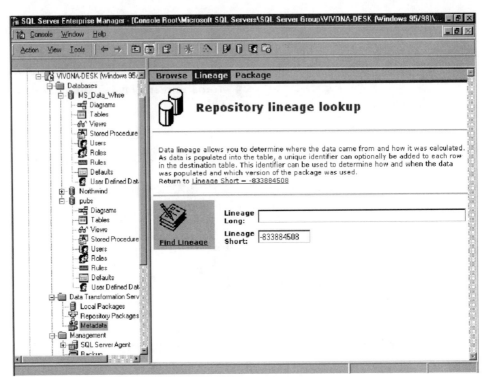

Figure 7.18   DTS package lineage.

part to using the various third-party tools available for data warehousing and reporting. To use OLE DB in an application, the application or related object needs to be inserted into the application workspace. Once the object is inserted, a connection needs to be established. Usually the connection information is stored as a control property or workspace property. When you access these properties, for example, for a Pivot Table, the property toolbox displays immediately, and you use the connection information property to properly establish the connection by selecting the appropriate OLE DB provider ad supplying the necessary connection information, as illustrated in Figure 7.19.

An OLE DB data provider exposes data from an underlying datastore or data warehouse. For example, the OLE DB Provider for ODBC exposes ODBC data sources, and the OLE DB Provider for SQL Server exposes Microsoft SQL Server 7. An OLE DB data consumer is something that consumes the data exposed by a provider. ActiveX Data Objects (ADO) is the definitive, language-neutral OLE DB consumer. However, because OLE DB itself is a COM specification, you could write C++ code to create

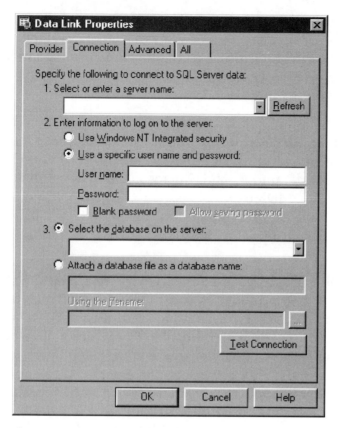

Figure 7.19 Data link properties.

a client that consumes an OLE DB data source. Finally, an OLE DB service provider sits between the data provider and consumer, offering some services not otherwise available. For example, DTS acts as an OLE DB consumer when it retrieves and manipulates data. It then acts as an OLE DB provider when it forwards data to SQL Server 7 for storage.

To use these items, any OLE DB-compliant application makes a call to a common library for OLE DB data source definitions. A dialog box is displayed to the user, who then fills in the appropriate connection information and continues using the application in a normal manner.

As discussed in Section I, OLE DB is not designed to replace ODBC but rather to extend its functionality by providing access to nonrelational data sources. ODBC technology and third-party tools have matured to a point where ODBC is an ideal technology for accessing SQL databases. Therefore, an integral part of OLE DB is a new OLE DB driver manager called OLE DB for ODBC, which enables OLE DB consumers to talk to ODBC providers. Using this provider allows a user or developer to continue using the various technologies deployed across the enterprise, while also taking advantage of the new capabilities available in the Microsoft Data Access Components.

OLE DB for OLAP is an OLE DB provider for OLAP cubes. When the Microsoft Data Access Components are installed or the SQL Server OLAP Services client, an OLE DB Provider called OLE DB for OLAP is installed. This provider understands Microsoft OLAP Services and how to access cubes using MDX expressions. Any OLE DB-enabled applications, such as Excel 2000 Pivot Tables, can access an OLAP cube using this provider.

Data providers and consumers can be written using any programming language capable of using and creating COM objects, including Visual Studio. But building a provider or consumer is not a trivial task because many conditions and error-handling routines must be enabled to create a fully functional provider. Microsoft provides a development toolkit called the Data Access SDK that enables developers to build OLE DB providers. The SDK comes complete with code samples and an OLE DB provider wrapper that enables developers to develop a simple OLE DB provider rapidly. For more information, see the Microsoft Web site at http://www.microsoft.com/data/oledb/.

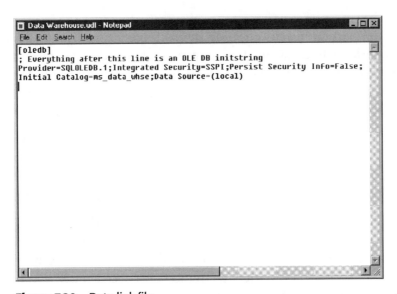

Figure 7.20 Data link file.

When ODBC was first created, one of the powerful features provided was the ability to create a single connection string of information and reuse it multiple times or to be able to deploy it across multiple desktops. OLE DB also provides this ability in a feature named Microsoft Data Links. The data link is a text file with the OLE DB connection information stored in it. These files can be copied to multiple desktops or deployed across a corporate server for use in product installations. They allow a product or user to define a connection once, and when using an OLE DB-enabled product, refer to the data link file (with a .UDL extension) to get the connection information. (See Figure 7.20.)

Desktop Tools for Data Access

Microsoft English Query

English Query gives developers the ability to deploy applications to end users that enable users to query data using plain English. English Query is an OLE automation API that can be interfaced with a Windows client application or, via Active Server Pages, a Web application. Once the entities and definitions of a SQL Server database have been defined, English Query can parse a natural language statement and generate SQL code. The SQL is submitted to SQL Server, which processes it and returns a response.

Developing the initial natural language search is relatively easy and typically requires a fraction of the effort required to build your overall application. The development process is more conceptual than traditional programming, and it can be mastered by nonprogrammers who have some database background (such as a database administrator or Web-content developer who works often with databases).

English Query ships with a set of component object models (COM) which convert a user's English question to a SQL statement. Microsoft provides samples that enable developers to rapidly create web sites and multiple data access methods.

Start the English Query author tool and on the File menu, click "New," and then select "Structure loaded from database." This initializes the database structure from your SQL Server schema, filling the Database tab with tables and fields. If tables are related to each other in the database schema, English Query will attempt to define joins between those tables. The joins usually are retrieved from the foreign keys defined in your database. However, if the necessary foreign keys are not discernible by English Query, you will need to add the joins manually inside the authoring tool.

When the database tables have been loaded into English Query, you are ready to start adding semantic entities. This consists of defining the "things" in your database and what tables or fields they are associated with. To create an entity, click on the Semantics tab, right-click "Entities," and then click "Insert Entity." In the New Entity dialog box, under Semantic Properties, enter a description of the entity, such as author or writer, in the words/phrases dialog box. In the Entity type box, enter a type. In the Table or Fields boxes, under Database Properties, identify which part of the database represents the entity. Major entities usually correspond to entire tables. If it is a major entity, then enter the fields that should be used to display the entity, such as name or address.

To create a relationship between major entities, select the Semantics tab, right-click "Relationships," and then click "Insert Relationship." In the New Relationship dialog box on the Entities tab, click "Add Entity." In the Select Entities list, click all entities that participate in the relationship.

Next, you will create phrasings for the relationship. Phrasing types include verb phrasings ("engineers support products") and subset phrasings ("some products are bestsellers"). Most trait phrasings ("products have cost") and name phrasings ("product names are the names of products") will have been created by Autotrait and Autoname. To create phrasings for a relationship on the Semantics tab, right-click "Relationships," and then click "Insert Relationship." In the "New Relationships" dialog box, on the "Phrasings" tab, click "Add." In the Select Phrasing dialog box, select a phrasing type.

After you have developed and tested the domain model to your satisfaction inside the English Query authoring tool, you are ready to build the application. "Build Application" (on the Tools menu) compiles the English Query domain (.EQD) file. The .EQD file and the English Query engine (the COM object called Mseq.Session) can be deployed as part of any COM-supporting application.

Office 2000

The introduction of Microsoft Office 2000 will bring about a new generation of OLE DB-compliant applications and development tools. All of the applications included with Office 2000 are OLE DB and COM enabled,

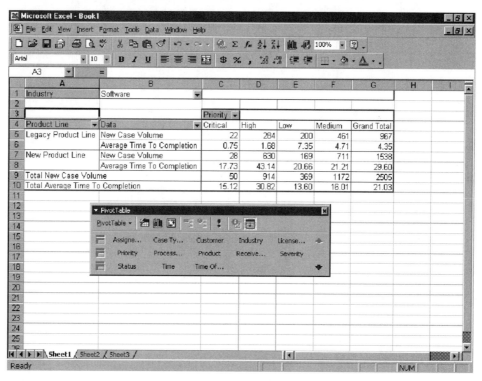

Figure 7.21 Excel 2000 worksheet with Pivot Table service.

which allows end-users or developers to include English Query, Pivot Table Services, and other data warehouse access methods.

In addition to the ability to host these objects in their native applications, each of the tools can publish their respective files as Web pages with built-in interactivity. This function will allow end users to customize the web pages they see but still maintain connectivity to the original data source. Figure 7.21 shows a sample Excel 2000 worksheet with an embedded Pivot Table ActiveX control. These controls can be used in any of the Office 2000 application or published to the Web using the Office Service Extensions and Office Web Components.

In this section, only a few of the many tools available for accessing the data warehouse have been described. Many more options and applications are available on the market today and even more are being developed now. When choosing a tool to deploy across the enterprise, always remember OLE DB-enabled applications allow these tools to access the data warehouse today and tomorrow.

Implementation

Throughout Part Two, we've discussed how to build a data warehouse and related applications using the various tools available. Once the application is developed, tested, and packaged the only item left to do before going live is the installation and implementation of the product. In order to do this a number of tools and software pieces need to be installed on the various computers involved with the product. In this chapter we discuss these pieces and which configurations are supported on the various platforms.

SQL Server and Client Tools

Before any applications are deployed, you need to install the database on the production machine and establish network connectivity. There are different installation options available depending on the operating system and version number currently installed. Table 8.1 lists these various options available for each operating system.

Various tools can also be used dependent upon the database version you install. For example, SQL Server Desktop does not have a SQL Server Performance Monitor, nor can a Windows 95 desktop monitor

Table 8.1   SQL Server Installation Options by Operating System

OPERATING SYSTEM	SQL SERVER CLIENT TOOLS	SQL SERVER DESKTOP	SQL SERVER STANDARD	SQL SERVER ENTERPRISE
Windows 95	✓	✓		
Windows 98	✓	✓		
Windows 2000 Workstation	✓	✓		
Windows 2000 Server	✓	✓	✓	
Windows 2000 Server Enterprise	✓	✓	✓	✓

the performance of SQL Server running on a Windows 2000 or NT Server. There are, however, two things that are common across all platforms:

- A common code base for the SQL Server database and related tools
- A common look and feel for Enterprise Manager with Microsoft Management Console (MMC)

One of the most interesting features of SQL Server 7 is the common code base, which allows you to develop a fix, integrate into the source code, and test it in one process instead of creating a unique fix for each platform. In addition to simpler fix process, the patch process for system administrators is now easier to install. With only one service pack version to download and install, the maintenance of an enterprise deployment of SQL Server allows administrators to focus on the data and objects, not on keeping the systems up and running.

NOTE
In late 1998 Microsoft announced that the next release of Windows NT would be named Windows 2000. In the spirit of this new naming convention, we use the term Windows 2000 Server to refer to both the new operating system, as well as Windows NT 4.x Server.

Installation Options

Even though there is a single code base for SQL Server 7, there are different installation options available which vary depending on the underlying platform that SQL Server 7 is being deployed on. Also, there are different versions of SQL Server 7, with varying capabilities. In this section we will review some of the more important versions of SQL Server 7, and discuss the differences between them.

Enterprise

The Enterprise installation of SQL Server 7 is designed with a lot of processing power and many users in mind. With support for more than 4 processors, 2-node clustering, and 250 or more users, this is the option to choose for single or multi-server, corporate-wide deployments. All of the tools can be installed and deployed, including Replication, Full-Text Search, English Query, and so on.

Standard

SQL Server 7 Standard Edition is designed for workgroups and smaller installations. Optimized for these environments, it provides the following features:

- Reduce the need for trained database administrators
- Make part-time maintenance easier
- Proactively monitor and resolve problems
- Provide Wizards for normal operations to reduce the learning curve

Typical installations for this edition include single-server, 1-4 processors with 250 or less users, which currently make up the bulk of the SQL Server user base. With the same tools and technologies as the Enterprise Edition, Standard makes a formidable database platform.

Desktop

SQL Server Desktop is designed for single user, desktop, or laptop applications that allow users to disconnect from the data center or departmental servers, but still have the power of a relational database with the tools necessary to synchronize and administrate with the main systems. The most notable features in this edition are:

- Reduced dependency on the corporate DBA for standard maintenance and operations

- Remove the levels of complexity for maintaining the server, with self-tuning and scheduled backups
- Transition tools for migrating from Access, FoxPro, and so on to SQL Server

Client Tools

The SQL Server Client tools, including the Microsoft Management Console, with the SQL Server Enterprise Manager snap-in, SQL Server Query Analyzer, and the Microsoft Data Access Components (MDAC), are the required components that allow users access to the data stored in any SQL Server database. These tools allow an administrator or user to manage or access multiple servers using a common, front-end tool. The MMC snap-in allows users access to a database server through either Windows NT Authentication or SQL Server logins, thus allowing a secured environment across the entire corporation.

Installation

To install any edition of SQL Server 7 and its tools, simply insert the appropriate CD-ROM into the CD drive. Once the CD has been inserted, the Autorun utility will begin the SQL Server installation utility. Depending on the CD inserted, a screen similar to Figure 8.1 appears.

Before proceeding to install SQL Server, make sure you read the release notes and install the appropriate SQL Server prerequisites from the CD.

Figure 8.1 SQL Server installation main window.

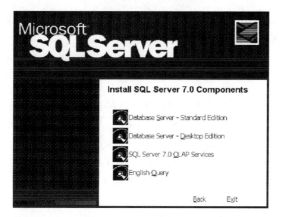

Figure 8.2   SQL Server 7 Component installation menu.

Once you have completed these steps, proceed to install the components, by selecting the component option from the menu.

Depending on whether you use the Standard or Enterprise CD-ROM, the appropriate sub-menu will appear. If the Standard Edition CD is inserted, the first menu item is Database Server - Standard Edition. If the Enterprise Edition CD is running, you see Database Server - Enterprise Edition as shown in Figure 8.2.

Select the appropriate database option, depending on which CD has been inserted. OLAP Services and English Query are covered later in this chapter. The installation application begins by presenting a list of options and components to install. If this computer is used only to access and administer remote servers, select only the Management Tools, Client Connectivity, and Books OnLine options from the menu. This installs the appropriate components to allow users access to the servers and databases. If this computer is used as a database server, select the appropriate Server Components from the list and proceed to install the product.

If you attempt to install SQL Server Standard Edition on a Windows 95, 98, or Windows 2000 Workstation computer the installation program only allows you to install the client access components. Additionally, if the appropriate prerequisites are not installed, such as Internet Explorer,* the installation does not allow you to proceed with the SQL Server

*Internet Explorer is used to display SQL Server on-line documentation.

installation. Before you continue, resolve the installation problem, then proceed to install SQL Server.

English Query

Similar to the SQL Server installation, there are two options for installing Microsoft English Query: Server and Developer. The server installation must be installed on a Windows 2000 or NT Server (Enterprise or Standard) which includes the core requirements and the development tools. The developer installation allows a user to develop English Query applications and models without being on the same machine as the query engine. Based upon which operating system is running, the installation will either install just the developer tools—for Windows 95, 98, and Windows 2000 Workstation—or allow you to choose server and tools for Windows 2000 Server. Once the English Query server has been installed, the sample application can be used to test connectivity between the engine and a Web Server using the supplied sample Active Server Pages.

SQL Server OLAP Services

SQL Server OLAP Services also has two installation modes: Client and Server. The server installation can be performed on Windows 2000 Server (Standard or Enterprise) and Windows 2000 Workstation, which gives a user the option to use OLAP Services on laptops and other types of personal desktop computers. The client pieces of OLAP Services, including MDAC and Pivot Table Services, give applications that use these technologies the ability to access the OLAP cubes using OLE DB for OLAP. OLAP Manager, an MMC snap-in that is installed during a server installation, allows remote administration of servers that run OLAP Services. This feature provides the system administrator with a variety of ways to administer desktop and multi-server platforms.

Data Warehouse

Once the database and related software are installed, the next major task to accomplish is to define the data warehouse. This includes building the tables, indexes, views, and so forth, which make up the components of a complete application. As discussed in Chapter 7, there are many ways to build your data warehouse, including: manually creating objects, creating Transact-SQL scripts, or using Visual Studio applications with ADO or Data Transformation Services (DTS) to copy objects from one database to another. Since application maintenance and version control is our primary concern, we're going to assume Transact-SQL scripts are used to create the data warehouse.

Create a new database as discussed in Chapter 7, which is big enough to contain the objects and their data. Once the database is created, start to create your objects using SQL Query Analyzer to run the Transact-SQL scripts. For each object created, Query Analyzer informs you if it was created successfully, or if an error occurred. If an error occurs (see Figure 8.3), Query Analyzer continues to process the remaining commands in the script. Once it has completed, review the results, determine how to resolve the errors, and run either the entire process over again or begin after the error point.

Once the database and its objects are created, it's time to install the Data Transformation Services (DTS) packages. DTS development is usually performed on a machine separate from the production databases. If this is so there are numerous potential configurations for the packages' production deployment. The most common configuration is

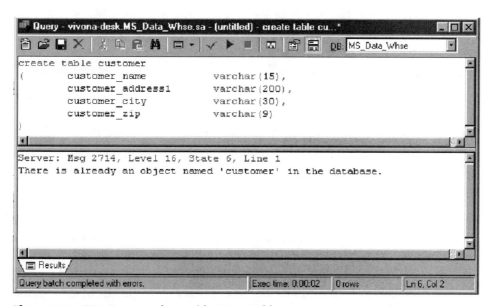

Figure 8.3 SQL Query Analyzer with Create Table error.

to save the packages from the development environment to a set of files, effectively exporting them. Once the packages are exported, an administrator can then move them into the production database for use. Another method for production deployment is to use a centralized production repository server, which acts as the administrator for each of the requests to use a package from the various servers. For more information on these deployment options, see the CD version of the SQL Server Repository books.

End-User Tools and Applications

Installing end-user query, analysis and reporting tools typically require the installation of components on the server and each desktop. Since remote deployment is usually a time-consuming process, starting as early as possible is usually a good idea. Before you begin to deploy applications, it's a good idea to make sure the installers know what they're installing and how to resolve application conflicts and installation problems.

When end-user tools and applications are deployed across your enterprise, the team has a unique opportunity to visit each of the desktops affected by the change. As long as they're there why not have them also perform all those corporate-wide administration tasks that have piled up on the list like virus file updates, security patches, and so on? To help with these tasks, determine what installations to automate and create a single application to deploy or run them from a central server.

Another option for remote deployment of end-user tools is to use the Microsoft Systems Management Console. This allows administrators to remotely install and update corporate computers, thus eliminating the need to visit each desktop in the enterprise. This deployment option saves both time and resources.

Regardless of which deployment method you choose there are a number of pre-requisite components that must be installed before you start to install the tools or applications required to access your data warehouse. For example, to access the data you need OLE DB, which is a component of MDAC. If MDAC is installed on a Windows 95 computer, then DCOM 95 needs to be installed. There is a very definite set of dependencies on each component. Make sure each of the components necessary for installation has its predecessors installed first.

Server-side component installations for the tools and applications usually present a different set of challenges, such as when to install, how much space is necessary, and so on. For end-user tools or n-tier applications various pieces may need to be installed. For example, you need to install MDAC on the Web server to use OLE DB with Web-based applications. Similar to a desktop deployment plan, each of the servers affected needs to have an installation plan that lists the software to be installed and the sequence to install it.

Office 2000 and Office 2000 Web Components

In the previous chapters we've discussed user access to data through Office 2000 and Web sites using pages developed with the various Office 2000 applications. A number of items need to be considered when deploying these applications and Web sites, such as Collaboration, the Office Web components, network firewalls, and so on. For example, if you install the Office 2000 Server Extensions your users can make comments on Web pages and data and have these comments stored in a database for review and comment by other users. These extensions allow users to interact with Office documents and each other in a Web environment. Since users that don't have Office 2000 installed on their computer may still need to view, through the Web, the documents and workbooks created using Office 2000, Microsoft provides a set of Web components that can be installed on a user's desktop to use these documents. These components are called the Office 2000 Web Components, and they provide the necessary ActiveX objects that allow users to access and interact with the data warehouse.

TIP

Before you install the Office 2000 Extension and Web Components, make sure the Windows 2000 Server Option Pack has been installed. The applications and updates contained in the Windows 2000 Server Option Pack are critical to the operation of Office 2000 on your Windows 2000 or NT server.

Data Conversion

Data-conversion planning and cut over is one of the most critical parts of an application going into production. Without the correct data, users can't analyze the information they need, which makes the system useless before it even starts. Make sure a set of representatives from the user community is involved each step of the way when designing and planning the data conversion process. This group can assist with the mapping process from one system to another, as well as testing the converted data at strategic points in time.

Testing

At key moments of the data-conversion development and design process a system test should be performed to ensure the conversion process is developed correctly. For example, the destination data source is checked for consistency and the number of converted records. Once each stage of the conversion is tested, a complete data conversion test should be run prior to scheduling final data cut over. DTS can be utilized to help track versions of the conversion routines. In addition, with DTS a data lineage tag (as discussed in Chapter 6) can be attached to each row in the database. This tag is searchable using the Microsoft Repository to help debug data conversion problems or to determine when data is actually populated into certain tables.

TIP

When testing converted data, perform a set of daily tasks against the data as well as period-end processes such as the closing of accounts at the end of a month or quarter. Ensure that all of the functions normally needed for business operations are available and verifiable such as month-end reports, quarterly statements, daily account reconciliation, and so on.

Cut Over

As the date for final applications go-live approaches, the project teams usually gets anxious about whether the final pieces of code are patched, the data conversion has performed properly, and the user training is delivered. When the data conversion begins, make sure no additional changes are made to the source system, in order to ensure data accuracy and correctness. Before you actually start, take a snapshot of the source system, both as a backup of the database and as a set of reports. Once the data conversion is completed, the same set of reports should be run against the final data to ensure the inputs to the conversion match the output to the conversion.

Each step of the conversion should be executed, the intermediate results checked for consistency, and the log files reviewed to ensure no errors occurred during processing. Once these items have been checked for each step, proceed with the next step in the conversion. After all of the data has been converted, review again all of the log files to make sure that any of the errors or messages are clearly explained and to ensure that no critical data has been lost or converted improperly. This requires a check of the number of records, as well as a check of the columns to verify that the data is correct.

Whether you are converting an existing data warehouse or creating one for the first time, each of these steps should be run with the final goal always in mind—create a repository for corporate data that is complete, consistent, and correct. Since the methods to convert the data to initially build the warehouse are usually the same processes for updating the warehouse, this also represents a good opportunity to test the various update processes at the same time.

During the conversion, we suggest that you keep both systems running to ensure that the data in one system is the same as in the new system. Before completing the conversion, get the users involved in testing the data, let them look at it, use it (but not change it), and generally review how the data was moved from the source to the destination. Once the users have accepted the data, and the conversion team has raised no issues, you can celebrate a successful conversion and data cut over.

After Go-Live

Usually the first work day after conversion, phone calls start to flow into the support desk by users asking where data is or how it's been converted from one system to another. Using the repository and DTS packages, the support or conversion team can quickly locate how data was converted and what its original source was. Additionally, the graphical display can be used to show general data flow and conversion to any end-user with access to the SQL Server database.

By using the various tools and documentation options available to the development and conversion teams, a comprehensive, error-free conversion can be performed. In addition any user issues with the data can readily be explained in a straightforward fashion with a highly traceable method for finding the origins of data from the conversion.

TIP

By keeping users involved in the conversion process, you can ensure that the entire community is represented on the design and conversion team. This helps users feel more connected with the team and less resentful for converting "their" data.

Training

Before any application is moved from development into production, a comprehensive training program needs to be developed to deliver key knowledge to users, administrators, and support staff. Each of these programs must be created with a specific set of tasks in mind. Don't combine multiple training topics into a single book or training curriculum. For example, applications administration and data maintenance should not be combined into a single training course. By focusing training topics on functional areas, the training can be implemented as discrete modules and delivered on an as-needed basis to the appropriate personnel.

Training is an evolving activity. There are always new people to train, people that require reference materials for their tasks, and new features added to the system. Make sure the documentation and training materials are synchronized with any new enhancements or process changes made to the system. It's also important to make available the latest version of the training materials to those who need them. You can do this by placing the documents on the network or intranet.

NOTE

One of the most common formats for publishing information in a platform-independent fashion is to use the Adobe Acrobat format. These files can be created from a variety of sources including Microsoft Word and Excel by using a set of tools. For users to view these documents, the free Adobe Acrobat reader must be installed on their computer. For more information on Adobe Acrobat, see the Adobe Web site at: http://www.adobe.com.

Application Operations and Support

Building operational and support training materials is a difficult task, at best. How can you tell people the solutions to problems that haven't even occurred yet? When creating operational materials, it's best to start with the basics of how the system operates from a business sense, then move into the technical details of how it actually accomplishes these tasks. For example, explain the month-end closing process along with, the type of output generated. Once the basic business flow is understood, a detailed look at how the tables and database accomplish these tasks can be reviewed by applying each process to a particular table or set of tables.

You can then establish and test processes and procedures that should be followed in a variety of common operational scenarios. Examples of routine activities include backing up the database; adding, modifying, or deleting user accounts; or performing routine database hygiene tasks such as running the integrity checker, reorganizing files to reduce fragmentation, or removing orphaned temp files. The next stage is to put together processes and procedures for non-routine, but unavoidable activities. These can include checking the database after it recovers from a system crash, restoring a backup to a failed drive, or reconfiguring the network after a network outage.

In order for administrators and support personnel to resolve data issues, they need to have access to up-to-date data process flow diagrams that show how the data moves from its source system into the data warehouse. For example, because understanding data lineage is useful in resolving some data issues, training on the various SQL Server Enterprise Manager management tools becomes important.

As administrators and support teams gain experience answering questions and resolving problems about the data warehouse, they will start to see a pattern for the most common questions. Once this pattern becomes apparent, develop a set of frequently-asked questions and publish it to the users on a regular basis. As people start to use this document, it can greatly reduce the number of calls to the support and administration teams.

Operations Execution and Recovery

Identify different people on the operations team for each process and system whose responsibility is to ensure that everything runs correctly. Supply the operations team with processing diagrams and notification rules so they can help resolve problems with minimal assistance from the administration team.

If the system uses DTS packages, make sure that success and failure messages are routed to the appropriate people and that they actually receive them. Give the operations team the ability to view the database and the running processes to help them verify that everything works properly. *Job Flow Diagrams* are the most common method for documenting DTS operations. They clearly show the recovery step instructions. Typically an online reference of error messages for job steps and recovery techniques is created to allow for an immediate response to any problems with process execution.

WARNING

Don't place your entire process and procedures documentation solely online. If a system crashes, you've lost your recovery procedures as well. Also, make sure that you don't secure the documentation in a locked office. It should be readily accessible to the people who need it at all times.

Once processes recovery has been started, the operations team should keep a log of which steps failed and how the recovery was performed. Administration and Support should review this log on a daily basis to determine when problems occur and how to improve the software to prevent them in the future. Also, these logs are useful in case recovery was performed incorrectly, because the administration team can use this information to "back-out" the changes made to the data and re-run the correct processes.

Just as with the other documentation and training materials, the operations manuals and job recovery processes and procedures should be reviewed and updated whenever changes are made to the system. This allows correct and current processing to continue and helps avoid off-hour phone calls.

Data Stewardship

To identify where data belongs and how it's maintained is usually a daunting task. Before go-live and deployment each piece of information fed into the data warehouse should have a clearly identified source and owner. Once this identification is accomplished a functional table should be established to document this information.

The people responsible for data maintenance should be trained on how to edit, add, delete, and otherwise modify the data in the source systems. They should also understand how the data entered affects both the data warehouse and reports that they and others use to make business decisions. When training data maintenance personnel it is always a good idea to research how they previously performed these tasks, and how the new systems alter their routines. Make sure to explain how the transformation processes from old system to new system, or transaction system to data warehouse, are used to accomplish specific goals. Also, when training data maintenance personnel, it is a wise to train more than one person on the same set of tasks, thereby creating a backup for the primary person.

End-User Access

End users need to access the data once the system is put into production. By providing short tutorials on how to retrieve data from the data warehouse using common tools and tasks, a large portion of end users can start to access the data immediately. When creating short tutorials, make sure the data in the data warehouse matches the data that resides in the tutorial. If not, the training rapidly becomes ineffective and eventually increases the number of calls logged into the support and administration teams.

End users typically want two types of information about a data warehouse: how do I access it and where is the data stored? When writing the documentation, make sure to include a simplified data warehouse map that describes each of the tables or relationships and how to retrieve the most typical types of information from the tables. Also consider creating a set of templates which provide a starting block for users. These templates can have basic connectivity already established with key fields represented. Providing these types of materials to users shows the value of the data warehouse almost immediately.

Just like every other piece of documentation and training material we've discussed, it's important to keep this information up to date to reduce the number of issues raised about the data and to keep your users happy.

Documentation

Similar to training materials, overall system documentation is an important part of any project. As part of a data warehouse project, the documentation should encompass all of the system's areas that affect data added to the warehouse and how data leaves the warehouse. Document each piece of the system consistently in both style and format. Try not to repeat sections of documentation. Instead refer users from one manual to another. This helps the documentation's maintenance by allowing changes to occur in one place instead of many.

As suggested with the training materials, an effective way to deliver documentation is to place it on the network or intranet depending on your infrastructure capabilities. Make sure everyone who needs access to the material has it, and that only the people that need to make changes actually do.

Using the Database Diagrammer

One of the first things to accomplish when building a database or data warehouse is to examine the various relationships between the data that resides in the database. To document these relations use the Database Diagrammer as discussed in Chapter 7. This tool allows an online view of how tables relate to each other and the keys that link them. By creating multiple diagrams, a system can be documented by functional area, but still maintain its overall relational focus. One of the key features of the Diagrammer is the ability to print the diagrams for use in hard copy documentation, or to use tools, such as Adobe Acrobat, to generate the diagrams in electronic format.

TIP Acrobat can be configured like a printer, similar to desktop faxing software. Using this feature, the print function in the Database Diagrammer allows you to create in-line diagrams for use in electronic documentation.

DTS Package Documentation

DTS packages are represented through graphical maps displayed on-screen. One of the features in the DTS Package Designer is the ability to insert text labels to identify data flows and key points in the package. By using these text labels, a cross-reference of documentation sections can be created to help with the project. By creating documents that describe both the package flow and how tasks are accomplished you allow for a comprehensive resource for the system. Typical documentation points for DTS packages in a data warehouse include:

- Source object definitions such as machine, database, user ID, etc.
- Each transformation that is performed and how it manipulates the data
- Destination for each data step, including interim data tables or in-memory storage areas
- Final data destinations and the steps needed to actually achieve success
- Job error event notifications, where in the process they can occur, and who is notified
- Job success event notifications, and who is notified
- External dependencies for each DTS package or step, such as files created, or backup completion, and so on.
- Any files created as output of the package such as input for other external systems
- When the DTS package executes like where it is time-based, event-based, and so on.

By documenting these items, the system can be easily and readily reviewed for modification impact and external process definitions that can change how packages are executed on the server. This documentation also serves as the detail behind the Job Flow Diagrams discussed in the next section.

Similar to the database diagrams and other documentation discussed in this chapter, various formats should be used to maintain accuracy. Since DTS packages are maintained on the server, teams should always check the database for the latest version of the package, rather than rely on the printed documentation, although every effort should be made to ensure all of the documents are maintained.

Job Flow Diagrams

Job Flow Diagrams maintain a set of tasks, the dependencies on each other, and execution timing. By combining these diagrams with the DTS package documentation, operations and administration can see how changes to a DTS package or other task can affect a set of data streams from source to destination. Figure 8.4 shows a simple example of a Job Flow Diagram.

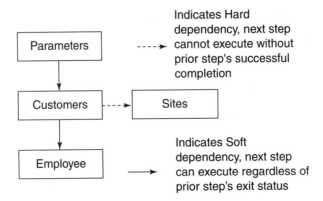

Figure 8.4 Job flow diagram.

Each of the boxes shown in Figure 8.4 represent a different DTS package which is executed. By showing the job dependencies and the sequence of execution errors and execution, problems can rapidly be tracked to determine the root cause of the problem. Since these diagrams do not contain the details of the individual tasks in a package or job, they are usually easier to maintain and publish to the appropriate teams.

Operations Manual

As each of the project pieces are completed, places where data needs to be maintained or where logs need to be checked start to be identified. Maintenance tasks and other upkeep of the system are the responsibility of the operations team. This team ensures that the system runs, provides the correct information to the users, and performs to agreed-upon levels. By creating this manual as an ongoing part of the project, these tasks can easily be documented and identified by the developers responsible for creating the system.

The key items to document when creating system administration manuals are:

- Performance tuning
- Data correction processes and procedures
- Audit requirements for system changes
- Applications-development, version-control guidelines
- Design issues—why were certain features or options removed from the design of the data warehouse

- Troubleshooting system usage

- Development issues raised during coding—items which seem feasible but were not implemented for specific reasons, such as performance issues, data integrity, etc.

- How to use the tools available in SQL Server Enterprise Manager and any other third-party tools as necessary

Along with all of these items, the operations team uses and modifies some of the other documentation. They should always understand how one change can impact the users or any other part of the data warehouse, and how to minimize the impact. By arming this team with valuable information, end users can use the information stored in the data warehouse without needing to continuously adapt to unexpected results from system changes.

User Guides

User Guides are one of the most important pieces to any system-documentation project. By keeping the users in touch with how the system should, and can be used, along with changes made, they can focus on using the data instead of constantly changing the methods by which they retrieve the data. These guides are generally used to provide training for end users either through online delivery or classic classroom-style training. Involving a team of end users in the guides and training materials process allows the deployment team to ensure the training they develop and use actually matches the users' expectations. Regular, training-development updates should be made to the end-user community to ensure that the materials always match the software. Typical end-user guides provide the following items:

- System overview, what it's used for and how it got there

- Task flow diagrams, graphical maps of how to accomplish tasks in the system

- Detailed transaction review, each function in the system has a specific task and explains how it works

- System access, how do users connect to the data warehouse

- How to create reports

- Third-party tool usage, this is a good place to discuss OLE DB-compliant applications

- Data maintenance responsibilities, a list of who provides what information to the warehouse
- Support contact information

It's a good idea in the user community to create a power user team that is deployed across the organization, each focusing on a specific set of functions. These people can act as a first-line support organization that allows users to ask questions of peers, instead of calling the support team all of the time. They can also help solicit input about new features to add to the system or ways to make it easier to access certain functions from people that use the system every day. Additionally, they can provide input for a list of frequently-asked questions, which can be published to the end users for assistance with commonly-used features.

Summary

In this chapter, we discussed how to deploy applications on an enterprise scale, including the server and desktop installation of required components. Training and documentation provide valuable links for the various teams that use and administrate the data warehouse and applications. They also ensure that the system is used in for the purpose of its original design.

Now that the data warehouse has been designed, developed, and deployed the next major task is to manage the ongoing maintenance of the data and its systems.

CHAPTER 9

Operations and Management

N ow that we have developed, implemented and deployed the application, we turn our attention to the activities required to manage the system once it is in production. Operations and management is primarily concerned with maintaining the integrity of the system. In this chapter we will discuss the various tasks that need to be implemented in order to keep the system running smoothly.

Protecting Data Integrity

Data integrity refers to the concept that the data must be logically consistent and physically intact. One of the primary tasks of the system is to provide tools, processes and procedures that will ensure the data is logically and physically intact. Protecting the data's integrity in the SQL Server database is the primary responsibility of the database administrator (DBA) and the system administrator. The DBA is ordinarily responsible for managing the database, while the system administrator's functions are focused on the operating system, applications, and system hardware. In many companies the same person fulfills both of these roles while in larger organizations the roles are delegated to separate individuals. Larger organizations also tend to have a separate network administrator who is responsible for the performance, reliability, and availability of the network and its infrastructure.

If the IT organizational structure assigns these functions to separate units or individuals, then the CIO, or senior IT manager responsible for the decision support application, must establish policies and procedures for coordination and communication to ensure that all operational and management activities are harmonized. Otherwise, the organization may find that the activities of one manager, such as a network upgrade, may cause a problem like a network outage that brings down the database and affects the DBA.

The operations and management team needs to focus on several areas to ensure that the system meets the needs of the organization, once it has been placed into production. These areas include:

- Maintaining data integrity
- Maintaining data security
- Maintaining system performance at acceptable levels
- Managing upgrades and system changes while minimizing disruptions

Data Integrity

Data integrity is vital to the success of the system. If the users feel that the data is unreliable, they will reject the decision support system. Data integrity must be managed as part of the data transformation and loading process, as well as within the database itself. Data integrity ensures that the data is complete, correct, and valid.

When we talk about *complete* data, we mean that all of the required application data is present for analysis. Incomplete data cause business managers to make poor decisions. An address field in a customer record, for example, should have a complete address, including street and building number, apartment or unit number, if applicable, city, state, postal code, and country. The name of the individual in the record should also be formatted appropriately.

Correct means the data is free of errors. A correct address is not only complete, but also contains data, such as a street address or name, that is free of misspelling and other errors.

Valid means the data reflects a real-world entity. Correctness and validity are similar, related concepts, but where correctness refers to the *content* of the data, validity refers to the *authenticity* of the data. In our address example, the address is *complete* if all of the address data is present, it's *correct* if it's spelled and formatted properly, and it's *valid* if that address actually exists.

These three data integrity concepts are under the control of the application. While they are important and must be considered during the application design, they are outside the scope of this chapter, which deals with how to maintain the internal logical and physical consistency of the data once the application has been deployed, among other issues.

Maintaining Database Consistency

Since its inception, SQL Server has had a utility called DBCC (database consistency checker), which is a tool that can be used by the operations staff to verify the internal consistency of the database. With the release of SQL Server 7 the need for DBCC has been significantly reduced, due to some architectural changes that have been made to the internal data structures managed by the database. As a result of these changes, Microsoft no longer recommends that the DBA run DBCC on a regular basis. Instead, the administrator can use DBCC only when there is a question about the internal consistency of the SQL Server 7 data structures.

TIP

Running DBCC against a large database will invariably result in spooling data pages to the `tempdb` database, especially if DBCC runs while users actively use the database. As a result, Microsoft recommends that you keep the `tempdb` table on a separate disk drive from the production database tables. This helps to reduce the time required to complete the DBCC run.

Constraints and Triggers

SQL Server 7, like most commercial relational databases, provides a number of features to help ensure the logical integrity of the data, including constraints and triggers.

A *constraint* is used to define a rule that specifies the values that are allowed within a column. SQL Server 7 supports five constraint categories, as described in Table 9.1.

Table 9.1 SQL Server Constraint Types

CONSTRAINT TYPE	DESCRIPTION
NOT NULL	It requires that the column contain a value.
CHECK	A Boolean test is applied, if the expression is FALSE, the data is rejected. A CHECK constraint can only validate data against an expression or another column within the same table.
UNIQUE	No two rows in the table can contain the same value for the column.
PRIMARY KEY	Each row in the table is guaranteed to have a unique primary key.
FOREIGN KEY	A row cannot be inserted with a FOREIGN KEY value if there is no corresponding primary key in another target table.

Where a constraint is used to enforce a database rule, a *trigger* is a special form of stored procedure that can be used to enforce a business rule. A trigger can be fired upon an INSERT, DELETE, or UPDATE operation, and more than one trigger can be defined for a table. A constraint can only reject a data value that fails the constraint test, but a trigger can execute any SQL command, including EXEC, which enables SQL Server 7 to run an external program. For example, a trigger can be used to perform some action, such as sending an email message, which would not ordinarily be part of the SQL command set.

A constraint is a verb that is used as part of either the CREATE TABLE or the ALTER TABLE command, whereas a trigger is created using the CREATE TRIGGER command.

Backup

The single most important step the system administrator can take to ensure the ongoing integrity and availability of the database is to define and implement a reliable backup strategy. Even if the database is stored on a RAID drive, a responsible system will always institute a backup procedure. This protects the organization from a hardware or software failure that can corrupt the database or an environmental event, such as a computer room fire or power outage, that can damage the system.

Defining a Backup Strategy

SQL Server 7 has added a number of features to improve the system administrator's ability to perform backups with a minimum of impact on users. Backup time is faster than with previous versions, and backups can be performed while the database is up and running. This last feature is critical for organizations with stringent 24×7 availability requirements.

There are three primary backup options available with SQL Server 7:

1. Full backup
2. Incremental backup
3. Transaction log backup

When you plan your backup strategy you should consider a number of failure scenarios, and build the backup procedures that will enable you to recover from any one of them. For example, what will you do if a user or application error results in the loss of a large volume of data? In this instance a transaction log backup may be sufficient. Similarly, no separate backup or recover procedure should be required if the database suffers from a system crash, as long as the file system remains intact. When the system is rebooted SQL Server 7 will automatically

---

Checkpoints

One way SQL Server 7 attempts to reduce the amount of time required to recover from a failure is *checkpoints*. The SQL Server 7 checkpoint process periodically and automatically forces all "dirty" pages (pages that have been modified but not written to the database) to disk. If SQL Server didn't periodically checkpoint the database there could conceivably be a very large transaction log file to apply to the database. A checkpoint record with a log sequence number is written to the log file, and SQL Server 7 can then initiate a recovery from the most recent checkpoint, rather than start at the beginning of the log file.

Note that a checkpoint does not mean it's OK to delete the transaction log file. You cannot afford to delete or reset the transaction log file until after the next backup. For example, if the disk that holds the transaction log file fills up, you should backup the database, then reset the log file, otherwise you risk losing data in the event of a failure.

recover the database. First, SQL Server will roll back any uncommitted transactions. Second, it will locate the last logical checkpoint (called the Minimum Recovery Log Sequence Number) in the transaction log file and apply all committed transactions from that point forward to the end of the transaction log. This restores the database to its state at the point of the failure, with the exception that uncommitted transactions will be discarded and must be reentered.

On the other hand, if a hard disk crashes then, at the very least, the file-group residing on the disk will need to be recovered. This assumes the hard disk is not mirrored. Any transactions in that filegroup that have occurred since the last backup will then need to be reapplied. Your backup strategy should also include a schedule for rotating and storing backups to an off-site location, along with a procedure for recycling older backup sets as they become obsolete and are no longer required. In certain instances, such as a need to meet regulatory, audit, or other legal requirements, older backup sets may need to be stored in a permanent archive. Older backup sets can also be helpful if you discover that a current backup set is physically or logically corrupted and you need to restore from further back in time. For example, a user or program error may delete critical records, and the error may not be detected until after the next system backup has occurred.

Full Backup

A *full backup* makes a physical copy of all the pages in a database. It includes system tables and user tables, as well as the transaction log files. A SQL Server full backup only copies pages that contain data; it does not copy empty pages within the database files. However, a restore operation recreates the database as it was at the point of the backup including allocated, but unused, pages.

When you plan a full backup, you need to consider the type and number of backup media to use, whether you are going to perform the backup with the database up and running or shutdown, and how much data needs to be backed up. You should also consider the frequency of performing full backups. Many sites run a full backup once a week, while others consider once a month to be sufficient. The main consideration is recovery time. If the database is completely lost, then the most recent full backup will need to be restored, followed by all the incremental backups, followed by all the transaction logs used since the most recent incremental backup. If the database is very large, or there are a large number of tapes that make up the full recovery set—full backup, one or more incremental backups, one or more transaction logs, then more frequently full backups are advisable.

WARNING

If you lose the transaction log files as a result of a hard drive crash you won't be able to recover the transactions that have occurred since the most recent backup. For this reason, transaction log files should be kept on a mirrored disk, which protects them from a hard drive failure.

Incremental Backup

An *incremental backup* or differential backup copies the database pages that have been modified since the most recent full backup. The advantage of an incremental backup is that it finishes faster and consumes fewer resources than a full backup. Many companies create multiple incremental backup sets between full backups. Recovery using an incremental backup set, however, does not restore the database to the point of failure, only to the point of the most recent incremental backup.

Transaction Log Backup

A *transaction log backup* copies the transaction log files. The difference between the incremental backup and a transaction log backup is that the former makes physical copies of the changed pages in the database, while the latter copies the logical operations like SQL statements in the log that have been executed.

If a system has stringent data availability requirements and cannot tolerate loss of data, then a combination of full, incremental, and transaction log backups is advised. A reasonable schedule, depending on the size of the database and the backup media available for the operations is shown in Table 9.2.

Table 9.2 Typical Backup Schedule

OPERATION	FREQUENCY
Full Backup	Weekly
Incremental backup	Daily
Transaction log backup	Hourly

If the database is not very large, or if there are sufficient backup devices available, then the full backups can be done daily, with the incremental backups done once per shift.

TIP

SQL Server 7 enables you to append backup files to a tape. This is useful when you create either incremental or transaction log backups, since you can run a recovery process without having to mount and dismount a tape for each backup file.

Offsite Storage

Backup tapes, especially recent ones, should always be stored in a secure location. This can be a commercial off-site facility, an off-site office of the same organization, or an on-site vault. If you store your backup tapes in the same building as the database system and a local disaster—fire, flood, tornado, or earthquake—occurs which can destroy both the computer systems and the backup tapes, then there is virtually no chance you can recover the data. Therefore, if you elect to store the backup data sets on-site, be sure that the room or vault you use is engineered to withstand a major disaster.

Implementing a Backup Strategy

Your backup strategy needs to consider the application availability requirements for the system you are backing up, and the number of times the database is updated.

If the availability requirements are stringent, then a combination of full, incremental, and transaction log backups can be done frequently. If availability requirements are less restrictive (the database is updated infrequently, or is read-only), then a full backup at infrequent intervals, with few or no incremental backups may suffice. A key element of the backup strategy is the recovery process. If you have many backup sets to restore, the recovery process will take longer. On the other hand, if you have daily full backups and hourly transaction log backups, then the process should complete faster. All this depends on the volume of data to recover and the number of tapes that must be managed.

If you use SQL Server 7 as a data warehouse, then you should consider performing a full backup every time the data warehouse is refreshed. Another alternative is to do a full backup once a month, and then do an incremental backup with each refresh cycle. To decide which backup would work for you consider how much data is updated, and how long you want a recovery cycle to take.

You also need to consider a number of likely failure scenarios and define a backup strategy for each of them. Some scenarios to consider include:

- Database or application errors that corrupt the database
- Disk drive failure
- Computer failure
- Network failure

Some failure scenarios, such as an operating system crash, can be resolved by rebooting the computer and allowing SQL Server to perform its own internal recovery process. When SQL Server 7 restarts it detects the fact that the database was not shutdown normally, and removes any incomplete transactions from the database. It then uses the transaction logs to reapply the committed transactions and bring the database back to a physical and logical state of consistency. Note that this process does not guarantee zero loss of data, since the data in uncommitted transactions is discarded. The only way to guarantee no loss of data is to deploy a truly, fault-tolerant system. However, even the best fault-tolerant box cannot protect against disasters that destroy the computer room.

Backup Tools

Microsoft provides a variety of tools to perform SQL Server 7 backups. You can use the BACKUP DATABASE command of Transact-SQL. You can write your own program that uses SQL-DOM. SQL-DOM is a collection of COM objects, implemented as a DLL, that encapsulate SQL Server 7 functions. SQL-DOM utilities must be written using C or C++. You can also schedule or run backup jobs automatically using Microsoft Management Console.

Using MMC you can define a backup schedule, or you can interactively backup the database. To perform a full backup, select the database from the SQL Server 7 Enterprise Manager window, right-click the database, point to "All tasks…" and click "Backup database." In the dialog box you will have the option to schedule the backup to occur at a later time.

The MMC backup application also gives you the option of backing up a filegroup. Filegroup backups can be useful if you need to restore just the data on a single disk. SQL Server 7 can also run several backup streams in parallel, with each filegroup backed up to a separate device.

Online Backup

Microsoft SQL Server 7 supports the ability to perform backups while users are online, actively using the database. This enables the system administrator to provide 24x7 availability during backups. Note that the database is *not* available during recovery operations. The backup process tracks all of the transactions that are applied while the backup is running. Once the database backup is complete, the transactions are backed up, providing a complete backup of the state of the database at the time the backup completed. There are a few restrictions that must be noted while online backup is running. The database files cannot be allowed to shrink, nor can files be added or deleted. You are also not allowed to create indexes or perform non-logged operations.

Recovery

The recovery process is intended to restore the database to a known state. There are three sets of files involved in the recovery process: the most recent full backup, all of the intervening incremental backup files, and all of the transaction log backup files created since the most recent incremental backup. These files can be used in a variety of recovery scenarios.

Recovery Scenarios

A CPU failure does not ordinarily require initiating a recovery process using backup files. As noted earlier, SQL Server 7 will attempt to automatically restore the database integrity using the existing transaction log files.

Safety Precautions

SQL Server makes some effort to minimize the potential for recovery errors. An interrupted recovery process can be restarted where it left off. This option is only available with removable media. The system does not allow the operator to recover a backup set if the target database exists and has a different name from the database in the backup set.

Recovery from hard disk failure is the most common recovery scenario. If you can't afford a RAID drive, which can protect against hard drive failure, then you must recover using a backup set, once the failed drive has been replaced.

When you recover a full backup set, SQL Server creates the database files and fills in the used pages. Unused pages are allocated, but are left empty. Once the full backup is complete, the incremental backup and transaction log backup files are applied in chronological order.

A special type of backup is a *filegroup backup*. If you manage a large database that spans many disk drives, then using a filegroup backup can be an effective way for performing many backups in parallel, since each filegroup can be backed up to a separate device.

NOTE

When you backup a filegroup, you must also do a transaction log backup. This is because a transaction may span multiple tables, and the filegroup may only have one of the tables involved in the transaction. When you restore a filegroup you need the transaction log backup to re-apply the transactions; otherwise, you may wind up with a logically inconsistent database.

The third major backup scenario involves recovery from a user or application error. In this scenario you may need to recover backups from farther back in time, since the error may not be noticed until considerable time has passed since it was first entered. This is one reason to save backup sets in an archive.

Restore Database

The restore process is similar to the backup process. You can use Transact-SQL to restore the database, using the RESTORE DATABASE command.

You can use the SQL Server Enterprise Manger by right-clicking the database, pointing to "All Tasks" and selecting "Restore Database..." The dialog box will give you a variety of options, including selecting the backup set(s), and deciding whether to apply transaction log files, or not.

The third alternative is to write your own customized backup program in C or C++ that calls the SQLRestore method in SQL-DMO.

Using a Hot Standby

Some site managers may consider making a copy of the database on a hot standby machine, rather than making a backup. When a failure occurs they can quickly switch users to the hot standby database rather than go through a complete backup and recovery cycle. The copy can be updated by applying transaction log backups, and the users can then access the database. However, this is not a good idea because once the copy is mounted and modified, you have lost your only backup of the database! If the hot standby system fails you have no backup to recover. If you elect to use this approach to availability, you should ensure you backup the hot copy before users are allowed to access it in the event you need to failover from a primary database.

Data Security

The backup and recovery process is designed to make sure that the data is available to the users when they need it. A security scheme is primarily concerned with two issues: authentication and authorization. Authentication verifies that the user is who he or she claims to be. Authorization has to do with the types of access the authenticated user has to the database. The goal of a security process is to make sure that only authorized users can access the data. There are multiple levels of security access and multiple types of access. Access levels (in descending order) are illustrated in Figure 9.1.

A user accesses the server, which authenticates the user with the password that the user supplies. The user is then granted access to SQL Server, which manages the users' privileges to perform certain tasks or access certain parts of the system.

SQL Server privileges include the ability to create databases, tables, or columns. Privileged users can also backup and recover database files, create and modify SQL Server accounts, and access system tables.

Two related and complementary security levels can be implemented for a SQL Server production environment: operating system security and SQL Server security.

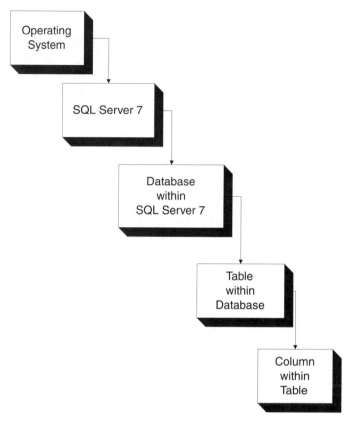

Figure 9.1 SQL Server security hierarchy.

Operating System Security

Windows 2000 Server has a robust security scheme that is compliant with the C-2 standard published by the U.S. Dept. of Defense. In many instances there are advantages to using Windows 2000 Server security to authenticate users. For example Windows 2000 Server enforces minimum password lengths, encrypts passwords, can force passwords to expire after a certain time, and can lock out users who have made multiple attempts to access the system using an invalid password.

Accounts and Privileges

The system administrator must create a Windows 2000 Server account in order for the user to access the computer system. This Windows 2000

Server account can then be mapped to a SQL Server 7 account. The user account can also be made part of a group within the Windows 2000 Server environment. This simplifies the process of managing multiple accounts, since users who fall into a common category such as marketing, production, or accounting can be granted similar privileges.

SQL Server Security

SQL Server 7 provides its own security scheme, in conjunction with Windows 2000 Server, for two reasons. First, to ensure backwards compatibility with applications written for previous versions of SQL Server. The other is to enable security for users who access the SQL Server 7 database from a non-secure source, such as a Windows 95/98 client or an Internet connection.

Database Privileges

A user who has logged on to SQL Server will also need a valid user account for each database that the user plans to access. This scheme enables the DBA to set up a single server with multiple databases that can be managed separately. For example, a single server may have databases for personnel, accounting, sales and marketing, customer self-service, and manufacturing. Each database requires its own security environment to ensure that external customers, for example, can't access sensitive accounting or payroll data.

The user account within the database ensures that the user has the appropriate privileges to access various objects within the database, such as tables, views, and stored procedures. Figure 9.2 shows the multilevel security architecture of SQL Server 7.

Users who have been granted access to a table have privileges that enable or prohibit them from modifying the table. Modification privileges for table include—in descending order of severity—read/write/delete, read/write, and read-only.

To grant a user access to a SQL Server database, you must create a Windows 2000 Server user account. You can do this from the Enterprise Manager by selecting a server, expanding "Security", right-clicking "Logins" and selecting "New Login." You can then select "Windows NT Authentication", enter the user name including an optional domain name, and optionally select the default database the user will connect to.

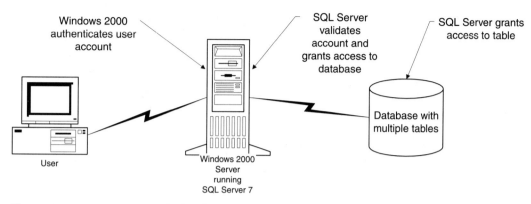

Figure 9.2 SQL Server security levels.

Database Roles

If the system administrator hasn't created a Windows 2000 Server group, and the application that you install on SQL Server doesn't require access to more than one database, you can create a database role. Users who are members of a database role are limited to access a single, identified database.

A Microsoft Wizard is available to help with the process of defining a login. You can run the Create Login wizard from the Enterprise Manager window by selecting "Wizards…" from the Tools menu. In the "Select Wizard" dialog box expand "Databases" and double-click "Create Login Wizard".

Privileges

Users are granted privileges to read, modify, create, delete objects, or to execute SQL statements within a database. Privileges are granted to identified user accounts or to roles. These privileges are granted using either the GRANT Transact-SQL command, or the Enterprise Manager application.

A user can be given privileges to create a table, procedure, rule, or view within a database. They can also be granted permission to execute the SELECT, INSERT, DELETE, or UPDATE SQL commands. These commands can be further restricted to specific tables, views, or stored procedures. The lowest level of granularity is limited access to specific columns within a table.

Certain privileges, such as the ability to create or alter a table, are limited to the role of the `dbcreator` (the user account that created the table), or the system administrator.

OLAP Security

Microsoft SQL Server OLAP Services also provides additional security services. These services can be used to manage access to OLAP cubes that run on the Windows 2000 Server platform. Access and privileges for SQL Server OLAP Services cubes is managed using access control lists (ACLs), which are integrated with the NTFS file system.

TIP

The FAT file system does not support ACLs. If you want to define a privilege scheme for your SQL Server OLAP Services cubes you need to install SQL Server 7 on a system that has the NTFS file system installed.

SQL Server OLAP Services authentication relies on the user having a Windows 2000 Server account. If a user wants to access a SQL Server OLAP Services cube, he or she must have an account within the same Windows 2000 Server domain where the server is installed, or come from a trusted domain. Users can be granted three levels of access to an OLAP cube: read-only, read/write, or administrative.

The process of establishing OLAP cube security is a little different from the process described for the SQL Server database. The concern with SQL Server is to manage access to SQL commands and to database objects. In the OLAP environment these concepts are meaningless, so a modification of the scheme is required. OLAP users are placed in a role, and a role is assigned to a cube. Thus, the system administrator must create a role for a database, which is done by combining user accounts and groups. Then the system administrator must assign the role to one or more cubes within the database.

These activities are performed using the OLAP Manager application, not the Enterprise Manager application that is used to manage SQL Server databases.

System Performance

Once the system availability has been ensured with a solid backup/ recovery scheme, and data security has been implemented with a reliable authentication and authorization scheme, you are ready to consider performance issues.

Monitoring Performance

Managing the performance of a sophisticated computer system can be very complex. In order to effectively manage a system you must monitor it.

NOTE
The first rule of system performance management is to measure system performance, establish a baseline, and then monitor performance against the baseline over time. Then, as you apply changes to the system, you can assess the impact of the changes by comparing them to the previously-established baselines.

System Resources

A modern computer system is a layered environment. One way to conceptualize the system is to envision an onion—each layer is supported by the layers beneath it. An application dependency stack (as seen in Figure 9.3) further illustrates this concept.

Any layer in this stack can cause performance or reliability problems. In the rest of this section, however, we focus on the server side of the performance management problem. It's outside of the scope of this chapter to discuss network or client-side performance management.

When you measure or evaluate performance issues on the server you need to assess the three major subsystems in the following order: memory, I/O, and CPU. If you have tuned these subsystems for maximum efficiency and you still have performance issues, you'll need to consider the application itself.

Memory Utilization

SQL Server, like most commercial databases, implements an in-memory cache that contains database pages. The pages in the cache are managed

NOTE
A modern client/server system is a layered environment. Each layer has an impact on overall performance. These layers include the network, the hardware configuration (including disks, I/O subsystem, memory, and CPU), the operating system, and, finally, the database configuration. You must understand how to monitor and modify each layer in order to obtain optimum performance.

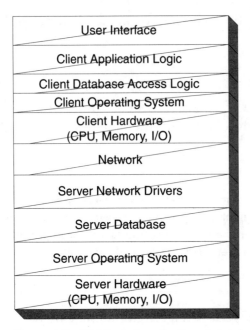

Figure 9.3   Distributed application dependency stack.

using a least-recently-used (LRU) algorithm. This algorithm attempts to ensure that once a page has been read into cache as a result of a client request, it is kept in memory as long as possible. When a page is modified, SQL Server doesn't always, immediately write it to disk, especially if multiple users are reading and writing the page.

SQL Server 7 will automatically allocate and release memory for the cache, as needed. If the system needs pages SQL Server 7 will release pages so that they can be used either by the operating system or other applications.

The most important, single memory utilization statistic to monitor is the *cache hit ratio*. The cache hit ratio is the percentage of logical page requests that are satisfied without requiring a physical I/O. A well-tuned system should be able to maintain a cache hit ratio of at least 80 percent. If the cache hit ratio is less than 80 percent on a busy system then either the cache is too small and pages are getting flushed out to disk, or the application is not designed and written to take advantage of the cache.

It is important to consider the size of the cache relative to total system memory size and virtual memory size. If the computer has 64 MB of physical memory and a 64-MB swap file, then 128 MB of virtual memory are available.

TIP

Microsoft recommends that system administrator's configure the Windows 2000 Server swap file to a minimum of 150% of physical memory. Therefore a 64-MB machine should have the swap file of at least 98 MB, which gives the operating system a total virtual memory of 192 MB. If you implement the full-text option, the swap file should be at least 300% of physical memory.

If the SQL Server disk cache was allowed to expand larger than the amount of physical memory available to it, the excess pages in the cache would be stored on disk in the swap file. Any I/O to those pages would require a physical I/O from the swap file. Because of this effect, SQL Server 7 always attempts to keep its cache smaller than physical memory. If another application starts and there are less than 5 MB physical memory available SQL Server 7 will release cache pages back to the operating system.

There are two memory parameters that can be adjusted, using the Enterprise Manager, to manually configure the amount of memory (in MB) that SQL Server 7 uses. The `Min server memory` option is used to define the minimum amount of physical memory allocated to SQL Server 7. The default value for this memory option is 0. The `Max server memory` option is the memory option that limits the maximum amount of memory SQL Server 7 can allocate. Its default value is 2,147,483,647 MB. It's highly unlikely that any computer system that runs SQL Server 7 in the foreseeable future will run on a computer with this much physical memory.

Database Resources

The database also consumes a variety of system resources, many of which utilize memory. These resources include buffers, locks, threads, and I/O blocks.

Buffers

The in-memory buffer cache maintained by SQL Server cannot be directly configured by the system administrator. SQL Server automatically builds the cache and maintains a list of available buffers. When a process or thread requires a page, SQL Server 7 returns the first available page on the list—structured as a single-linked list. Any time a SQL statement affects a page, SQL Server 7 increments a counter in the page header. Periodically, SQL Server scans the entire buffer list and decrements the page counter. Once the page counter has reached 0, that indicates no activity has occurred recently with the page. If the page is dirty or a checkpoint occurs, and another thread requires a buffer, SQL Server 7 writes the dirty page to disk, and frees up the buffer for the other job to use.

As mentioned previously, SQL Server 7 automatically and dynamically allocates and releases pages for its buffer list. When SQL Server 7 requires more pages and there are no more buffer pages available, it checks the free list to see if there is sufficient free memory. The free list is the list of available pages maintained by the operating system. If at least 5 MB of memory is available SQL Server allocates the additional memory and places them on the free buffer list. If the system doesn't have at least 5 MB free, SQL Server 7 forces some number of dirty pages to disk, and links those pages to the free buffer list.

Conversely, if the system or another application requires memory, SQL Server 7 will release pages to the free list, after first ensuring that they have been written to disk.

Locks

Locks are used to ensure the integrity of the data. SQL Server 7 automatically grants a lock on a resource—row, table, page, key, range of keys, etc.—based on SQL statements. The intent of a lock is to ensure that no two processes modify the same resource in an uncoordinated fashion. The granularity of a lock is exclusively controlled by SQL Server 7, and cannot be directly affected by an application.

SQL Server attempts to maintain a balance between resource consumption and concurrency when deciding the appropriate lock to grant for a resource as shown in Figure 9.4. Locks taken at the table level, for example, result in relatively fewer locks, but at the cost of reduced concurrency, since no other users can modify the table while it is locked. At the other end of the spectrum, locks that are granted at the row level, which is the most granular lock category, result in greater concurrency, since more users can modify the table, but consume more resources since more locks must be managed.

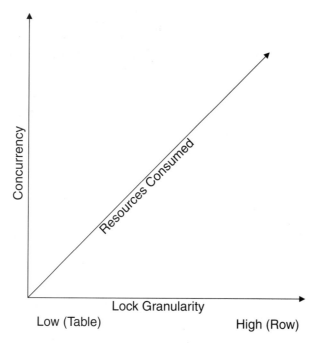

Figure 9.4 SQL Server lock resource consumption.

There are several categories of locks that can be taken out, such as shared, update, exclusive, intent, and schema. Shared locks are used if the SQL statement does not modify an object (SELECT statement). A shared lock stops another process from modifying the object while it is read, but must be upgraded to either an update or exclusive lock before the job that holds the shared lock can change the object. An upgrade occurs when an UPDATE, INSERT, or DELETE SQL command is executed. An intent lock is used as an enhancement performance. A process can take out an intent shared or intent exclusive lock on a table. Another job that wants to modify the table can then test to see if an intent lock is held. If it is, the testing job knows another job is about to modify the table, without having to scan the entire lock table to see if a row or page lock is held.

You can monitor the current locks using the Enterprise Manager. Expand a server, then expand "Management". Expand "Current Activity", and select either "Locks/Process ID" to view locks per process, or "Locks/Object" to view the locks currently held for each object.

One locking issue all DBAs need to consider is *deadlocks*. A deadlock should not be confused with a process that is blocked on a single lock.

As soon as the locking process releases its lock the blocked process can resume processing. The deadlock situation, by contrast, is characterized by two processes that each want a lock on a resource the other process has locked. By definition, the two processes will wait forever. A deadlock arises if ProcessA holds a lock on ResourceA and attempts to obtain a lock on ResourceB, while ProcessB has a lock on ResourceB and it attempts to obtain a lock on ResourceA. Neither job can release its current lock until it obtains the requested lock, which is held by the opposing process.

SQL Server 7 has built-in deadlock detection and breaks the tie by forcing one job to rollback its transaction. Naturally, this is an expensive process that should be avoided.

TIP

Avoiding deadlocks is primarily an application-logic issue. The application developer should ensure that resources are always accessed in the same order. If two applications are going to take locks out on the `customer` and `sales_order` tables, they should both do so in the same order. This approach will alleviate the potential for deadlocks.

User Threads

Threads are lightweight execution streams that can run in parallel. SQL Server and the operating system both manage the creation and execution of threads. Thread management is limited under Windows 2000 Server. There are a few options that can be set using Enterprise Manager, including an affinity mask option and maximum worker threads option. The affinity mask option enables the system administrator to restrict a process or application to a specific CPU on an SMP platform. This may be useful in a mixed workload environment, but is generally not recommended. The maximum, worker threads option enables SQL Server to establish a pool of threads that can be used to accept incoming connection requests. Establishing a thread pool can help performance by reducing the processing required to create a new thread. SQL Server has a default value of 255, which should be adequate for most systems.

Managing I/O

It has been the experience of the authors that most performance problems found with database applications are related to I/O. The typical database application becomes I/O-bound before it becomes CPU-bound—assuming sufficient memory is available to the application.

There are several types of I/O issues that need to be addressed to ensure adequate performance. The first issue is to configure the database in such a way that no single disk can become a hot spot. The classic table category that causes this kind of problem is an application queue. In this type of application the application maintains a counter of some sort. When a user requires a service, the application takes a number from the counter and increments it by one. This simple "take a number" algorithm requires the application to retrieve the current number, lock the table or row, increment the number by one, update the counter, and release the lock. The counter is then used as a pointer to a row (usually the next available row in another table) where data is stored. This is a classic queuing technique used to create a stack, also known as a first-in/last-out (FILO) queue.

With this type of data structure, a commit occurs every time the counter is incremented, which can force a disk I/O. SQL Server 7 attempts to reduce disk I/O in this situation in two ways. First, if the counter is accessed frequently, it is likely to be memory-resident. Second, when the commit occurs SQL Server 7 attempts to flush the commit record to the transaction log file, rather than write the database page to disk. However, if the load on the system is heavy enough, this type of application data structure can cause a disk hot spot.

There are other types of disk hot spots that can emerge as a result of the logical or physical design of the database. However, SQL Server also provides a variety of techniques for addressing these issues.

The second type of I/O issue, which is one of the most common disk I/O problems, arises as a result of insufficient memory. Both Windows 2000 Server and SQL Server 7 allocate memory for processes, buffers, and system working space. When the computer is under-sized with respect to memory, the system is forced to swap out pages to the swap file. This swapping overhead can be extensive and can result in a significant slow-down of the system. Eventually, if the load on the system becomes excessive, the system may begin to thrash, or it may stop completely, especially if the swap file is full and there is no more disk space to expand it. Thus, if there is a performance problem and the Windows 2000 Server system monitor indicates a high degree of swapping, you should probably increase physical memory in the computer.

One way to deal with disk I/O problems, especially if there is a very active table, is to use *mirroring* (RAID 1). Mirroring makes two spindles available to respond to I/O requests. Mirroring can improve I/O performance for reads. However, it will not improve performance for writes, since the I/O must complete to both spindles.

Another way to improve I/O performance is to use filegroups and to place frequently accessed tables in a separate filegroup stored on a separate spindle. This allows the system to evenly distribute the I/O load represented by multiple tables. You can also place the transaction log files and index file on spindles separate from the data files. Another way to evenly distribute the I/O load is to use *striping* (RAID 0), which evenly distributes the database pages across a range of disks. See Chapter 5 for a more detailed discussion of the various types of RAID configurations.

CPU Utilization

There is very little you can do directly to manage or affect CPU utilization of a particular application. On most representative Windows 2000 Server platforms, the CPU is primarily consumed with either managing memory and processes or executing system and application code. A good rule of thumb is that a balanced system spends no more than 20 percent of the CPU cycles for overhead work and 80 percent, or more, for application processing.

The issue of the ratio between system to application work can be important in a symmetric multi-processing (SMP) environment. All SMP machines have a certain amount of overhead associated with coordinating the activities of the various processors. While it may be tempting to simply add another few processors when CPU utilization is high, you should be aware that you won't be able to get 100 percent of the new CPU working on behalf of the applications.

However, this is not to say you shouldn't add more CPUs where it makes sense, since SQL Server 7 is designed to take advantage of an SMP environment by creating parallel execution plans, and using operating system threads to run the plan components on all available processors.

TIP

Windows 2000 Server manages access to the CPU by assigning jobs a priority level, which ranges from 0 to 31. In general, jobs with a higher priority run before jobs with a lower priority. However Windows 2000 Server is not a pre-emptive operating system, so a process is not forced to release control of the CPU until its time slice expires.* SQL Server 7 runs at a default priority of 7 on a single processor computer and 15 on an SMP machine, which is sufficient for most applications. If your system is dedicated to SQL Server and does not run any other applications, you might consider boosting SQL Server 7's priority, by changing the `boost priority` option from 0 to 1. This increases SQL Server 7's priority level to 15 on a single CPU machine, and 24 on an SMP box. This option should be exercised with caution, since other important processes may not run on a busy system. See the documentation for further details on how to set this option.

One nice feature that SQL Server has is the ability to run background jobs whenever the CPU utilization rate has fallen below a certain percentage for a period of time. This allows the system administrator to schedule non-critical jobs to run whenever the system is idle.

Before you can take advantage of this feature you must define the job, using the Enterprise Manager. Once you have defined the job, it's a good idea to find out how much CPU the job requires. You can do this by using either the SQL Server Profiler or the Windows 2000 Server Performance Monitor to observe server traffic and collect statistics. Once you have this information you can determine how much idle time should pass before the job(s) are activated.

You do this by running the SQL Server Agent. Right-click the Agent, and select "Properties". In the dialog box that is displayed click the "Advanced" tab. Set the CPU idle condition as a percentage below which the average CPU usage must remain for a specified time, defined in seconds. When this time is exceeded, SQL Server Agent starts the jobs defined to run when the CPU is idle.

On the other hand, if the CPU is running at close to maximum, then you will need to investigate which jobs are consuming the CPU and what kind of work the CPU is performing to determine if there are any

---

*If a process runs longer than the system time slice option, the operating system assumes it is stuck in a loop and terminates it. This brute force approach to thread management argues against modifying the `time slice` option, unless absolutely necessary.

inefficiencies in the system that can be corrected. It's a good idea to do this analysis before the users start to complain about slow performance.

There are several tools that you can use to monitor and analyze the system behavior, including the aforementioned SQL Server Profiler and Windows 2000 Server Performance Monitor tools.

SQL Server Profiler is used to analyze database events. You start the Profiler from the Enterprise Manager window. It doesn't collect any data until you define a trace (or import a trace file). Once you define a trace it collects the required data and stores it in a trace file. The trace file can be used to replay the system events on another system. There is a full range of event classes that the Profiler can trace. These classes include errors and warnings; lock events, including deadlocks; events associated with creating, modifying or deleting objects; scans; sessions; transactions and stored procedures. SQL Server 7 supplies a Create Trace Wizard to help define traces for the most common types of event classes. Using the Profiler you can monitor the activity of users, by user name, identify and analyze slow-running queries, or detect deadlocks. To start the Create Trace Wizard you select "Wizards..." from the Tools menu of the Enterprise Manager.

The other important tool to use is the Windows 2000 Server Performance Monitor. This tool can be used to monitor the activity of the operating system and hardware. It provides a long list of counters that can be graphically displayed to analyze many aspects of system behavior. Performance Monitor is also extensible, and SQL Server adds a number of events that it can monitor. These include:

- SQL Server I/O
- SQL Server memory utilization
- SQL Server locks
- SQL Server replication activity
- SQL Server users

Since Performance Monitor uses remote procedure call (RPC) technology you can use it to monitor a remote system on the network, without having to be physically present at the computer.

Tuning

Tuning is the process of optimizing the utilization of system resources for maximum efficiency and performance. In the SQL Server environment tuning can be performed at the query level, the database level, and the system level.

Query Optimization

In order to run a query on behalf of a client, Microsoft has implemented a prepare-and-execute strategy. Ordinarily the client OLE DB or ODBC driver sends a SQL statement to SQL Server 7 through its API. The SQL Server query optimizer evaluates and compiles the statements into an execution plan and returns a response to the client with a handle that points to the location of the plan. This completes the prepare phase. The client then sends a request to SQL Server to execute the query and return the result set. This requires two network roundtrips—first to prepare the statement, and the second to execute it.

If the query is only used once, then this process runs to completion and the generated plan is cached for a period of time before it's discarded. SQL Server can reuse a query that has compiled, as long as the query doesn't change. For example a query like the following could be submitted to the system.

```
Select * from customers
Where customer_id = 256
```

The next time another user runs this query the value of `customer_id` will be different, forcing SQL Server to recompile the query. If the query can take a parameter, it can be generated and the parameter bound to a variable, which is passed to the query at runtime. Using this capability improves performance in two ways. First, the resources required to evaluate and compile the query are used only once. Second, the two network roundtrips referred to previously are avoided, since all the client needs to do is pass the appropriate parameter and request execution.

A parameterized query would look like the following:

```
Select * from customers
Where customer_id = ?
```

SQL Server 7 has algorithms to automatically locate and run a pre-compiled plan if it exists in memory. This capacity can be very useful for routine queries that are used as part of decision support reports.

Tuning Queries

Query tuning can be a worthwhile exercise if a query is complex or is frequently used. The key to tuning queries is to clearly understand the impact the query has on the system. You can use this understanding to either modify the query, or modify the database, so that the query can run more efficiently, while producing the result expected by the user.

Queries are processed and controlled by the query optimizer, which is the core of the RDBMS. You can evaluate the plans created by the query optimizer and modify the query using the Query Analyzer.

Query Analyzer

The SQL Server Query Analyzer is a graphical tool that is invoked from the Enterprise Manager. It has a query text editor that's used to dynamically modify and execute a query. Query Analyzer can also present color-coded query text to help with your analysis of the query parts. The heart of the Query Analyzer is a display window that shows the logical steps of the execution plan. The DBA can analyze these steps to isolate slow-running portions of the query. This information can be helpful to determine how to improve performance.

The Query Analyzer window provides a lot of information about a query in a graphical format (See Figure 9.5). Each node on the display represents a logical step or operator that is executed. If you place the mouse over a node, a popup window will show information about the node.

Establishing Query Limits

The system administrator can establish an upper boundary on the amount of time a query is allowed to run. This allows the administrator to preclude run-away queries. This limit is modified using the query governor cost limit option. If the option value is set to a positive, non-zero integer value, the system does not allow a query to run if it determines that the query will run longer than that interval, in seconds. Thus a value of 300 causes SQL Server 7 to terminate a query that it determines will take longer than 5 minutes to execute. The default value is 0, meaning there are no limits.

The option can be enabled system-wide, using Enterprise Manager, or set for a specific query by executing the SET QUERY_GOVERNOR_COST_LIMIT statement.

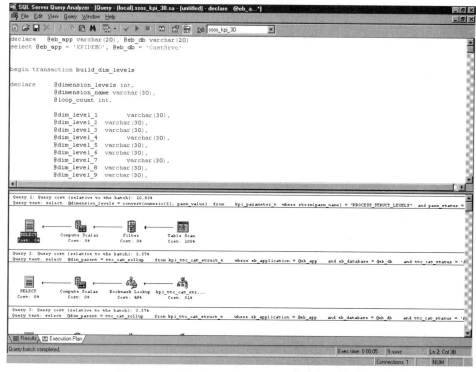

Figure 9.5   SQL Server Query Analyzer.

For example, if the node is a SELECT operation, the display window will show information about:

- The estimated number of rows that will be returned
- The estimated size of the rows
- The estimated I/O cost of the operation
- The estimated CPU cost of the operation
- The number of times the operation was executed during the query.

Other details are available for different categories of operations.

Once you have obtained the operation details for the various steps within a query, you can now perform some analysis for the best way to optimize the step's operation. You should identify and focus on those steps that have the highest I/O cost first, then concentrate on steps with the highest CPU cost. There are two major types of optimization that you can use to tune the system for maximum performance. One is to evaluate and optimize joins. The second is to use indexes and aggregate tables appropriately.

Statistics

It's important to provide up-to-date statistics to the optimizer. As the database is used, current statistics can be invaluable to the optimizer as it considers various execution plans. SQL Server automatically collects statistics for indexed columns. Statistics for non-indexed columns can be collected either by enabling the `auto create statistics` database option in the Enterprise Manager, or by executing the `CREATE STATISTICS` command in t-SQL.

Joins

A join is the result of a SELECT statement that retrieves rows from more than one table, based on a keyed relationship between the two tables. There are two major types of joins that SQL Server supports: nested loop joins and hash joins.

A simple *nested loop join* loops through two tables and selects zero or more rows, by comparing the value of a specified column in the row with a comparison operator. The comparison operator typically evaluates a column value. A lot of the work that went into the SQL Server 7 optimizer was focused on improving the performance of nested loop joins. For example, if there is an index that SQL Server 7 can use, it does, rather than perform a table scan.

A *hash join*, on the other hand, goes through two stages. In the first stage SQL Server 7 scans the table and builds an in-memory hash table with the column's values that it's search is currently on. The equality predicate—the expression used to search for the column values—is used to generate the hash key. Each row is put into a hash bucket. If the table grows to exceed physical memory, SQL Server partitions the hash table and moves it to disk files. In the second stage SQL Server 7 uses the hash values to probe into the joined table to locate rows with matching column values. The hash scheme is inherently faster than others, but can also consume more system resources if the hash table becomes too large.

The system automatically selects the most appropriate join tactic, but the DBA can also use hints to force the usage of a hash join.

Tuning the Database

The database itself can also be configured to improve performance.

Filegroups

Filegroups were discussed previously in the context of a backup and recovery strategy. Filegroups are also useful in helping to partition the database across multiple disk drives, which can improve I/O performance by balancing the workload across spindles.

You create a filegroup, and then create the tables that go into the filegroup, using the CREATE DATABASE command with the FILEGROUP qualifier. An example looks like:

```
CREATE DATABASE customer_data
ON PRIMARY
     (NAME=Customer Primary,
     FILENAME=c:\mssql7\data\CustPrim.mdf,
     SIZE=4,
     MAXSIZE=10,
     FILEGROWTH=1),
FILEGROUP Customer_FG1
     (NAME = Customer_FG1_data,
     FILENAME = c:\mssql7\data\CustFG1.ndf,
     SIZE = 1MB,
     MAXSIZE=10,
     FILEGROWTH=1),
     ( NAME = Customer_FG2_data,
     FILENAME = c:\mssql7\data\CustFG2.ndf,
     SIZE = 1MB,
     MAXSIZE=10,
     FILEGROWTH=1)
LOG ON
     (NAME=CustFG_LOG,
     FILENAME=d:\logs\Customer.ldf,
     SIZE=1,
     MAXSIZE=10,
     FILEGROWTH=1)
```

Note that the log file is *not* part of the filegroup. For availability purposes, it is a good idea to store the log files for a database on a separate disk, unless the disk is mirrored.

Once you have created and placed a database on a filegroup, you can create tables or indexes in the filegroup, using the CREATE TABLE command with the ON option, which is used to specify the filegroup.

Data Partitioning

Placing a table on a specific set of disks is one way to allocate the I/O load to improve performance. Another way is to partition the data *within* a table across multiple disks. This is a much more granular approach to partitioning than placing the entire table.

If you decide to partition the table by the column value, you do this by creating a horizontal partition scheme. This approach can allow a logical partitioning of data by some meaningful unit, such as date, identifier, or a range value. For example, a sales management database may partition data based on the months of the fiscal year, with a separate partition for each month.

There are several performance benefits for a horizontal partition. One is that multiple disks can work in parallel. For example, if a sales manager performs a comparative sales analysis for several months, each partition can be scanned independently of the others. Another benefit is workload isolation. If the manager wants to analyze sales data for a specific month, only the affected disk is utilized, leaving other disks free to handle queries from other users.

It's important to understand how the data is used. If a table is partitioned using this scheme, but most queries retrieve data from multiple months, the overhead for all of the UNION operations required can be substantial, overwhelming the performance advantage gained by other queries.

To create a horizontal partition you create a table using the CREATE TABLE command for each month of the year, and apply a CHECK constraint on the column of interest. For example:

```
CREATE TABLE JanuarySales
    [define various columns...]
    OrderMonth INT
        CHECK (OrderMonth = 1),
    [define more columns...]
```

The CHECK constraint limits data in the OrderMonth column to month #1 (January). If you then want to look at data for the year, you create a view that looks like this:

```
CREATE TABLE YearSales
AS
    SELECT * FROM JanuarySales
        UNION ALL
```

```
SELECT * FROM FebruarySales
    UNION ALL
[add the rest of the partitioned tables...]
```

Once you have created the view YearSales, then any query against the view that limits OrderMonth will only access the appropriate monthly table.

Indexes

Indexes are probably the first line of defense when addressing database performance. An index, by definition, inverts the data in a column in some sorted order. SQL Server 7 takes advantage of indexes in a number of ways. For example, when it performs a nested join it searches the inner join table, for each row of the outer join table, using the index of the inner table.

Clustered Indexes

A *clustered index* is a special type of index. A table's data rows with a clustered index are stored in sorted order and the table's pages are linked to each other using a *doubly-linked list*.* The index is stored as a B-tree. Use a clustered index in situations where most of the queries search on a column in sorted order. The advantage is that if a page is read-in and the other data rows on that page are scanned, the page is already memory resident. The read-ahead abilities of SQL Server also enhance the likelihood that the next page, in order, is resident in memory when the query thread is ready for it.

NOTE

▬▬▬ Because a clustered index forces the ordering of data rows there can only be one clustered index per table.

Up to 256 non-clustered indexes can be used on a table, whether it uses a clustered index or not. Tables that use only non-clustered indexes are

---

*SQL Server stores data in pages that are each 8 KB. Each page has a header block that contains information about that page. If a table has a clustered index, the header block contains two pointer fields. The *forward pointer* is the number of the next page, in sorted order. The *backward pointer* is the number of the previous page. These two pointers are a *doubly-linked list*. The first page's backward pointer and the last page's forward pointer contain a NULL value. When SQL Server scans a sorted table and detects a NULL value in the forward pointer field, it knows it has reached the end of the table.

not stored in sorted order. However, the index, itself, is sorted, and there can be multiple indexes on different columns for the same table.

Aggregate Tables

There are two types of aggregate data structures that you can create in the SQL Server 7 environment. The first is the dimension tables associated with a star schema. The second is the multi-dimensional database you set up using SQL Server OLAP Services.

The configuration process for these two data structure types is described in Chapter 3. To build the star schema tables, you invoke the Enterprise Manager, expand the database, right-click Tables, and select "Create Table". You can also create tables using the CREATE TABLE command in Transact-SQL, or by writing a C/C++ program that calls SQL-DMO.

The next step after you have created the table is to define how the table is populated. You do this by creating a Transact-SQL script, which summarizes detail data from the fact table and inserts the summary records into the appropriate dimension tables. Alternatively, the DTS script you use to populate the database can be modified to automatically populate the dimension table at the same time the fact table is built.

Once the star schema has been defined, you can proceed to create one or more SQL Server OLAP Services cubes that users can access for their analysis purposes. SQL Server 7 automatically populates the cubes once you have defined them. At regular intervals you can define a procedure for updating the cubes, which Microsoft refers to as *processing* the cube. Remember that in certain instances users are not allowed to access a cube while SQL Server is processing it, so you want to be sure that processing only takes place during off-hours.

Buffers

Buffer management is another area where Microsoft SQL Server does most of the work on behalf of the system administrator.

As noted earlier, SQL Server 7 dynamically allocates buffer pages from the available memory of the computer. SQL Server makes every attempt to ensure that the buffers are memory-resident. It does this by continually checking to see that the system has 5 MB of available memory before requesting additional pages.

TIP

Wherever feasible, run the SQL Server production environment on a dedicated machine. SQL Server attempts to allocate its cache using as much memory as possible. The memory requirements of the operating system and other applications, and the goal of minimizing page swapping regulate the amount of memory SQL Server can allocate. If other applications are allowed to run on the same machine, the overall performance of both SQL Server and the other applications is affected, particularly if SQL Server is forced to frequently release and reallocate pages due to other applications starting and stopping.

As described earlier, the system administrator can control the maximum and minimum amount of memory available to SQL Server, through the `min server memory` and `max server memory` options. However, these options should be left at their default values unless there is a compelling, documented reason to modify them.

Locks

There is no mechanism for an application or user to directly modify the database's locking mechanism. The only option available is to set the size of the lock table, using the `sp_config` system procedure. The default value is 0, indicating that SQL Server 7 will dynamically allocate memory for the lock table. SQL Server 7 allocates lock table space, up to the point where doing so would cause paging at the operating system level.

SQL Server implements a lock architecture based on shared locks. Both readers and writers take locks on the data, depending on how they plan to access it. This ensures that a reader only views committed data, and that a writer does not overwrite data that is currently viewed by a reader. This architecture, however, can result in one application blocking another from acquiring a shared lock.

There are several scenarios where applications can cause blocks to occur. Blocking usually occurs when locks are not released in a timely fashion.

One scenario is where an application submits a long-running query and performs a DELETE or UPDATE operation that affects many rows. If SQL Server escalates the locks to the table level, the query can block other queries that access the same table. This problem can be resolved by optimizing the query, such as adding indexes, or breaking up a large query into smaller queries.

Another scenario that results in blocking is where an application that uses ODBC issues a SQLCANCEL statement to cancel a query, but does not issue the appropriate COMMIT or ROLLBACK statements. SQL Server does not cancel locks acquired within a transaction unless the transaction is committed or aborted, so the locks remain outstanding forever, or until the server is shutdown.

Finally, when an application submits a query to SQL Server, it must retrieve all the rows returned by the database. If the application fails to fetch all of the rows from the database, locks may be left intact on the tables, which can block other users.

Tuning Data Loading

DTS is implemented as a collection of COM objects. Here are a few hints to optimize DTS performance.

The DTS Data Pump, for example, is an OLE DB service provider that is used to move data from source to target. In general, you should use the Data Pump as part of the DTS package with reasonable performance. Microsoft claims that Data Pump performance is comparable with the bcp utility as discussed in the next section, Bulk Loading.

The Data Pump provides a number of interfaces, including the Set FetchBufferSize method, which can be used to increase the Data Pump input buffer from its default value to 1 to some larger number of input rows. DTS also provides support for managing the level and granularity of locks.

Use ActiveX scripts as part of the transformation process with discretion, particularly if they are written in PerlScript or Jscript. Scripts can be up to two to four times slower than straightforward copy operations. Also, when you map similar transformation functions to multiple columns, consider mapping all of the transformations into a single invocation, if possible. This runs the transformation script only once, rather than multiple times, which can improve overall throughput.

DTS performance can be affected by modifying the DTSFastLoads constants. The default values are listed in Table 9.3.

Bulk Loading

Data cannot be rapidly added to the SQL Server database using the INSERT command. When large volumes of data need to be added to

Table 9.3 DTS Load Option Constants

DTSFASTLOADOPTIONS CONSTANT NAME	DEFAULT VALUE
DTSFastLoad_CheckConstraints	Enabled - constraints are checked
DTSFastLoad_KeepNulls	Enabled - nulls are inserted, rather than the column default value
DTSFastLoad_NoOptions	Disabled - options are enabled
DTSFastLoad_TableLock	Enabled - locks are taken at the table level

the DBMS, resort to a *bulk loading* technique. There are two ways to bulk load data. The first is to use the old bcp utility. The second is to use the BULK INSERT command. Microsoft recommends using BULK INSERT, because it's faster.

For example bcp formats OLE DB rowsets which it sends to SQL Server. SQL Server, in turn invokes the query optimizer to load the data. The query optimizer can generate an optimized plan to insert the data, update the indexes, check constraints, and generate parallel load threads.

BULK INSERT, on the other hand, loads the data directly into the database without these steps. BULK INSERT cannot be used to transform data, since it is limited to importing data from a file, nor can it update an index. Therefore data that needs to be transformed should go through the DTS Data Pump, and bcp should be called from within DTS to insert the data, while data that does not need to be transformed can be moved using the BULK INSERT command. Alternatively, DTS can generate a BULK INSERT file using formatted data.

There are some considerations when using BULK INSERT. A column can have a default value defined as a constraint. However, if the input data field is blank, you have the option of allowing SQL Server to use the default value, or a NULL. The KEEPNULLS qualifier allows BULK INSERT to insert a NULL, otherwise, SQL Server fills in the field with the default value.

SQL Server treats the entire input file as a single transaction by default. If you want to limit the number of rows that are considered part of a single transaction, use the BATCHSIZE = (# of rows) option.

If the table has a clustered index, the input file should be sorted on that column, especially if the index size is less than, or equal to, 30 percent of

TIP

Consider turning off logging during the bulk-load operation. The transaction log can fill up as a result of the large number of updates applied from a bulk load. In order to turn off logging, the `select into/bulkcopy` option for the database must be altered from its default value of "false" to "true". If the option is not set and a bulk copy operation is initiated SQL Server generates an error message and logs the transactions.

the table size. When the data is loaded into the table, use the ORDER hint, which speeds up the loading process. If any non-clustered indexes are present, they should be dropped before the bulk-load process starts. It's generally faster to drop an index, load the data, and then rebuild the index than it is to load the data and update the index simultaneously.

Also, use the TABLOCK hint, which forces a lock on the table, rather than the individual rows as they are inserted. This reduces the number of locks that SQL Server must manage during the load process.

WARNING

If you disable transaction logging during the bulk-load process, it's imperative that you backup the database files and re-enable transaction logs before allowing the users access to the system. Otherwise, if there is a subsequent failure, SQL Server cannot reinsert the bulk load data, since the transactions are not present in the log file.

Updating OLAP Cubes

Updating the SQL Server OLAP Services cubes in your decision support system is somewhat different from updating the SQL Server database. Where you can load data into the SQL Server database using bulk-loading utilities, such as bcp or BULK INSERT, you must synchronize the SQL Server OLAP Services cubes with the data warehouse.

The synchronization and update process can be somewhat complicated, due to the highly-aggregated nature of the cube, and the intertwined structure of the dimensional tree within the cube. As noted earlier, users are not allowed to view a cube that is synchronized, because the system cannot ensure that the user will see consistent information. There are three types of synchronization update scenarios: rebuild, refresh, and update. Regardless of the method used to synchronize the cube, if a cube is online, it remains online while a copy is built. Once the copy is complete, the online version is replaced with the new cube.

Cube Rebuild (Process)

A *rebuild*, which Microsoft refers to as *processing*, completely reloads the cube with data. Processing is required to initially populate the cube, and if you make a subsequent structural change to the data warehouse linked with the OLAP cube.

Cube Refresh

The *refresh* synchronization method is used when the underlying data in the data warehouse has changed, but the structure is unchanged. In this instance, you rebuild data within the cube, without the need to modify the dimensional structure. This scenario can be invoked when errors are discovered in the data warehouse, and the errors need to be removed from the data warehouse and the OLAP cube.

Cube Update

The most common scenario is an *update*. This occurs when new, incremental data changes are moved from the data warehouse to the OLAP cube. The new data is added to the cube and dimension members are recalculated. This updated data is stored in a separate, temporary partition while the update process is active. Once the update is complete, the temporary partition is merged into the cube.

In either the refresh or update scenario, any online users are automatically connected to the new cube. If you run a rebuild process, however, any users who are connected to the cube are disconnected when the process is complete. They must then re-connect with the cube to access the new cube.

NOTE

If a shared dimension's *data* is updated, then any cube that accesses that dimension becomes unavailable to the client's workstations and must be processed before users can access it. If the shared dimension's *structure* is modified and saved, but not processed, it's processed as soon as any cube that uses that dimension is processed at which time all other cubes that share in the shared dimension become unavailable and must be processed. For this reason, you should plan to update any shared dimensions first, before updating any other cubes, especially if you modify the shared dimension structure.

To process a cube, start the OLAP Manager window. Select a database and expand the Cubes folder. Select a cube and right-click it, and then click "Process." In the Process A Cube dialog box that comes up, click "Process" and then "OK."

OLAP Partitions

An OLAP cube can be carved up into separate, but related, partitions. These partitions can be placed in separate disk drives, for performance and management reasons. Partitions can be merged into each other, as long as they contain the same structure.

Partitions are also used to manage the storage implementation. Each type of cube—MOLAP, ROLAP or HOLAP—is stored in its own partition.

Partitions should be designed precisely, since duplicate data in multiple partitions can be double-counted unless the designer is careful. In general, OLAP partitioning can be extremely useful, but it should be carefully planned, implemented, and tested because of the potential for reporting erroneous data to users.

To update or refresh a cube, click "Incremental Update" in the Process A Cube dialog box. This starts the Incremental Update Wizard. You then select the partition to update, identify the source and fact table, and, optionally, create a filter expression to limit the data that is moved into the cube. If the cube contains only one partition then the partition selection step is skipped. Otherwise, you need to run the Wizard for each partition in the cube.

Role of Microsoft Repository

Microsoft Repository plays an important, yet evolving, role in the ongoing administration of a decision support system using SQL Server and SQL Server OLAP Services. The Repository contains information about the applications, metadata, and information models used to define the data structures in the system. It also stores the DTS packages used to populate and update the data in the SQL Server database. Information is stored in the Repository as collections of objects that have relationships with each other.

The primary value of using the Repository is to build an over-all information model that links your production-oriented transaction processing systems with your multi-dimensional decision support applications and database. This model can be very useful as your information system needs change and evolve, by enabling you to visualize, document, and capture all of the objects that make up the model. The model can then be used to verify the logical correctness of the applications during the design and development process. Another attribute of Microsoft Repository is that it enables you to track versions of the various objects, which enables you to make some changes and then rollback to a prior version if required. This capability can be useful if a software modification has gone awry, and the developer needs to restart using a known, trusted baseline.

Summary

Since a complete decision support system contains multiple parts, the personnel who care for those systems need to understand the complex relationships between the various parts, and how to optimize reliability and performance. In this chapter we discussed some of the important tasks that must be executed to ensure that the system operates smoothly and provides the best possible response time for the end users.

CHAPTER 10

Analytical Applications

As popular and as necessary as data warehouses and OLAP cubes are, they are merely the first step to making better, more informed decisions. The revolution in corporate effectiveness associated with decision support technology is actually based on the ability of companies to effectively utilize such systems. Knowing what you should do with the information contained in the warehouse is as important as making that information available.

In this chapter, we explore the complexities for understanding the business side of data warehousing. We discuss the data warehouse from the user perspective, criteria for effective information analysis, and provide some interesting examples of multi-dimensional data analysis.

What Is a Data Warehouse?

By now, you have a pretty good understanding of what a data warehouse is, and how to build one. However, do you know what the data warehouse means to the people who will use it?

A data warehouse is nothing short of a revolution in the way knowledge workers perform their jobs. It offers a tremendous opportunity for them to execute what they currently accomplish in a fraction of the time, freeing up valuable resources to delve deeper into other problems.

Today's business environment is not only fast-paced but, increasingly, faster-paced. The speed of change is increasing. Competition has become more fierce and gone global. Customers and end users demand more and require instant delivery for higher-quality goods and services. Constant innovation is the norm, and the edge achieved from being innovative lasts for less time. Important decisions are made every day, every hour, virtually every minute.

In this incredibly dynamic environment, there are fewer and fewer resources to achieve increasingly difficult goals. Demands on people's time are increasing. Companies continually ask their employees to do more with less. People perform multiple jobs, work harder, and longer hours. The rapid pace of the business environment requires that lower-level employees make key decisions, since there is no time to wait for senior managers to respond. They need to do more, react quicker, look for opportunities and avoid threats, all without the resources required to do so.

It is also widely agreed that an organization's effectiveness is directly proportional to the effective use of information. Companies make good business decisions when they are based on facts. The idea of making a decision on "gut feel" is yesterday's news. An organization cannot survive in today's hectic environment unless they make effective use of information.

However, taking advantage of information takes time, resources, and knowledge of how to turn information into insight. It takes time and effort to research decisions. It takes resources and domain expertise to delve into the issues. To use information requires an understanding of what information to use and how. The frequency of decisions and the scale of their importance exacerbate the problem.

Two opposing forces are squeezing employees. On one hand, they are pressured to react faster to the environment and make more effective business decisions. On the other hand, they have fewer and fewer resources with which to be effective.

From a business perspective, a data warehouse is a reservoir for knowledge about corporate performance. It is a centralized database of statistics that is highly tuned for decision-making purposes. Corporations need a data warehouse when:

1. There is a lot of data available for their employees to make decisions with.

2. The marketplace changes so quickly that decisions must be made rapidly in order to stay one step ahead of the competition and client demands.

3. Information is scattered throughout the organization making it difficult to retrieve. The organizations core applications all have stand-alone databases that effectively create information stovepipes.

4. There is no commonality to the information each department looks at, and there needs to be. For example, different departments have different definitions for what a sale is. It can be defined as either when a customer orders or when the product is shipped. Both are correct, from the perspective of the department.

5. The information resides in a format that is difficult to work with.

6. The demands for the use of this information are sophisticated enough, or change enough, that a fixed-reporting solution is unfeasible.

As we stated previously, a data warehouse is nothing short of a revolution. It is a tool that can help users manage the pressure from opposing forces. With a data warehouse, people can make better, more informed decisions faster, without the need for more resources. It allows an organization to create an information-centric environment, where information is at the hub of all decision making. At the same time, it allows individuals to become more effective, and to further refine their decision-making processes without the burdens associated with research.

A Data Warehouse Business Justification

There are tremendous benefits to implementing a data warehouse. This is particularly true from a business user perspective. Data warehouses help users become more effective with fewer resources. Before we discuss these business benefits, let's first look into how data warehouses came about.

History in the Re-Making

A data warehouse centralizes decentralized systems. Over the course of the past 10 years, companies have decentralized their information services to individual departments. Initially, one, highly centralized department took care of all information processing at companies. However, over time, sales became responsible for order-entry systems, marketing for competitive intelligence and consumer consumption data, finance for general ledger systems and profit and loss statements. The thought was that these individual departments were best able to control and maintain information that was part of the department's core competency.

Recent trends are re-centralizing these decentralized systems. Companies have started to see the benefits for having cross-departmental communication of information. Departments are not islands onto themselves. They are part of the larger organization. Hence, all departments should strive for a centralized goal: improve corporate profitability and increase shareholder value. Utilizing information is one of the founding elements of improving corporate profitability.

Companies have come full circle. At first, centralized systems were decentralized into departmental responsibilities. Now, decentralized departmental responsibilities are re-centralized into corporate objectives. Everything old is new again. Centralization is in fashion.

However, information systems are much like the fashion industry. Every few years, old fashions come back into vogue, but they never look quite the same as the way they did before. Lapels are wider, buttons are more numerous, or colors are different. You cannot go into your closet and dig out the old stuff.

The same is true with respect to data warehouses. While they are a reincarnation of centralized systems, they do differ in one respect. A data warehouse is focused on the output of information for decision-making purposes, not on the input of that information. While information is centralized into a data warehouse, the individual departmental input systems like order entry or general ledger systems remain in place. A data warehouse addresses getting information *out*, not getting information *in*.

Most data warehouse projects concern themselves with the centralization of data. In order to blend data from different sources, many things need to happen, including:

- Accessing the decentralized systems
- Downloading their information into a centralized location

- Cleansing the data from each system, so that it can be compared to other data sources

- Aggregating data so that it is at a level that is conducive for analysis—too much data at too low a level can be overwhelming

- Organizing the data into a format that is (1) conducive for use, and (2) fast to retrieve

The idea of "getting information out" is paramount to the success of a data warehouse. The centralization of information is one thing, the use of that information is another. A successful implementation of a data warehouse concerns itself as much with the tools those users use to retrieve data as with the back-end technology used to centralize the information.

The Business Benefit of a Data Warehouse

There are many benefits to a data warehouse. A data warehouse allows you to focus less on bad stuff, and frees you to focus more on the good stuff that should be done in organizations as shown in Table 10.1.

Table 10.1　Data Warehouse Benefits

LESS BAD STUFF	MORE GOOD STUFF
Wasting processing time required to pull together analyses	Understanding data, finding out what the information means
Typing/transcribing results from hardcopy reports to spreadsheets	Making decisions based on facts, rather than on "gut feel"
Running around gathering information from multiple sources	High-end analysis of information such as importance analyses, rankings, shopping basket analyses, etc.
Making assumptions on how pieces of data are related if they came from multiple sources	Availability of quality presentation vehicles to communicate findings like summary reports, graphs, spreadsheets, models, web sites, etc.
Frustration arising from doing grunt work	Value added to customers via improved relationships based on benefits that you bring to their business, and the ability to teach them something that they did not know

(continued)

Table 10.1 Continued

LESS BAD STUFF	MORE GOOD STUFF
Miscommunication of information because of lack of understanding of that information	Faster results—daily or weekly—that are more in time with marketplace dynamics
Erroneous assumptions about the data's relationships	Company integration and cohesiveness from everyone using the same data, and sharing information, key findings, and successes
Data transcription errors (mis-keying entries)	Sales—as positive trends are capitalized on, and negative trends are minimized
Confusion from consulting too few (or too many) sources of information	Profit—as products, promotions, and customers are rationalized, and as the costs associated with processing information is reduced
Cost, in terms of hours spent typing, calculating, and reporting information	The time saved by entering data once and reusing it multiple ways
Paper waste and costs used for printing standard reports that are obsolete as soon as they are delivered	The ability to have instant electronic access to online, up-to-date data

What Users Can Do with a Data Warehouse

The next thing to consider is what users can, or should, do with the data you provide them. This is likely to be different than what you think. Transforming an organization into an information-centric office is more than providing data and having it available. It involves using that information effectively.

There are two primary ways to retrieve data from a data warehouse: standard reporting and ad-hoc analysis.

Standard Reporting

Standard reporting involves providing users with pre-retrieved, pre-processed information. It involves the attempt to speed up analysis by having a computer run, on behalf of the user, analyses that don't change over time. These analyses are generally quick to run, but inflexible in nature.

Standard reports can be an asset to an organization because they limit the choice for users when it comes to researching decisions. By telling the users what they should be looking at, the designer of the standard reports removes the burden of deciding what is important and what is not. Users can only look at certain data in certain ways. This data is brought to the user's attention quickly and efficiently, generally at the click of a button or two.

Problems with Standard Reporting

Although standard reports are an efficient way to retrieve fixed information, they do present several problems.

First, taking into account the chaotic, fast-paced environment in which most businesses operate, standard reports potentially become a drag on organizational effectiveness. Any benefit gained by fast data retrieval is lost to the inflexibility of the reporting environment. Standard reports are based on yesterday's issues. When a report is built, it is built at a point in time, with particular business issues in mind. They are also used at a point in time that is different than when they are built. In other words, someone builds reports, then a user uses them from that point on. Therefore, reports are built for historical issues. Given the nature of the business environment, and the speed of change, reports that are built based on yesterday's news are usually not relevant for more than a fleeting instance.

The second problem associated with standard reporting is that reports are generally plagued with the "broken-telephone" syndrome. The person who builds the report is normally not the person who needs to use it. The user of the information describes the nature of the report. Someone else takes these specifications and attempts to build a report out of them. The draft of the report is given to the user for approval. Because of the inefficient nature of human communication, the report builder usually doesn't get it right on the first try, and is sent off to add some enhancements. This iterative cycle continues until one of three things happen:

1. The builder gets it right.
2. The business need for the report has changed, making the current report obsolete.
3. The report builder gets pulled onto another project, and the report is never completed.

The fact that different categories of users have different business needs presents the third problem with standard reporting. The head of the engineering department has very different needs for marketing and competitive intelligence reports than the head of the marketing department. A standard report designed to meet the needs of multiple categories of users will almost certainly meet the needs of none of them.

Finally, users will almost never feel confident that they have all of the information that they require, no matter how many reports are built. There are always other factors to look at, other ways to approach the data, or other questions that are brought up by an existing report, but which are not addressed by it. Users rely so heavily on the report writer that they become a support burden. It is the report writer that must react every time another question comes up, and of course, other questions always come up.

Ad-Hoc Analysis

A more efficient approach for data retrieval is to make users self-sufficient for their information needs. This is *ad-hoc analysis*. Providing them with the data in the form of a data warehouse is the first step. The next steps involve giving them the tools and the knowledge to handle their own information requirements.

The Right Tools

Earlier in this book, we discussed the fundamental principles of a good data warehouse implementation. We described how a data warehouse relies heavily on the quality of the data access and analysis technology in the desktop environment. Collectively called Business Intelligence (BI) technology, this quality of the desktop tools can make the difference between a data warehouse that is used and a data warehouse that is mothballed.

Selecting Business Intelligence Technology

A successful selection of business intelligence technology requires an understanding of several issues from a business perspective. When selecting the tools your users will use, ask yourself these questions:

1. Can the user follow a typical analysis path—start at the big picture and work down towards the specifics?
2. Can the user look at the data from multiple perspectives?
3. Can the user frequently change their mind when looking at the data?

4. Can the tool retrieve at the "speed of thought"?

5. Are the tools mobile, allowing the user to work from a customer site, home, the road, and so on?

6. Can the tools export information to spreadsheets, or link the analysis to presentation tools?

7. Do the tools contain features that help in analyzing information such as exception reporting, ranking, graphing, and so on?

8. Are the tools simple to use, but powerful enough to be consistently relevant?

9. Can the tools suggest what is relevant in the information like automated data mining?

10. Do the tools allow for custom calculations that are not currently in the data set?

11. Can a user easily build cross-tabs, and nested cross-tabs?

Answering "no" to any of these questions casts a negative light on the data warehouse implementation because users demand these benefits.

Multi-Dimensional versus Relational

If you look at the types of analyses and reports created by knowledge workers, several factors become apparent. First, views of information are generally cross-tab in nature. They compare one data element in relation to another data element in the rows and columns of the report. Common reports include products by time, channel, and channel by time, which are all cross-tab style reports.

Second, typical analyses are normally at a high level of detail. Summaries of the year, product groupings—department, brand; customer groupings—region, customer type, channel, and so on are the norm. The only exception to this rule is a ranking report. Ranking reports start at a low level of detail, but eventually the information that is important jumps to the top of the list. Ranking reports are described in greater detail in the next section.

Third, there are often calculations in the rows or columns of the analysis. Calculating segment sub-totals, percent change between periods, or share/importance of the business are important to the users.

Finally, while not often used, graphical displays of information usually appeal to end-users and organizations should explore the use of more graphics in their analyses.

Relational-database queries are sufficient for list style reports. Displaying a list of records that meet a specific series of conditions (filters), organized according to values on the report (groupings or sorting), with sub totals are the traditional type of results from a relational query. These list style reports are only a fraction of the information views demanded by the end-users.

Since cross-tabs are one dimension crossed against another, displayed in rows and columns, multi-dimensional databases allow for quick and efficient creation of cross-tab reports. The concept of drill-down normally associated to multi-dimensional databases allows for a top-down approach to reporting. Rows and columns can easily be calculated using this type of technology by targeting specific categories contained within a dimension. Finally, most multi-dimensional clients allow for fast creation of graphical displays, with interactivity that allows a user to drill-down and pivot those graphs quickly and efficiently.

It becomes apparent, given these similarities in information views that a business user relates more to multi-dimensional analysis tools than to query tools. Business users can easily perform the kinds of analyses they require using multi-dimensional analysis tools because of the way these tools look at information.

Creating an Information-Centric Analysis

The final step to a successful implementation of a data warehouse is the knowledge of how to use the data contained in that warehouse. The following section details the criteria for an effective information analysis, and presents a few helpful ideas about some different types of analyses.

Fact-based decision making evolves an understanding of market conditions at the time decisions are made. It requires a flexible, quick, and powerful analytical process that will lead the decision-maker towards an understanding of the marketplace. It involves doing an *information-centric analysis*.

The reality, however, is that many companies have not, to date, performed information-centric analyses. Instead, they've concentrated on the collection and distribution of information, not on the digestion of said information. The reasons are simple—digesting information requires the knowledge of how to find the critical elements hidden in corporate data, and the time to sort those issues out. You need to know what data is important to look at and when, and what is not. To use a mining example, you need to separate the gold from the slag. Information-centric analyses are the cornerstone to effective data analysis.

The solution to the problem plaguing companies today lies in teaching people how to do an effective, information-centric analysis. With these skills, employees can make better, fact-based decisions without wasting a lot of time looking at non-relevant information.

Myths About Average Users

Throughout this book there has been much talk of "users". They are, in fact, the reason why data warehouses are built in the first place. However, without an understanding of what drives an end-user, the data warehouse cannot meet its intended goals.

While it is impossible to accurately define every end-user, there are several common misconceptions about them. Some of these misconceptions are shown in Table 10.2.

Table 10.2 Myth versus Fact Regarding End-Users

Myth	Users like features. They like all of the bells and whistles that come with software, and are attracted to a software package that offers the best set of these features.
Fact	Users are attracted to *benefits*. Unless the user knows how the software package will help them do their job better and/or faster they are not interested.
Myth	Users know how to analyze information.
Fact	Users don't know what an effective data analysis is, because nobody has taught them how to do an effective data analysis.
Myth	Users have time to explore and analyze issues.
Fact	Users have absolutely no free time to do anything except breath. Unless they can explore data quickly, and in such a way that it derives a more in-depth understanding of their business, they are not interested.
Myth	Users don't mind waiting for answers.
Fact	Because the business environment changes so quickly, users cannot wait for periodic data downloads, batch runs of reports, or scheduled delivery of answers. They want information as soon as there is a need to use it. They want "speed-of-thought" answers to ad-hoc questions.

(continued)

Table 10.2 Continued

Myth	Users like reports.
Fact	Users like anything that provides the answers to the ever-changing set of questions they have. As soon as a report cannot supply the answers they are looking for, the love affair is over. Because reports answer "yesterday's" questions, users become disenchanted with them very quickly.
Myth	Users like it when answers are handed to them.
Fact	Interestingly enough, users are rarely happy when an answer is handed to them. They want to know how the answer was produced, verify the numbers, and change the question on purpose, just to exercise control over the situation. Users want to control the information themselves.
Myth	Users understand databases.
Fact	Users understand business. Databases are a technical thing. They tend to understand how databases can help them in their business, but not what that database is.
Myth	Users can be easily taught to program in such languages as SQL, for example.
Fact	SQL is a complicated language to teach a non-programmer. If given the choice, many users would rather use a graphical tool to build analyses, and not a programming language.

As you can see, addressing the needs of users is a complicated process. They want instant answers to constantly-changing questions. How they use technology relates to the benefits it provides, not the features contained in the technology. How they use data also relates to the benefits they derive from it, not in how fast they received it.

Therefore, your data warehouse implementation has to keep these criteria in mind. Providing users with data, or reports, is not good enough. The users need lots of flexible control to build ad-hoc analyses, and expect sub-second response time. A data warehouse implementation that does not take this into account is doomed to failure.

Now that we have an understanding about what a data warehouse is, how it can benefit end-users, and what those end-users want, we can now turn our attention to defining the criteria for an effective information analysis. This is the one piece of the puzzle that is often overlooked when implementing a data warehouse. Most end-users don't know how to analyze data effectively, and therefore will likely not derive many benefits from the data warehouse unless the concepts of effective information analysis are presented to them.

Information-Centric Analysis

As discussed earlier, creating an effective system for multi-dimensional data analysis is the cornerstone for making effective business decisions. Making effective business decisions is at the cornerstone of a successful data warehouse implementation. Creating this effective analysis requires an understanding of five key concepts, or facets of an effective analysis. These five concepts are collectively referred to as an *information-centric analysis* and described in Table 10.3.

Information-centric analysis is simply a methodology you can use to make fact-based decisions. It can guide you towards an understanding of significant factors embedded in data by outlining the criteria for effective information analysis. It can help you improve the bottom line by taking the guesswork out of decision making, and can make the time your users spend analyzing data more efficient. With these concepts in place, a person has the intellectual tools necessary to do effective information-centric analysis. We now explore each of the five concepts in greater detail.

Benchmarking

Benchmarking compares one fact to another. It implies that a fact in isolation does not mean very much, until you relate it to something else. If you know that your volume is up 100 percent versus a year ago, is that good? Most people would say yes, but, in truth, it really depends. What if the market was up 500 percent, you would be losing ground (the market would be outpacing you). What if a competitor is up 500 percent? What if the plan called for 500 percent growth? What if the year before

Table 10.3 Information-Centric Analysis Processes

PROCESS	DESCRIPTION
Benchmarking	Compare a tracking variable to something else.
Limiting	Look deeper and deeper at specifics, and keep the analysis simple, by looking at one issue at a time.
Highlighting	Cause answers to jump out.
Trending	Indicate what may happen in the future, or is happening in the present, based on what happened in the past.
Communicating	Present data in a way that everyone can understand.

last you were up 500 percent? Knowing a fact in isolation is not enough. You have to be able to compare performance to a benchmark.

Potential Benchmarks

There are good and bad benchmarks. When selecting a benchmark, you must be careful to choose something that compares reasonably to the variable you are tracking. A meaningful benchmark is one that contains some similarities to the variable you are tracking.

A benchmark can be almost anything. A number of potential benchmarks are described in Table 10.4.

What Is a Good Benchmark?

There are no hard-and-fast rules when it comes to selecting a benchmark. As discussed, a benchmark can be anything that proves a point.

Table 10.4   Potential Benchmarks

BENCHMARK CLASS	DESCRIPTION
A competitive or similar product	Compare one brand's performance to another, particularly if that benchmark brand is a competitor or, at least, within the same industry or target segment.
Time	Compare the variable you are tracking to itself, looking at changes between periods. Reasonable comparison time periods are 1. Versus a year ago 2. Versus the previous period 3. Versus the average of several periods such as the last 12 months, or fiscal year-to-date.
Targets	Compare performance versus expected performance (plan, budget, etc.). This is likely the best benchmark because it conveys what needs to be done to achieve expectations. However, target information is rarely used in benchmarking because it is usually unavailable, or unavailable at the same level of detail that the tracking variable is at. For example, budgets are generally created at a yearly level, but monthly tracking of performance is important, which makes it difficult to relate the two.
Other levels	Compare performance to performance in a higher level of detail. For example, comparing brand performance to performance of the company, a segment, or a package size, etc. as a whole.

The only rule that comes into play when selecting a benchmark is that the benchmark must effectively communicate performance of the tracking variable by looking at it when compared to something similar.

A Sample Analysis Using a Benchmark

Figure 10.1 illustrates an analysis that uses three benchmarks.

Limiting

Limiting examines increasingly-detailed points of data, in order to investigate the root causes of performance hidden in the data. Limiting helps you to understand the underlying issues that are not apparent when looking at summary information. Many people also refer to limiting as *drilling down.*

Starting with summary information gives us an overview of *what* has happened, but does not tell us *why* it happened. Looking deeper into the data allows us to see the detail behind the summary information.

However, if you start to look at the root causes behind all summary items, you can easily waste a lot of time. The key is to investigate the

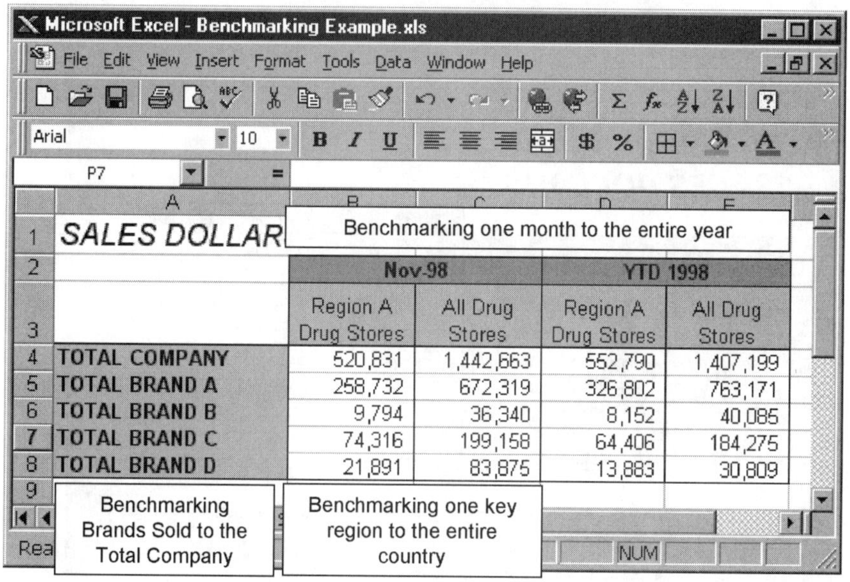
Microsoft Excel - Benchmarking Example.xls
File Edit View Insert Format Tools Data Window Help
Arial
10
P7
SALES DOLLAR
Benchmarking one month to the entire year
Nov-98
YTD 1998
Region A Drug Stores
All Drug Stores
Region A Drug Stores
All Drug Stores
TOTAL COMPANY 520,831 1,442,663 552,790 1,407,199
TOTAL BRAND A 258,732 672,319 326,802 763,171
TOTAL BRAND B 9,794 36,340 8,152 40,085
TOTAL BRAND C 74,316 199,158 64,406 184,275
TOTAL BRAND D 21,891 83,875 13,883 30,809
Benchmarking Brands Sold to the Total Company
Benchmarking one key region to the entire country
NUM

Figure 10.1 Benchmarking analysis example.

detail behind a summary item that catches your attention (for whatever reason), and divorce yourself from the other summary items. This involves *limiting* your analysis.

There are two important things to remember when limiting for effective analysis. First, focus on the specifics, without losing sight of the big picture. Look at the detail behind a summary item, but keep the summary item in your analysis. Second, limit the data in your analysis. As you drill down on a specific issue, it's tempting to keep your eye on the other issues that you haven't drilled down yet. People often try to build reports that contain detail for all possible issues, cramming them on to a couple of pages. It's important to focus on one data issue at a time.

An Example of an Analysis Using Limiting

Figure 10.2 illustrates an example of an effective analysis using limiting. Notice how the analysis starts at a high level of detail, and with each

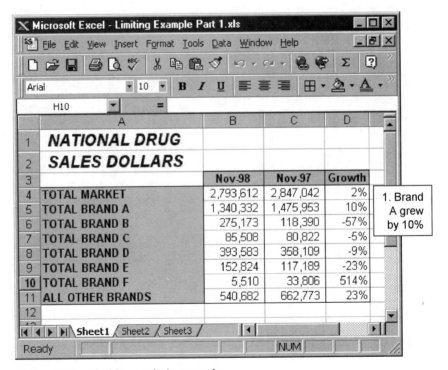

Figure 10.2 Limiting analysis example.

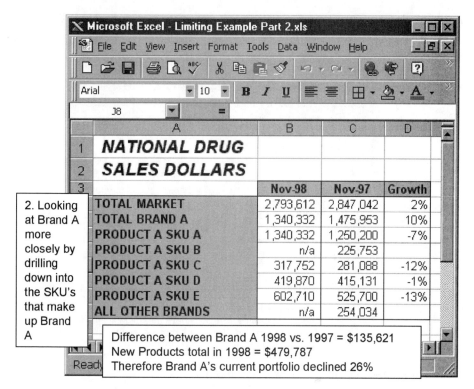

Figure 10.3 Drilling down.

iteration, looks at lower and lower levels of detail. The example does not try to analyze what occurs in the entire data set. It only tries to explain the suspect performance of Brand A.

We now focus our attention on one specific brand—Brand A—however we still maintain the Total Market benchmark, as illustrated in Figure 10.3.

In Figure 10.4 we focus our attention on one specific SKU—SKU E—and look at this SKU from a different perspective. For now we won't try to look at other SKUs, but will wait until we've fully explored this one.

Now let's look at one SKU in a couple of markets (See Figure 10.5). We want to keep the scope of our data set small, and fully explore it. However, it's important to benchmark items to check for relevance. In this case, one of the benchmarks we use is a region.

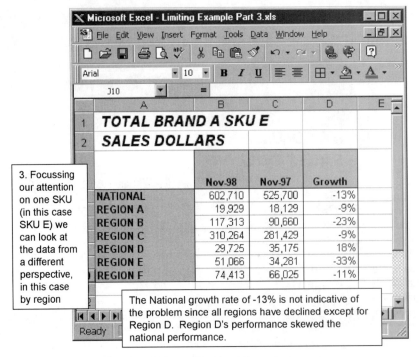

Figure 10.4 Pivoting to analyze SKU by region.

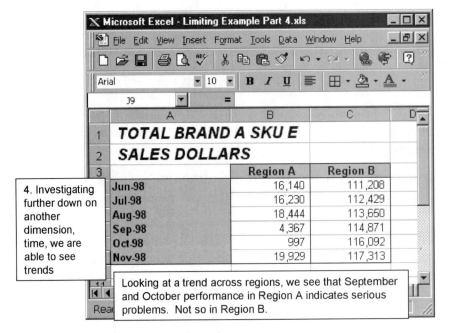

Figure 10.5 Identifying regional trends.

Highlighting

Highlighting brings to light the key issues found in the data. By employing highlighting concepts, it becomes very obvious what you should focus your attention on, and what is safe to ignore. Highlighting takes analysis a step beyond a report. It is the evolution into a synthesized piece of information that draws the reader towards an effective decision.

There are three types of highlighting concepts: ranking, exception reporting, and segmenting. Within each of these concepts there are also several analysis sub-categories that can be performed as shown in Tables 10.5 to 10.7.

Table 10.5 Ranking Sub-Categories

SUB-CATEGORY	DESCRIPTION
General	Sort a set of rows in an analysis from highest to lowest, or vice versa based on a specified piece of information found in a column.
Single Column	Add rank numbers that indicate which item is first, second, etc.
Multi-Column	Add in a second column of rank numbers that indicate the rank of a benchmark column.
With Limits	Limit the analysis to the top or bottom X.

Table 10.6 Exception Reporting Sub-Categories

SUB-CATEGORY	DESCRIPTION
General	Color code an analysis based on specified criteria.
Winners and Losers	Indicate in a specific color those products where growth is greater than zero.
Different Than Benchmark	Indicate in a specific color those items that are significantly different than a benchmark—+ or − 10% off the benchmark.
Rank Difference	Indicate in a specific color those items that have their first-rank column different from the second rank column in a multi-column ranking analysis.

Table 10.7   Segmenting Sub-Categories

SUB-CATEGORY	DESCRIPTION
General	Group rows of information together that meet a specified condition by adding a column into your analysis, and sort or group on that column.
Classifying	Add a column into your analysis that indicates if something is good or bad news. An example of this is to add in a column "Good News" if growth is over X%, and "Bad News" otherwise.
Sizing	Add in a column that indicates whether or not a sale is good or bad. An example of this is to add in a column "Big Sale" if a sale is larger than $X and "Small Sale" otherwise.

An Example of an Analysis Using Highlighting

Figure 10.6 shows an analysis using highlighting and illustrates three of the highlighting concepts: exception reporting, multi-column ranking, and ranking with limits.

As you can see from Figure 10.6, highlighting makes the negative growth of SKU B and SKU E readily apparent.

Trending

Trending allows you to see what has led up to a certain situation. By looking at the history of an issue, you can better understand the reasons why

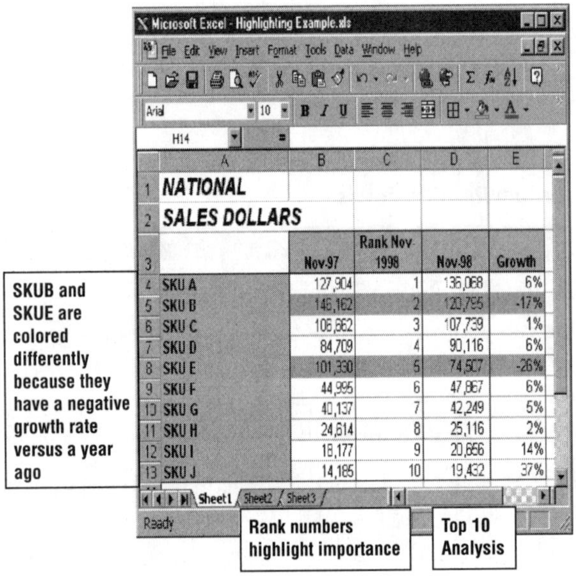

Figure 10.6   Highlighting analysis example.

something happened. Knowing the past experiences of a situation will also help you make a more accurate determination about what will happen in the future. Trending is also useful to see the causes of events. Looking back in time allows you to see a picture of events as they unfold. It is particularly useful when factors in the marketplace, besides performance, are relatively static—things aren't changing too much, or are changing at regular intervals, so you can isolate performance from the other external influences.

You can trend any type of periodic data, including hourly, daily, weekly, or monthly statistics. The finer the level of detail, the more data you need to see a true trend.

You must be careful to not get overzealous with the length of trend you look at. The more number of periods you use, the more confusing your analysis can become.

Types of Trend Analysis

Many types of trend analysis are possible. The major categories are described in Table 10.8.

Table 10.8 Trend Analysis Categories

TYPE OF TREND	DESCRIPTION
Simple Trend	An analysis that shows each period's data over a set of periods, displaying seasonal[1] irregularities,[2] and all.
Rolling Trend	An analysis that adds a new period to the end, and drops the oldest period from the beginning. Therefore there is always the same number of periods in the analysis. For every new period added, an old period is dropped. The term *rolling* implies that the trend period rolls forward in time, but does not get bigger.
Gain Analysis	An analysis that subtracts the current period's data from the previous year's data, for each period available, and trends the gain/loss over time. An example of this is a trend of (Jan 96 minus Jan 95), (Dec 95 minus Dec 94), (Nov 95 minus Nov 94), etc. This is an interesting analysis that shows improvement rates over time.
Smoothing Trend	An analysis that creates an average over a time period in the past, for each period available and then trends the average. An example of this is a trend of (the average of Jan 95 to Jan 1996), (the average of Dec 94 to Dec 95), (the average of Nov 94 to Nov 95), etc. This analysis shows a trend that smoothes the seasonality in the data, and shows a true trend irrespective of period-over-period blips.

[1]Seasonal is a factor of trend analysis that shows patterns in performance depending on the time of year. This pattern repeats itself each and every year. For example, sales of sun tan lotion are very seasonal because each summer, sales shoot up.

[2]Irregularities occur when something new occurs in the marketplace, and causes a change in the trend. Significant increases in advertising expenditures, for example, affect sales and cause trend irregularities if similar expenditures are not carried on each year.

Trend Period

Generally, it's a good idea to trend over a period of time where market conditions remain relatively constant. However, there is usually little need to look at a trend longer than three years. Trending over more than three years is unreliable because there are too many variables that can change over the trend period.

Displaying Trends

Trends display best as a line graph. Showing a trend as a series of numbers makes it difficult to see the patterns in the trend.

An Example of a Trend Analysis

Figure 10.7 illustrates two trend analyses.

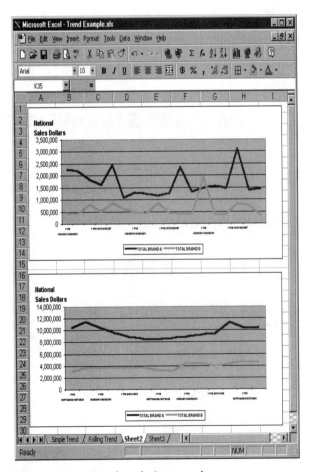

Figure 10.7 Trend analysis example.

The Rolling-6-Period Trend sums the six previous periods together in order to smooth the trend, and to remove the period-to-period spikes. In Figure 10.7, less periods are used in the rolling trend analysis because fewer periods are available to sum.

Notice that the "Rolling-6-Period-Trend" graph is smoother than the "Simple-Trend" graph. It's easier to see the absolute trend in the second graph.

WARNING

One caveat about trending: just because something happened in the past does not necessarily mean that it will continue to happen in the future. As described earlier, marketplaces change very quickly. History cannot always be an indication of performance. If the external factors that affect performance change on a frequent basis, or are about to change dramatically, then trend becomes less relevant.

Take for example a situation where a competitor decides to go on a marketing blitz, and floods the airwaves with television commercials. Their goal is to increase share by increasing advertising expenditures. In this case, trend analysis is not effective because something has happened to cause a disruption in the trend. The increased expenditures from the competitor's advertising causes a blip in your performance, which makes comparing today's performance to yesterday's less relevant.

Communicating

Finally, you can cap off an effective information-centric analysis by *communicating* your findings to other stakeholders who are affected by your decision. In general, this means making your analyses extremely easy to read.

Making analyses easy to read is very important. In fact, even the best analysis, that conveys the perfect piece of information, will not lead to effective business decisions if the decision-maker is unable to understand the work. Analyses that are not easy to read are also prone to misinterpretation. Therefore, it is critical to cap off a good, information-centric analysis with a well-presented, easy-to-read analysis.

You can create an easy-to-read analysis by using the five points described in Table 10.9.

With the five facets of an information-centric analysis in place, users can get an in-depth understanding of the data. With this understanding, they are better armed to make effective business decisions.

Table 10.9 Easy-to-Read Analysis Points

ANALYSIS POINT	DESCRIPTION
Make issues obvious	An easy-to-read analysis is one where the issues you want to communicate jump right out. By employing different fonts, colors, bordering, and shading, you can draw a reader's attention to the issues of the analysis.
Indicate assumptions	The analysis must indicate all of the pertinent information. A reader should know exactly where the analysis came from. By putting assumptions into the titles, headers, footers, or text boxes, a reader can understand all of the assumptions that are made, and which may affect future decisions.
Label report elements	Everything on an analysis must be labeled. All scales, measures, and so on must be visible to the reader.
Use common terms	It is a good idea for analyses to contain the language commonly used within the company. Terms like "profit", "share", "sales", etc. are usually prone to misinterpretation. For example, does "profit" mean net of taxes or not?
Use graphs	It is generally better to show an analysis graphically than numerically. People can digest information found in graphs faster than information found in tables. Elements like trends and benchmarks show best as graphs.

Likewise, users are not burdened with developing an increased understanding of data. Conducting an information-centric analysis saves time because it focuses the user on an analysis path that will likely pay off. Little time is wasted exploring irrelevant issues, and insights become apparent very quickly.

With this in mind, we can now turn to different analysis types that utilize the concepts of an information-centric analysis.

Multi-Dimensional Data Analysis

Now that we understand what an information-centric analysis is, we can explore various types of analysis that are possible when these concepts are put to use.

The following section deals with some interesting types of analysis that are valuable but not often performed in companies. View them as examples or different ideas to employ when conducting an information-centric analysis.

Seven different types of multi-dimensional data analysis are discussed in this section. They are:

1. Growth Trend
2. Importance
3. Customer Retention
4. Shopping Basket
5. Over-and-Under Developed
6. Dual Ranking
7. Industry Benchmark

Each of these data analysis explores multi-dimensional databases in a unique way, and yields valuable insights into the data. Each analysis type allows a user to look below the surface issues, exploring what is really going on in the data.

Growth Trend Analysis

To prove that sales of one product are consistently growing faster than other similar products, one can do a *Growth Trend Analysis*. A growth trend analysis takes each product or a product grouping's total performance in a given period, calculates a percent change versus the prior year, and trends those growth rates. Period-over-period percent change—called growth—is calculated according to the formula: Current Period – Older Period/Older Period.

For an example, let's take a look at the graph in Figure 10.8.

This graph shows an analysis that calculates the growth, or percent change, between each quarter and its prior-year quarter and then graphs the results. First 1998 Q1 is subtracted from 1997 Q1, and then that result is divided by 1997 Q1 to get a growth rate. Then 1998 Q2 is subtracted from 1997 Q2, and then that result is divided by 1997 Q2 to get a growth rate, and so on. These results are then graphed to see the trend of growth rates.

Growth trends illustrate something very interesting. They illustrate the pace of change for a given product or set of products. Products with a positive trend in growth rates are growing faster and faster, which illustrates more than a static, one-period change. We can then benchmark one product's pace of change to another to see which products accelerate.

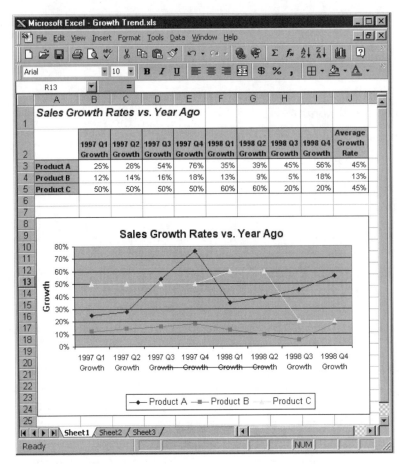

Figure 10.8 Growth trend example.

Products with accelerating growth will likely continue to do well as momentum carries the product forward in the short to medium term. Products with accelerating declines need immediate attention.

An extension to this type of analysis is to actually calculate the growth rate of the growth rates. In this case, we calculate the percent change between the newer and older growth rates. Calculating the growth of growth rates gives us an indication of the pace of change in a numerical format.

Importance Analysis

In order to prove that a given department has become more important to a company as a whole, one can do an *Importance Analysis*. An importance analysis determines how significant one set of products is to a higher level of benchmark like an entire department or company. The term *importance* is also known as *share*. In this case we calculate the importance or share of business a set of products has on the entire department or company.

To calculate product importance, we take one product's performance and divide it into total performance. We can then benchmark the product's performance to other products, and for comparison purposes, across time as illustrated in Figure 10.9.

Notice from the analysis shown in Figure 10.9 that Product A has become increasingly important to the company as a whole. True, Product B's performance is also strong, but not as strong as Product A. Product A's importance to the company increased faster than Product B.

One interesting use of this type of analysis is at performance review time. A case can be made that the product manager of Product A should be compensated more than other products because Product A has become more important to the company as a whole. More important means more resources, more responsibility, and more compensation.

The opposite is also true. A department with a lower share of expenses (department expenses divided by the total company expenses) year over year performs better (presumably) than its counterparts.

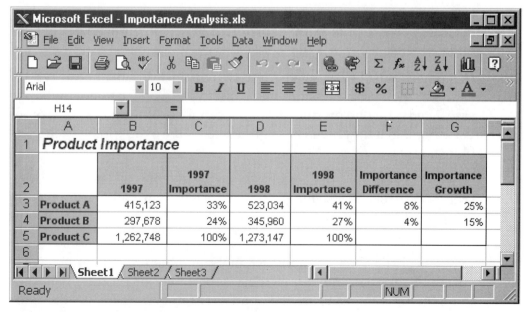

Figure 10.9 Importance analysis example.

Another way to use this type of analysis is when looking at a customer's business. A customer that has become increasingly important to the company—as a percentage of the company's total business—should be monitored. A customer with increasing importance to the company is not necessarily a good thing. A company that has too much business concentrated in the hands of a few customers is very vulnerable to demands by those customers.

If the figures are available however, it is extremely interesting to know what percentage of your customer's business you supply. If you sell to a retailer, for example, it is valuable to know what percentage of their purchases (in a given category) is given to you. If you find out that you supply an extremely high percentage of a given category, then this gives you negotiating clout when setting prices, discounts, and so on.

Customer Retention Analysis

In order to prove that customers enjoy dealing with a company or department you can perform a *Customer Retention Analysis*. A customer retention analysis benchmarks the trend of customer sales in one product to another.

To do a customer retention analysis, you need to look at the average customer's sales trend, and benchmark this trend to another product or group of products. You start with producing two lines of data. The first trend line is the average of all customers who bought a particular product, the second line is the average of all of customers who bought another product.

Customers must be segregated into two distinct groups. In this type of analysis, the two groups are mutually exclusive. Customers who are associated with one product grouping cannot be part of the other product grouping. If they are in both groups, then the overlapping customers blur the analysis.

Customers can be segregated based on many criteria. The segregating criteria are irrelevant, so long as it is consistent. Normally, customers are segregated based on a perception of which product a customer buys most often.

First you create a trend for all customers, and then calculate an average customer, grouped into appropriate department or product. You then graph these averages to see the trend over time.

Notice in Figure 10.10 that the gap between Product A's average customer's dollar volume and Product B's is growing. Product A's customers tend to buy more than Product B's, and the gap is widening. Product B's customers are not loyal, in the sense that their dollar purchases tend to decrease. This is very important to the long-term survival of the company as a whole. Having a customer base that increased its purchases over time helps to insure the overall success of the company.

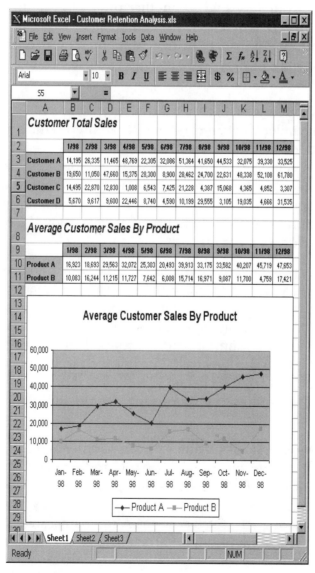

Figure 10.10   Customer retention analysis example.

Shopping Basket Analysis

Knowing that an average customer buys more than another customer is one thing, but most customers tend to buy more than one product at one time. To see the interaction of customers relative to multiple-product purchases, you can do a *Shopping Basket Analysis*.

A shopping basket analysis looks at the average size of a customer's *total* purchases when a given product was purchased, versus the average size of a customer's *total* purchases when another product was purchased. The issue is not as simple as a customer retention analysis because often customers buy multiple products at one time, making it difficult to segregate them into mutually exclusive groups. Often it's the overlapped purchases that are important to both groups.

The concept of a shopping basket analysis is something that is particularly important to retailers. Retailers often sell certain products at a loss (below cost) in order to stimulate sales in general. This concept is called *creating a loss leader*. A loss leader is a product whose profit is sacrificed in order to stimulate sales of other products. Looking at the transactions as they pass through the checkout scanner yields valuable insights. A retailer can look at the size or profitability of a transaction if a particular product was included in that sale.

An example of this is the selling of diapers. Diapers are often sold at a loss in order to bring Moms and Dads into the store. Presumably, Moms and Dads buy other products—film, baby accessories, infant formula, etc.—which are more profitable than diapers. Therefore, the total shopping basket purchased by Mom or Dad is profitable in the aggregate, even if the diapers are sold below cost. The question is, how profitable is that entire basket, and would it be more profitable if diapers were not sold at a loss, or if discounting other products could stimulate profits even more.

The concept of a shopping basket analysis can be extended to a manufacturer as well. Customers buy many types of products. For any given purchase, there can be multiple products on a given invoice. If we treat the invoice as a transaction, it can be used in the same way as a shopping basket going through the retail scanner. A company can look at the size or profitability of an invoice if a particular product was included in that sale.

To do a shopping basket analysis, you need to examine transaction-level data, summarized to a very high level of detail, according to multiple criteria. To look at tremendous amounts of data at the aggregate level, according to multiple factors, is something that is ideally done in a multi-dimensional database.

The first step is to determine which customers bought a given product, Product A (whether or not they bought Product B) and which customers bought Product B (whether or not they bought Product A). You start with the transaction data, and retool the data in a particular way. Using a query tool we can manipulate the data before it's brought into a multi-dimensional analysis tool.

You need to get to the point where you have a query that looks something like Figure 10.11.

Figure 10.11 shows a query that lists sales transactions at the atomic or lowest level of detail. In the case of a retailer, sales are indicated at the

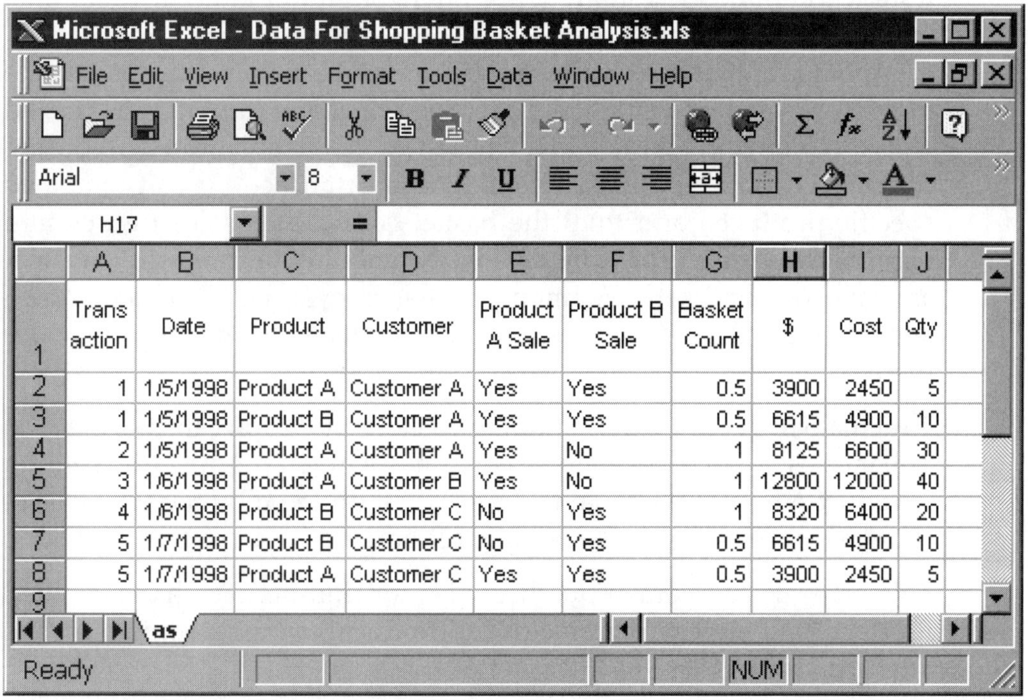

Microsoft Excel - Data For Shopping Basket Analysis.xls

	Trans action	Date	Product	Customer	Product A Sale	Product B Sale	Basket Count	$	Cost	Qty
1										
2	1	1/5/1998	Product A	Customer A	Yes	Yes	0.5	3900	2450	5
3	1	1/5/1998	Product B	Customer A	Yes	Yes	0.5	6615	4900	10
4	2	1/5/1998	Product A	Customer A	Yes	No	1	8125	6600	30
5	3	1/6/1998	Product A	Customer B	Yes	No	1	12800	12000	40
6	4	1/6/1998	Product B	Customer C	No	Yes	1	8320	6400	20
7	5	1/7/1998	Product B	Customer C	No	Yes	0.5	6615	4900	10
8	5	1/7/1998	Product A	Customer C	Yes	Yes	0.5	3900	2450	5
9										

Figure 10.11 Shopping basket analysis example.

transaction level, or, in other words, at the "products-passing-through-the-scanner" level. In the case of a manufacturer, it is at the invoice-line level, or, in other words, at the "products-passing-through-the-company" level.

The query is flagged according to a point-in-time transaction. The first column indicates customer purchases, which can contain multiple entries. Notice that some numbers are repeated due to multiple items purchased.

Two fields are added to the query. They are used to flag whether or not a transaction contained a product or not. A second query is used to uniquely identify transaction numbers (the first column) if they have a particular product. This second query is then joined to the main query. We are left with a set of rows that indicate all rows of transactions, if any of those rows contain a particular product. The process is then repeated across all products that you need to track. The fields entitled "Product A Sale" and "Product B Sale" are examples of these kinds of columns.

Finally, a field is added to the query that counts customers (or baskets). To do this, you divide the number "1" by a count of rows, grouped by transaction number. You are left with a column of either a 1, or some fraction of the number 1 that, when you add together the fractions, you get a count for that basket. The goal is to count each purchase as a single purchase, even if it contained more than one item. The column is called "Basket Count" in Figure 10.11. Once the data is transformed according to these criteria, you can then isolate specific transactions that contained specific products, and total the basket counts and sales figures into higher levels of information. Taking the data into a multi-dimensional analysis tool, and setting, amongst other things, the "Product A Sale" and "Product B Sale" columns as dimensions, you can easily produce these totals.

To actually investigate the shopping basket results you can take the total dollar sales of purchases, which contained a given product (the column "Product A Sale" was equal to "Yes"), and divide it by the total basket count of purchases, which contained Product A.

This gives us an average purchase size for transactions that contained Product A. Repeating the process for Product B, you get something like what you see in Figure 10.12.

Looking at these results yields two insights. First, when looking at 1998, the average purchase when Product A was in the basket was $4.81

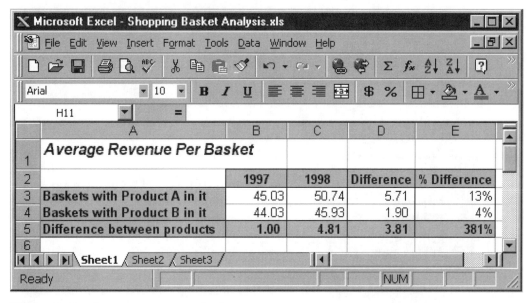

Figure 10.12   Average revenue per basket.

higher than when Product B was in the basket. Second, the gap between the two scenarios has widened over time. It seems that customers who bought Product A were more valuable in their entirety than customers who bought Product B. It would be good for the company to encourage customers to buy more of Product A, because when they do they tend to buy more in general.

Over-and-Under Developed Products Analysis

In order to prove that there are opportunities for future improvement in sales of a given product, you can look at performance by region, versus the company as a whole, in terms of a percentage of sales. This illustrates the potential areas for improvement (or lack thereof).

To conduct an Over-and-Under Developed Product Analysis you need to take a series of regional sales and divide it into the total for all regions. You obtain a regional importance (similar to a product importance analysis) by product. In order to benchmark product performance across region, you can include the total company.

The analysis in Figure 10.13 indicates there is room for improvement for Product A in Region B and Region C. Product A sales were under-

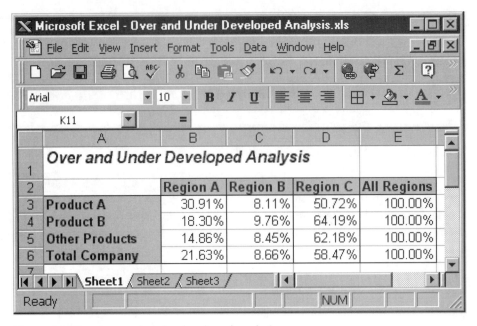

Figure 10.13 Over and under developed analysis.

developed in these regions, because these regions accounted for a lower percentage of sales for Product A then they did for the company as a whole. For instance, Region C accounted for only 50.72% of sales for Product A, but 58.47% for the company as a whole. Product A could have done better in Knottingham if benchmarked to the entire company, so there was room to grow. In the same region, Product B's performance was overdeveloped because they sold a disproportionate amount in this region versus other regions compared to sales for the company as a whole.

The fact that a region is underdeveloped is simply an indication for improved performance, not an absolute in and of itself. There can be good reason why a region is underdeveloped. For example, a clothing company may be underdeveloped in terms of bathing suit sales to Canada in January, compared to the entire company sales to Canada in January if the company sells both heavy and light clothes. Underdevelopment with respect to bathing suits in Canada for January is unlikely to be an opportunity for improved performance because most smart Canadians don't purchase too many bathing suits at that time of year, unless they're vacationing to a warm locale.

The opposite is also true. A region can be overdeveloped for a good reason as well. A company can have a strong customer base in a region (perhaps their home region), which is not necessarily a problem. A region can be more profitable to sell in (take for example a region with relatively low distribution costs), and therefore it's worthwhile to be overdeveloped. Overdevelopment is not necessarily a problem, but something to keep an eye on.

The argument for potential performance improvements from under-development is a particularly powerful argument to make with custo-mers. If a customer's share of business is lower in a particular customer versus the market to which that customer belongs, then a case can be made to that customer that there is reason why their share of business differs within the customer versus outside the customer. Possible reasons for underdevelopment include a lack of advertising, poor consumer pricing, other buying incentives, or simply a stock—out situation—the customer does not buy enough to satisfy market demand. Saying that your customer can improve their performance if they help your product achieve the same share of business within the customer as the share of business within the market is a powerful argument for stimulating sales of your product within that customer.

Dual Ranking Analysis

Another interesting analysis is a *Dual Ranking Analysis*. A dual rank-ing analysis looks at the change in rank position between two bench-marks. Creating a dual ranking analysis can illustrate interesting changes in performance either across time, between regions, or versus other dimensions.

To create a dual ranking report we produce a sorted set of rows based on one criterion. We then put in a column of rank numbers (1, 2, 3, etc.) to indicate rank position. We then re-sort the list, including the rank numbers, based on the new criteria, and add in a new column of rank numbers. The first set of rank numbers is no longer in numerical order; it is in the order of the second rank criteria.

We can then see how the rank changed between criteria. We are left with something similar to "this week on the bestseller list, last week on the bestseller list". Rows that have significantly changed rank position (either up or down) should be monitored.

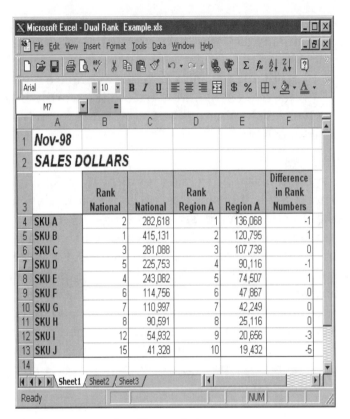

Figure 10.14 Dual ranking analysis.

An extension to the analysis is to calculate the difference between rank positions, and then re-sort the list based on the difference in rank position. This way, we can see the items that have significantly changed rank position easily, because they will be at the top and bottom of the analysis.

Industry Benchmark Analysis

The last type of analysis to discuss compares performance to a bigger perspective, the entire market.

To conduct an *Industry Benchmark Analysis*, you need to incorporate data from a trade association, market research company, or from government statistics. The goal of industry benchmark analysis is to know your performance vis-à-vis your competitors.

There are many market research companies that can be of assistance in understanding the total market's performance. In the consumer-packaged-goods world, there are two primary sources for market-level data: AC Nielsen and Information Resources. Both companies purchase scanner data from a variety of sources such as supermarkets, drug stores, and mass merchandisers, process this tremendous quantity of data into definable categories of information, and then sell this data back to manufacturers who in turn sell it in the channels they collect from. Therefore, purchasers of this data know what sold (for their products and their competitors), where it sold (by region, account, etc.), when it sold (by week, or collection of weeks), and why it sold (causal statistics like advertising, pricing, or marketplace prevalence). Comparing a product's performance to the entire market is extremely insightful information.

There are two primary things that you can look at. The first is to compare performance to the market in terms of percentage called *market share*. The second is *market growth*—looking at the growth rate of the market between certain periods. The two concepts are also interrelated.

Take, for example, the analysis shown in Figure 10.15.

Notice that the absolute performance of Product B was significantly stronger year over year (26% growth rate) than was Product A (16%

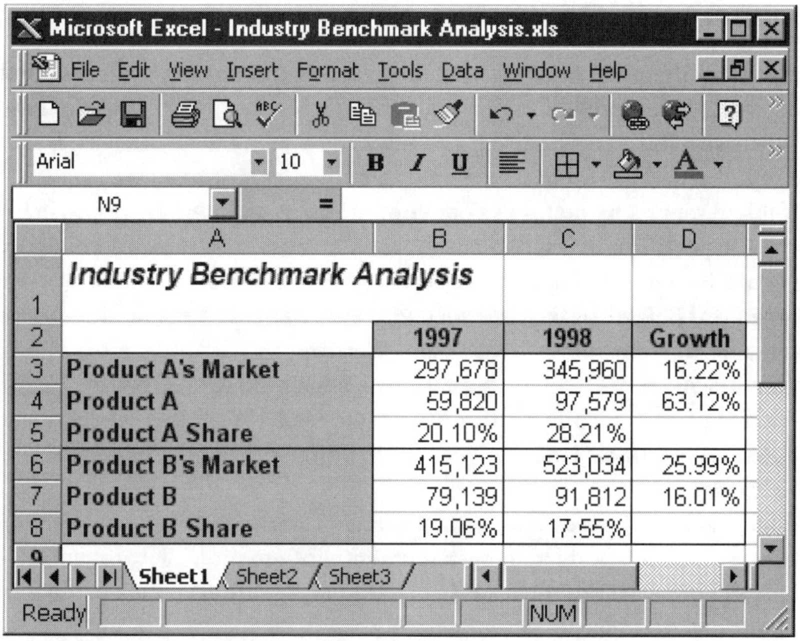

	1997	1998	Growth
Industry Benchmark Analysis			
Product A's Market	297,678	345,960	16.22%
Product A	59,820	97,579	63.12%
Product A Share	20.10%	28.21%	
Product B's Market	415,123	523,034	25.99%
Product B	79,139	91,812	16.01%
Product B Share	19.06%	17.55%	

Figure 10.15 Industry benchmark analysis.

growth rate). However, Product B captured only 19.06% of the potential market in 1997, and even less than that in 1998—17.55%. Product B actually lost ground to its competitors, because it lost market share.

Looking at Product A's performance, we see that market share increased 8.11% versus last year. Product A captures more of the market, and hence did better than its competitors.

Market share is related to growth rate. If a product grew sales faster than the market—had a higher growth rate than the market, then that product will likely increase its share. The entire market was strong in 1998, but Product A's sales were extremely strong. Product B's market was even stronger than Product A. Product B's growth did not keep pace to the market. It actually lost ground to the competition.

Therefore, it is not enough to know performance within a company; it is critical to know performance relative to what is transpiring in the market. Performance can be strong, or seem to be strong, but if the market outperforms this good performance, then that performance is not very good.

A Note About Standard Reports

Despite all of the problems with standard reports, the bottom line is that they do exist in companies today, and that many people feel comfortable using them. It is in that context that it is important to spend a few moments discussing how standard reports can be used to create an information-centric analysis.

Standard reports by themselves are not the bane of an information-centric analysis. Reports can be used in such regard. However, most standard reports are simply a deluge of information. They attempt to cover every possible situation, and every possible analysis a person could ever want. As a result, they become unworkable, and are generally not used effectively.

By employing some or all of the concepts illustrated earlier, standard reports can be more targeted and effective. This new breed of standard reports can be produced on a periodic basis for wide distribution, drawing out the issues inherent in the data.

Therefore, if the idea of standard reporting is warranted in a given situation, then use standard reports; only turn them into information-centric standard reports. Draw the user of the reports toward the significant issues in the data by employing the concepts outlined in this chapter.

Summary

Too often people make bad decisions because they rely on superficial numbers found in unreliable reports. These reports are generated by people who lost the art of looking deeper at the information because they had too much work to do, and not enough time to do it all. They put their data analysis projects on the back burner, and often never really got to them at all.

This is a tremendous mistake. Without proper analysis, numbers by themselves do not mean much. In fact they can often lead to bad decisions. Bad decisions cost money, and leave opportunities for your competitors to snatch away a piece of your business.

If people have little time to analyze data, the solution is to make better use of their available time, not to do less analysis. There are two ways to make time for better analysis.

The first involves using the right technology. To do the kinds of analyses required by the business community, a company must invest in multi-dimensional technology such as SQL Server 7 and SQL Server OLAP Services. Multi-dimensional databases and multi-dimensional analytical software give business users the ability to perform a tremendous amount of high-level analyses in a fraction of the time that it would take to do the same analyses using two-dimensional technology. All of the analyses discussed in this chapter were done with Cognos' PowerPlay, a multi-dimensional analysis tool. Multi-dimensional databases and analytical tools are targeted directly at the fast-paced business person.

The second way to improve your analysis time is to develop an understanding of what makes an effective, information-centric analysis. Focussing on effective analyses will yield better decisions, without additional time required to research decisions.

The concepts for creating an effective information-centric analysis are in this chapter. Information-centric analysis is an analysis that incorporates five criteria. They are:

1. Benchmarking
2. Limiting
3. Highlighting

4. Trending

5. Communicating

Several examples of information-centric analyses were also presented, including:

- Growth Trend
- Importance
- Customer Retention
- Shopping Basket
- Over-and-Under Developed
- Dual Ranking
- Industry Benchmark

With the two requirements for proper analysis in place, users can expect to make better, more informed decisions, in a fraction of the time.

This is a selective list of books, articles, research reports, online resources, and white papers that we found useful while researching this book.

Adamson, Christopher and Michael Venerable, *Data Warehouse Design Solutions*, New York, NY: John Wiley & Sons, Inc., 1998.

Barquin, Ramon and Herb Edelstein (ed.), *Building, Using, and Managing The Data Warehouse*, Englewood Cliffs, NJ: Prentice-Hall, 1997.

Boar, Bernard, *Constructing Blueprints for Enterprise IT Architectures*, New York, NY: John Wiley & Sons, Inc., 1999.

Bowman, Judith, Sandra Emerson, and Marcy Darnovsky, *The Practical SQL Handbook: Using Structured Query Language, Third Edition*, Reading, MA: Addison-Wesley, 1996.

Craig, Robert, "Packaged Apps Meet DSS," *Database Programming & Design*, June 1998.

Craig, Robert, *Enterprise Metadata Management*, Hurwitz BalancedView Report, Hurwitz Group, Inc., December 1998.

Craig, Robert, *Enterprise Reporting Systems*, Hurwitz BalancedView Research Bulletin, November 1998.

Craig, Robert, *Decision Support In The SAP Environment*, Hurwitz BalancedView Research Bulletin, October 1998.

Craig, Robert, *DSS Requirements for Enterprise Customer Management*, Hurwitz BalancedView Research Bulletin, September 1998.

Craig, Robert, *Change Data Capture In The DSS Environment*, Hurwitz BalancedView Research Bulletin, August 1998.

Craig, Robert, *Requirements for ETML Tools*, Hurwitz BalancedView Research Bulletin, July 1998.

Craig, Robert, *Decision Support for Packaged Applications*, Hurwitz BalancedView Research Bulletin, June 1998.

Craig, Robert, *Browser-Based Decision Support*, Hurwitz BalancedView Research Bulletin, January 1998.

Craig, Robert, *Data Warehouse Categories*, Hurwitz BalancedView Research Bulletin, December 1997.

Craig, Robert, *The Data Mart Alternative*, Hurwitz BalancedView Research Bulletin, December 1997.

Craig, Robert, *Decision Support Software Market Segmentation*, Hurwitz BalancedView Report, Hurwitz Group, Inc., December 1997.

Craig, Robert, *Evaluating DSS Benchmarks: Part II*, Hurwitz Balanced View Research Bulletin, August 1997.

Craig, Robert, *Evaluating DSS Benchmarks: Part I*, Hurwitz BalancedView Research Bulletin, July 1997.

Craig, Robert, *Decision Support for Packaged Applications: No Silver Bullet*, Hurwitz BalancedView Research Bulletin, June 1997.

Craig, Robert, *Decision Support Scalability*, Hurwitz BalancedView Research Bulletin, May 1997.

Craig, Robert, *Data Warehouse Management Framework*, Hurwitz Balanced View Report, Hurwitz Group, Inc., March 1997.

Craig, Robert, *The Metadata Muddle*, Hurwitz BalancedView Research Bulletin, March 1997.

Craig, Robert, *The Data Warehouse Business Value Cycle*, Hurwitz Balanced View Research Bulletin, February 1997.

Corey, Michael and Michael Abbey, *Oracle Data Warehousing*, New York, NY: Osborne McGraw-Hill, 1997.

Dunbar, Vernon, et al., *The Oracle Data Mart Suite Cookbook*, Oracle Corporation, 1998.

Gillett, Frank, *The Business Payback of AT&T's Successful Data Warehouse Effort*, Hurwitz BalancedView Report, Hurwitz Group, Inc., September 1997.

Gillett, Frank, *Web-Based Analysis Is Emerging But Immature*, Hurwitz BalancedView Research Bulletin, November 1997.

Gillett, Frank, *Microsoft's Windows NT: An Emerging Data Mart Platform*, Hurwitz BalancedView Research Bulletin, February 1997.

Gillett, Frank, *Microsoft's Data Warehouse Strategy: Promises with Promise*, Hurwitz BalancedView Research Bulletin, October 1996.

Gillett, Frank, *The New Data Warehouse Development Cycle*, Hurwitz BalancedView Research Bulletin, August 1996.

Gill, Harjinder and Prakash Rao, *The Official Client/Server Computing Guide to Data Warehousing*, Indianapolis, IN: QUE, 1996.

Hackney, Douglas, *Understanding and Implementing Successful Data Marts*, Reading, MA: Addison-Wesley, 1997.

Hernandez, Michael, *Database Design for Mere Mortals: A Hands-On Guide to Relational Database Design*, Reading, MA: Addison-Wesley, 1997.

Inmon, W.H., J.D. Welch, and Katherine Glassey, *Managing the Data Warehouse*, New York, NY: John Wiley & Sons, Inc., 1997.

Inmon, W.H., Ken Rudin, Christopher Buss and Ryan Sousa, *Data Warehouse Performance*, New York, NY: John Wiley & Sons, Inc., 1999.

Kelly, Sean, *Data Warehousing: The Route to Mass Customisation*, Chichester: UK, John Wiley & Sons, Ltd., 1994.

Kern, Harris and Randy Johnson, *Rightsizing the New Enterprise: The Proof, Not the Hype*, Sun Microsystems, Inc., 1994.

Kimball, Ralph, *The Data Warehouse Toolkit: Practical Techniques for Building Dimensional Data Warehouses*, New York, NY: John Wiley & Sons, Inc., 1996.

Kimball, Ralph, Laura Reeves, Margy Ross and Warren Thornthwaite, *The Data Warehouse Lifecycle Toolkit: Expert Methods for Designing, Developing, and Deploying Data Warehouses*, New York, NY: John Wiley & Sons, Inc., 1998.

Lozinsky, Sergio, *Enterprise-Wide Software Solutions: Integration Strategies and Practices*, Reading, MA: Addison-Wesley, 1998.

McCarthy, Jim, *Dynamics of Software Development*, Redmond, WA: Microsoft Press, 1995.

Melton, Jim and Alan Simon, *Understanding The New SQL: A Complete Guide*, San Francisco, CA: Morgan Kaufmann Publishers, Inc., 1993.

Microsoft SQL Server: Getting Started with SQL Server 7.0, Redmond, WA: Microsoft Press, 1998.

Peppers, Don and Martha Rogers, Ph.D., *The One To One Future: Building Relationships One Customer at a Time*, New York, NY: Doubleday, 1996.

Radding, Alan, *Hurwitz Group Data Analysis Framework*, Hurwitz Balanced View Report, Hurwitz Group, Inc., December 1997.

Radding, Alan, "It's in the can: Analytical applications simplify back-end datamarts," *PlugIn Datamation*, January 1999.

Russom, Philip, *Data Models for Data Warehouses*, Hurwitz BalancedView Research Bulletin, November 1998.

Russom, Philip, *Frameworks for Knowledge Management: Part I*, Hurwitz BalancedView Research Bulletin, September 1998.

Russom, Philip, *Frameworks for Knowledge Management: Part II*, Hurwitz BalancedView Research Bulletin, October 1998.

Russom, Philip, *Balanced Scorecards: Management Method and Software Automation*, Hurwitz BalancedView Research Bulletin, September 1998.

Silverston, Len, W.H. Inmon and Kent Graziano, *The Data Model Resource Book*, New York, NY: John Wiley & Sons, Inc., 1997.

Simon, Alan, *Data Warehousing for Dummies*, San Mateo, CA: IDG Books Worldwide, Inc., 1997.

Sobel, Ken, *The Challenge of Information Access: ODBC Enables Multi-Source Analysis*, Hurwitz BalancedView Research Bulletin, December 1996.

The Windows Interface Guidelines for Software Design, Redmond, WA: Microsoft Press, 1995.

Thomsen, Erik, *OLAP Solutions: Building Multidimensional Information Systems*, John Wiley & Sons, Inc., 1997.

Useful online resources include the following Web sites:

WEB SITE	UNIVERSAL RESEARCH LOCATOR
Alta Plana: Online Analytical Processing (OLAP)	http://altaplana.com/olap/
CIO Magazine Data Warehouse Research Center	http://www.cio.com/forums/data/
Data Administration Newsletter	http://www.tdan.com/
Data Warehouse Institute	http://www.datawarehouse.org/
Data Warehousing	http://www.datawarehousing.com/
DM Review	http://www.datawarehouse.com/
Hitchhikers Guide to Decision Support	http://members.aol.com/hhg2dss/
Ken Orr Institute - Data Warehouse	http://www.kenorrinst.com/datawh.html
Meta Data Coalition	http://www.mdcinfo.com/
Microsoft SQL Server home page	http://www.microsoft.com/sql/
Microsoft Universal Data Access home page	http://www.microsoft.com/data/
Microsoft Repository home page	http://www.microsoft.com/repository/
Microsoft Developer Network home page	http://msdn.microsoft.com/developer/
Microsoft Research Lab home page	http://research.microsoft.com/barc/
OLAP Council	http://www.olapcouncil.org/
OLAP Report	http://www.olapreport.com/
PlugIn Datamation IS Managers Workbench - Data Warehouse	http://www.datamation.com/PlugIn/workbench/dwhouse/dwhouse.htm
Rational Corporation UML Resource Center	http://www.rational.com/uml/index.jtmpl
Strategic Enterprise Knowledge Centers	http://www.knowledgecenters.org/

Interesting and useful white papers included:

Architecture and Implementation Techniques Used in Building the MS Sales Decision Support System. Microsoft Corp., 1998.

Armstrong, Rob, Data *Warehousing: The Fallacy of Data Mart Centric Strategies.* NCR Corp., 1996.

Blum, Adam, *Developing with Microsoft English Query*, Microsoft Corp., 1998.

Developing with Microsoft English Query in Microsoft SQL Server 7.0. Microsoft Corp., 1998.

Ebel, Doug, *Technology Doesn't Kill Data Warehouses, People Do.* NCR Corp., 1998.

Flanagan, Thomas and Elias Safdie (ed.) *A Practical Guide To Achieving Enterprise Data Quality.* The Applied Technologies Group, 1998.

Flanagan, Thomas and Elias Safdie (ed.) *Building A Decision Support Architecture for Data Warehousing.* The Applied Technologies Group, 1997.

Flanagan, Thomas and Elias Safdie (ed.) *Delivering Warehouse ROI With Business Intelligence.* The Applied Technologies Group, 1997.

Flanagan, Thomas and Elias Safdie (ed.) *Putting Metadata To Work In The Warehouse.* The Applied Technologies Group, 1997.

Fryer, Ron, *Questions You Should Ask Today (or You'll Wish You'd Asked Tomorrow).* NCR Corp., 1996.

Graefe, Goetz, Jim Ewel, and Cesar Galindo-Legaria, *Microsoft SQL Server 7.0 Query Processor.* Microsoft Corp., 1998.

Lau, Henry, *Microsoft SQL Server 7.0 Performance Tuning Guide.* Microsoft Corp., 1998.

Meltzer, Michael, *Using the Data Warehouse to Recreate Customer Intimacy for Profit.* NCR Corp., 1998.

Microsoft SQL Server 7.0 Data Warehousing Framework. Microsoft Corp., 1998.

Microsoft SQL Server 7.0 OLAP Services. Microsoft Corp., 1998.

Microsoft SQL Server 7.0 Storage Engine. Microsoft Corp., 1998.

The Microsoft Data Warehousing Strategy: A Platform For Improved Decision-Making Through Easier Data Access And Analysis, Microsoft Corp., 1998.

What Is Microsoft Repository?, Microsoft Corp., 1998.